DOMINION AND AGENCY: COPYRIGHT AND THE STRUCTURING OF THE CANADIAN BOOK TRADE, 1867–1918

The 1867 Canadian confederation brought with it expectations of a national literature, which a rising class of local printers hoped to supply. Reforming copyright law in the imperial context proved impossible, and Canada became a prime market for foreign publishers instead. The subsequent development of the agency system of exclusive publisher-importers became a defining feature of Canadian trade publishing for most of the twentieth century.

In *Dominion and Agency*, Eli MacLaren analyses the struggle for copyright reform and the creation of a national literature. Using previously ignored archival sources such as the Board of Trade Papers at the National Archives of the United Kingdom and the Macmillan Company of Canada Fonds at McMaster University, MacLaren addresses the foundations of the Canadian publishing industry. A groundbreaking study, *Dominion and Agency* is an important exploration of the legal and economic structures that were instrumental in the formation of Canadian literary culture as it exists today.

(Studies in Book and Print Culture)

ELI MACLAREN is an assistant professor in the Department of English at McGill University.

T0339286

ELI MACLAREN

Dominion and Agency

Copyright and the Structuring of the Canadian Book Trade, 1867–1918

UNIVERSITY OF TORONTO PRESS
Toronto   Buffalo   London

© University of Toronto Press 2011
Toronto Buffalo London
www.utorontopress.com

Reprinted in paperback 2022

ISBN 978-1-4426-4321-5 (cloth)
ISBN 978-1-4875-2770-9 (paper)

Publication cataloguing information is available from Library and Archives
Canada.

We wish to acknowledge the land on which the University of Toronto
Press operates. This land is the traditional territory of the Wendat, the
Anishnaabeg, the Haudenosaunee, the Métis, and the Mississaugas of the
Credit First Nation.

University of Toronto Press acknowledges the financial support of the
Government of Canada, the Canada Council for the Arts, and the Ontario
Arts Council, an agency of the Government of Ontario, for its publishing
activities.

This book has been published with the help of a grant from the Canadian
Federation for the Humanities and Social Sciences, through the Aid to
Scholarly Publications Program, using funds provided by the Social Sciences
and Humanities Research Council of Canada.

Canada Council for the Arts · **Conseil des Arts du Canada**

ONTARIO ARTS COUNCIL
CONSEIL DES ARTS DE L'ONTARIO
an Ontario government agency
un organisme du gouvernement de l'Ontario

Funded by the Government of Canada · Financé par le gouvernement du Canada · **Canadä**

For my family

Contents

Acknowledgments

It takes a community to make a book.

My research would not have been possible without financial support from various quarters. I gratefully acknowledge funding received from the Social Sciences and Humanities Research Council of Canada and the Advisory Research Council of Queen's University. I am equally grateful for the support of the Department of English at Carleton University. The New Scholars Prize of the Bibliographical Society of America allowed me to present my work to a meeting of that august institution in New York, and the Bibliographical Society of Canada not only supported my participation in a number of key conferences but also served as an intellectual home.

Many librarians, archivists, and rare book dealers were of indispensable assistance. I wish especially to thank the staff of the Thomas Fisher Rare Book Library at the University of Toronto; the United Church / Victoria University Archives; the Wilson Library at the University of North Carolina at Chapel Hill; Library and Archives Canada; the W.D. Jordan Special Collections and the Archives at Queen's University; the National Archives of the United Kingdom; the Elizabeth Dafoe Library at the University of Manitoba; the William Ready Division of Archives and Special Collections at McMaster University; the Archives and Special Collections at the University of Guelph; and David Mason Books of Toronto. The history of publishing depends on the outstanding work of collecting and preserving rare books *in their original form* and the various papers associated with them.

Many people influenced the writing of the manuscript. I am indebted to all those who read and commented on it in whole or in part at various stages of its development: Heather Murray, Nick Mount, Pat Fleming,

Laura Murray, Deidre Lynch, Will Robins, Carl Spadoni, Ian MacLaren, Jody Mason, Margaret MacLaren, Trevor Howard-Hill, Kathleen Garay, Christl Verduyn, George Parker, and the assessors engaged by the University of Toronto Press. Many others have heard some version of the argument and, in reacting to it, altered it: Oliver MacLaren, Julia MacLaren, Jeff Matt, Sandra Alston, Josée Vincent, Marie-Pier Luneau, Tobi Kozakewich, Marta Straznicky, Heather Jackson, Richard Landon, Yannick Portebois, Michael Groden, Colin Hill, Christine Wiesenthal, Judy Donnelly, Glenn Willmott, Margaret Lock, Tracy Ware, Gerald Lynch, Janice Fiamengo, Cynthia Sugars, Travis DeCook, Sarah Brouillette, Daniel O'Leary, Mark Simpson, John Considine, Terry Belanger, Greta Golick, Jonathan Rose, Sydney Shep, Brian Johnson, Suzanne Waldman, Gwendolyn Davies, and Carole Gerson. Thanks also go to Clarence Tang, Joseph Fridman, Brendan Klug, Bob de Frece, James Calkin, Jean-Noël Rocher, Hartmut and Elisabeth Zimnol, Jean Chia, Tariq and Hala Gordon, Bill and Linda Mason, Doug Gordon, Caroline Dolny Guerin, Dave Gordon, Dorene Inglis, Alison Gordon, Corey Mihailiuk, Sheila and Wendell Alton, and Tom, Janet, Andy, Debbie, Jim, Tim, and Bev MacLaren for their unfailing support.

The commitment of the University of Toronto Press to publishing Canadian book history has been an indispensable framework within which to work. Both the acquisitions editor, Siobhan McMenemy, and the editor of the Studies in Book and Print Culture series, Leslie Howsam, expressed interest in the project from an early date. For obvious reasons I am very aware of the role of the publisher in bringing a book to fruition, and the completion of this study is a tribute to the Canadian publisher who has been bold enough to take an interest in it.

The publication of parts of the manuscript along the way was equally important to the maturation of the project. Chapter 5 was originally published in the *Journal of Canadian Studies / Revue d'études canadiennes* 40, no. 2 (2006): 139–62, and chapter 6 was published in the *Papers of the Bibliographical Society of America* 101 (2007): 507–31. I am grateful to both for connecting me with their discerning readers. It is true that books germinate in periodicals.

Finally, thanks are due to the patient readers of this book, present and future, without whom its words would cease to live.

DOMINION AND AGENCY

Introduction

Isolation, financial distraction, and the temptation to emigrate hounded Canadian writers in the decades following Confederation. Despite the acute desire for a literature that would mirror and fulfil the nationhood promised in the British North America Act of 1867, the Dominion of Canada was no more attractive a place to cultivate the art of letters than had been the former colonies. The second volume of the *History of the Book in Canada,* which runs to the year 1918, describes a country that, because of education, urbanization, and mass production, was increasingly able to read and write but not correspondingly able to support the careers of literary authors: 'for both men and women the price of success was often expatriation, if not forever, at least for a substantial portion of their professional life.'[1] Nick Mount has measured the depth and extent of this literary exodus, estimating that as many as half of Canada's aspiring writers left the country in the 1880s and 1890s, most for the American magazine boom centred in New York.[2] David Bentley's study of the Confederation Poets argues that the partial and short-lived cohesion of this group was due to the promotional efforts of one man – Charles G.D. Roberts – the nexus disintegrating after he too threw over the attempt to make a living as a writer in Canada.[3] Nor did the domestic writer's lot suddenly improve after the First World War; in the third volume of the *History of the Book in Canada,* Frank Davey states, 'with the notable exceptions of journalists and a few commercially successful novelists, until 1960 Canada's best-known writers all followed other careers.'[4] Far from charting a simple line of progress parallel to other industries in a modernizing economy, professional literary authorship in Canada in the period after Confederation generally struggled to establish itself at all, and most of the literary works that have been recovered from this time in the interests of cultural nationalism should be construed as remarkable individual achievements against overwhelming economic odds. If the adjective is understood to denote residence, the *Canadian* author was a rare bird.

Yet the literary field was teeming with activity. 'Canada has produced no author who is a classic in the sense of possessing a vision greater in kind than that of his best readers,' judged Northrop Frye as critic in his 1965 conclusion to the *Literary History of Canada*; however, in the same breath as cultural historian he upheld the *Literary History*'s findings – namely, that 'what is really remarkable is not how little but how much good writing has been produced in Canada.'

If literature itself was thriving in Canadian society, and there are countless indications that it was, what prevented the maturation of the author in Canada? What obstructed the formation of the long career in letters, in which the novice turns expert within a rising spiral of vocation, accessing higher points of view and testing new forms of expression with each return to the task of writing, through the criticism of his or her own prior accomplishment? To broach this question is to look into the socio-economic factors of creativity. For his part, Frye professed a calculated ignorance of such factors, nodding to the problem of object and matrix but staying firmly with the object: 'I stress our ignorance of the laws and conditions of cultural history for an obvious reason. The question: why has there been no Canadian writer of classic proportions? may naturally be asked. At any rate it often has been. Our authors [the contributors to the *Literary History*] realize that it is better to deal with what is there than to raise speculations about why something else is not there. But it is clear that the question haunts their minds.'[5] This approach underlies the whole of the *Literary History*. By focusing on extant works, Frye and his collaborators sidestepped the paralyzing complaint that Canadian literature was not great, and so broke the circular argument that it therefore should not be studied. But Frye protests too much. He is evidently interested in the question of the matrix and cannot hide his conviction that the elements surrounding an aspiring writer do play a major role in nurturing the creation of which he or she is capable. What the best conditions might be the 1960s literary critic does not risk saying, but he probably entertained a few hypotheses. The question is indeed haunting. Put it this way: if *As for Me and My House* is a great work of literature, why did Sinclair Ross achieve only one?

As important as it is, the reading of literature is only part of the analysis, and the new interdisciplinary approaches to literary studies have offered complementary methods for the explication of the causes, the form, and the effects of texts. At their origin, literary objects do emerge from environmental matrices, not only incarnating an individual's thoughts but being formed by social forces and bearing the mark of industrial and commercial processes, and for this reason important literary questions sometimes have non-literary answers. Why did so many aspiring writers abandon the Dominion of Canada? Part of the answer lies in the economic milieu – the book trade – in which authors and publishers made the choices they did. At the heart of the book trade lies the law of copyright, which, because it defines property in texts, determines the way in which they are offered, bought, transformed, and used. The argument of the present study is that copyright compelled the book trade of the Dominion of Canada into modes of operation that were more or less incompatible with original publishing. Although there were many isolated publishing moments before the First World War, as well as a thriving newspaper industry, a number of magazines anchored to a national church, and government-authorized textbooks, there were, bluntly put, no general literary publishers. The law of copyright precluded aspirants to this role from stably occupying it for any length of time. If, in Browning's words, the triumph was 'to reach and stay there,' none triumphed. Hemmed in by copyright, the businesses that supplied literary books to Canadian readers essentially remained distributors or retailers rather than becoming full-fledged publishers.

The distinctions are important. A *publisher* or *specialist publisher* is the principal who, cultivating a relationship with the author, initiates, organizes, and finances the transformation of a manuscript into an edition, both managing its production and advertising and wholesaling it in one or more markets. A *distributor*, by contrast, has no necessary dealings with the author, being the one who wholesales but does not create the edition. The *retailer*, of course, is the one who sells single copies to readers.[6] Specialist publishers emerged in Britain and the United States in the nineteenth century, but they struggled to do so in Canada, and the role they eventually settled for was that of the *publisher-agent*, one who controlled the distribution of a foreign edition to the English-Canadian market, invariably from a base in Toronto. For reasons of nationalism and prestige, publisher-agents did dabble in original publishing, but this activity was very limited, and they entertained no illusions about existing off it alone. (In French Canada, the main player was long the *grossiste*, or wholesaler, who imported books from Europe but did not formally monopolize distribution to the local market as the

English-Canadian publisher-agent did.)[7] As a result of this structural lack of literary publishers, the Dominion lacked the infrastructure to foster and retain authors.

Many have recognized that copyright presented something of a barrier to Canadian literature. In his presidential address to the Royal Society of Canada in 1893, John George Bourinot observed that a book published in Canada had a small local market and that its access to the larger British or American markets, if not blocked, was not facilitated by British or American publishers, who preferred to sell their own editions directly. Bourinot consequently recommended that 'an author of ambition and merit should perforce look for publishers outside his own country if he is to expect anything like just appreciation.'[8] However, in order to pass swiftly on towards a Ruskinesque call for art to transcend its circumstances, Bourinot touches on the matter only lightly. The challenge is to stop and explain the technicalities of the way in which copyright impeded Canadian publishing, with reference to statutes, cases, and actual books. It is only then that causality, if not proven, may be persuasively suggested.

Nineteenth-century Canada was contested territory. It developed at the confluence of two English-speaking imperial powers whose people mingled and jostled for position within it. The Anglo-American friction that Susanna Moodie captured so memorably at the level of character in *Roughing It in the Bush* – 'How I wish those odious people would give us possession of the home which for some time has been our own!' thinks the English settler indignantly of the Yankee squatter[9] – also manifested itself in the rival copyright policies of these two states, which struggled with each other for control of the interstice. Both British and American laws were thus responsible for placing obstacles before an independent Canadian book trade.

One obstacle was the prohibition by the British Copyright Act of 1842[10] against unauthorized reprinting. Everywhere in the empire, it was forbidden to reproduce without permission the many books and magazines first published in London. Canadian printers therefore could not on their own terms take advantage of the immense colonial demand for works from their centre of culture – that centre where many settlers had been born and to which they collectively referred in order to posit an identity in the face of the immense alterity and the profound cultural fractures of their adoptive country. In 1868, Canada undertook copyright reform on the authority of its new constitution with the aim of liberalizing textual property in order to stimulate national printing and publishing. Debate ignited on the question of whether and how the unauthorized Canadian reprinting of British copyright works might be permitted. The combatants traced copyright back to its first principles and arrived at a concept of it that balanced authorial property with public access and regional development. However, although John A. Macdonald's ministry succeeded in persuading the appropriate department of the British government, the Board of Trade, of the justice of a plan of licensed Canadian reprinting, the London publishers successfully diverted the reform to their own end to the detriment of Canada's interest. When a new law finally arrived in the Canadian Copyright Act of 1875, it was confusing; a robust reprint industry started up in Toronto, only to be cut short by the judgment in *Smiles v. Belford* (1876–7), which clarified that the 1842 act remained immovable. This renewal of imperial copyright was a sharp disappointment both to the proponents of Canadian publishing and to the advocates of cheaper books for Britain; as for those who had seen the birth of a new nation in the British North America Act, it gave a repressive twist indeed to the meaning of *dominion*. *Smiles v. Belford* reinstated the London publisher's nominal control of the Canadian market, drove south those Canadians who were set on competing seriously in the North American publishing arena, and had an important negative impact on the development of Canadian publishing. This crucial debate and its legal aftermath are the subject of the first three chapters.

The 1842 act, repealed in the United Kingdom in 1911, was replaced in Canada by the Canadian Copyright Act of 1921,[11] but the prohibition against reprinting never vanished, for by then the Berne Convention for the Protection of Literary and Artistic Works was well established, and Canada had adhered to it by virtue of British ratification in 1886.[12] The Berne Convention remains in effect in Canada today under the auspices of the World Intellectual Property Organization. Canada thus never enjoyed a period of unauthorized reprinting. The 1842 Act, followed by the Berne Convention, made Canada a place where literary books were imported and not freely reprinted, and this encouraged bookselling but depressed printing, thus effectively cutting off one path to independent publishing.

There is, of course, a leap from the reprinting of existing works to the publishing of new ones. The developmental link between the two may be doubted, but significant precedents exist to indicate that original publishing tends to take root where book production is first allowed to flourish. In the 1730s, Scottish booksellers began to reprint books originally published in London. The London establishment sued them for piracy, asserting a common-law right to the perpetual monopoly of copies, but in the 1740s the Scottish Court of Session ruled that the re-printing was quite legal. As a result, the Scottish book trade blossomed, soon adding original publishing to the practice of reprinting, and dis-tributing both new and old titles throughout Scotland, into England, and to destinations overseas.[13]

In Ireland a one-man 'patent' controlled the circulation of print in the sixteenth and seventeenth centuries. During this time, with some exception due to the Interregnum, the king's printer in Dublin was the only person allowed to print, bind, or sell books. Officially this monop-oly lasted until 1732, although it had effectively broken down around 1680, and when it vanished, the Irish book trade grew geometrically, especially in printing. Subject to its own customs and conventions but not to any law of literary property, it thrived for the better part of a century. Although officially debarred from entering Great Britain, Irish reprints in practice supplied both British and Irish readers, and original Irish publications soon ensued. Then, towards the end of the eighteenth century, the government began to crack down. Threatened by the revo-lutions in America and France, it instituted oppressive taxes on news-papers and pamphlets to destroy the opposition press, and shortly after Ireland was subsumed by the United Kingdom in 1800, the island be-came subject to British copyright. In consequence, the Irish trade in the early nineteenth century once more shrank into the mere retailing of imported books.[14]

The same pattern is evident when one turns to the United States. From the seventeenth to the late eighteenth century, British copyright law restricted printing in the North American colonies. Most original American imprints from the pre-Revolutionary period served the local needs of government, religion, and agriculture, with newspapers and pamphlets increasing in the mid-eighteenth century; the few reprints that survive, of educational texts or novels for example, suggest that little printing occurred without authorization. This changed dramati-cally when the American Revolution did away with British copyright and replaced it with the federal Copyright Act of 1790, which expressly permitted the unauthorized reprinting 'of any map, chart, book or books, written, printed, or published by any person not a citizen of the United States, in foreign parts or places.'[15] This sudden access to the entire body of English literature past and present resulted in an imme-diate boom in production. In the last decade of the eighteenth century,

Americans printed at least fifteen thousand different works – as many as in the previous two centuries combined. Out of this explosion of reprinting eventually arose a solid national publishing industry, which by the end of the nineteenth century rivalled that of Britain itself.[16]

In all of these cases, freedom from copyright was a major factor in the rise of a local publishing industry, and it is therefore reasonable to imagine that this would have arisen more rapidly in Canada too if the Dominion had become a separate copyright zone. Most of us are so-cialized from an early age to fear copyright and to repeat the logic of the discourse of author's rights, without ever understanding the pri-vate-public balance that underlies copyright as its sole justification. Draconian intellectual-property policy contributes to the uneven de-velopment of private enterprise and affects the vitality of cultural dif-ference worldwide. As long as developing regions are bound by 'strong copyright,' they will be exploited as markets, forced to purchase the permission to distribute and reproduce influential texts from foreign publishers. The expansion of the international copyright jurisdiction, combined with the lengthening of the term and the strengthening of penalties, helps maintain the global economic and cultural disparities that are so profitable to centres of industry. In light of this analysis, it is not surprising – perhaps it is justifiable – that aspiring publishers on the margins of power turn to piracy.[17]

Piracy is a morally charged term, but what it designates is much more than mere theft. Like radio interference, piracy is a liminal phenom-enon; what may at first appear to be an annoying anomaly in the trans-mission of content turns out to be friction between colliding orders of regular signalling. The complex subjectivity of piracy is manifest in its mutual recriminations: for every charge of rapacious infringement, it seems, there is an equal but opposite one of rapacious monopoly; for every defence of property, a demand for liberty. The legitimacy of both is less intrinsic than circumstantial.[18] This friction may be traced back to the origins of copyright itself. The lapse of the English Press Act in 1695 exposed the tightly self-governing group ('conger') of London booksellers to the threat of outsiders reprinting their books. The book-sellers reacted by lobbying for a new act based on the idea of property arising out of the labour of the author. In 1710 the British parliament acted on the matter, but instead of merely adopting the concept of lit-erary property, the new act limited it to a fixed term, thereby substan-tially redefining it as privilege bestowed by the state.[19] The 1710 act formed the premise upon which Scottish reprinting flourished, but the

London conger resisted it by obtaining injunctions against such activity in England with arguments to common-law rights of property. By the mid-eighteenth century, debate had ignited over whether the right of the author (only now called *copyright*) was perpetual or not, and each camp vituperated the other for piracy, the London booksellers accusing the Scots of stealing, the latter in turn blaming the former for withholding knowledge from the public. In 1774 the House of Lords, judging the case of *Donaldson v. Becket*, struck down perpetual literary property, proclaiming the statute rather than the common law to be the sole basis for copyright in Britain. Nevertheless, rather than putting an end to the matter, the eighteenth-century copyright debates produced intense and elaborate arguments both for and against the principle of authorial property, arguments to which we continue to have recourse in attempting to distinguish the proper from the piratical use of a text.

The eruption of piracy upsets the normal relations of authorship and trade, often leaving them in a profoundly altered state. Surveying the long history of piracy, Adrian Johns concludes that contests between pirates and their persecutors 'strained relations between creativity and commercial life, and at critical moments caused them to be reconstituted.'[20] Johns does not examine the case of Canada, but it fits his argument very well. At the formative moment of modern Canada, property and piracy clashed so intensely as to call into question the very constitution of the new state, and in the aftermath a new norm of commercial relations among authors, publishers, and readers was forged.

Besides the illegality of reprinting under British copyright law, another obstacle to Canadian publishing was the protectionism of American law. The United States protected its printers by explicitly granting them the liberty to reprint British books. This had an adverse effect on Canadian book production. The cheap books of the United States found a ready market in Canada, and regardless of the relative size of that market it was in the interest of American printers and publishers to continue to supply it. American reprints were abundant from the end of the eighteenth century on, and Canadian bookselling soon organized itself around importing them. The 1842 act prohibited such importation, but the British Foreign Reprints Act of 1847[21] suspended the prohibition, once more allowing unauthorized American reprints into Canada. The 1847 amendment was originally passed at the request of British North America so that the colonists, who could not afford British editions, would nevertheless continue to read British authors.[22] However, the lasting effect of this law was that Canada became a place where multiple editions of the same work circulated competitively; until 1900 it was often the case that both the British edition and any American edition could legally be sold in Canada. This unpredictable competition undermined the growth of Canadian wholesaling. Without control of the national market, retail booksellers had trouble becoming wholesalers, and success in wholesale bookselling was another possible path to original publishing.

Dominance in the supply of British-authored literature to Canada was one aspect of American protectionism; the other concerned original Canadian publications, a small category that was negligible on the world stage but highly significant to Canadians. The United States did not recognize Canadian copyright until the later-twentieth century. From 1790 until 1962, editions first published in Canada automatically forfeited copyright protection in the United States. This was the North American copyright divide, a massive impediment that Canada was powerless to remove. Before 1891 an author had to be an American citizen or resident to receive American copyright; after 1891 authorship became irrelevant, but a manufacturing clause applied: the work had to be printed from type set on American soil and deposited at the Library of Congress before being published anywhere else. Owing to these measures, the independent Canadian publisher could not control an edition in the American market, which was not only nearby geographically and culturally but also more than ten times larger than the Canadian one; in fact, if an original Canadian edition proved at all successful, the publisher could reasonably expect to see it reprinted without permission in the United States. Charles Dickens is the best-known example of an author who lost control of his works in the American market and looked on enviously as they sold there, but the list also includes numerous Canadians, including Thomas Chandler Haliburton, Susanna Moodie, William Kirby, Ralph Connor, and Stephen Leacock.

The causal relation between unauthorized reprinting and authorial fame has been persuasively demonstrated by William St Clair in the cases of Shelley and Byron and by Meredith McGill in the case of Edgar Allan Poe, and the list above suggests that it has also helped form the Canadian canon. However, whereas Canadian authors might ultimately reap some benefit from American reprinting, as lost profits converted themselves into wider renown, Canadian publishers did not; the person who financed an original edition only suffered when that edition was superseded and undercut by a cheap reprint, which besides selling in the United States could also be smuggled into Canada. Canadian publisher-agents adapted to the North American copyright divide by arranging for a new Canadian manuscript to be printed and published in the United States, reserving for themselves the role of distributing this American edition in Canada. In that they dealt with the author, they approached the role of the specialist publisher, but it should not be forgotten that finding an American partner was the key to the enterprise, and if no such partner could be found, the project could well falter. The United States did not offer reciprocal copyright to Canada until it signed the Universal Copyright Convention in 1954. Canada, long inured to the copyright divide and its disadvantages, struck a royal commission headed by J.L. Ilsley to study the convention three years later. Canadian ratification of it in 1962 finally secured the American market to Canadian editions and levelled the divide – unless the author was a Canadian who lived for part of the year in the United States, in which case the manufacturing formalities still applied. This last complication evaporated in 1989 when the United States, having signed the Berne Convention the previous year, finally brought American copyright law into accord with it. So it is not unfair to say that Canadian editions did not constitute stable property on their home continent until 1962, or in some cases 1989, and that serious investment in Canadian publishing could not occur until this status as property had been clarified. The North American copyright divide is the subject of chapter 6.

The Dominion of Canada did not possess a specialist book-publishing industry. Still, there were many firms who in newspaper advertisements and on the title pages of their books presented themselves as Canadian 'publishers': Belford Brothers, William Briggs, George N. Morang, the Macmillan Company of Canada, and the Westminster Company, which were five of the most prominent before the First World War and all located in Toronto. If we took their self-representation as being publishers at face value, we might look for the beginnings of a national literature among their publications, and some have attempted to do precisely this, ignoring the expatriate fact – that Canada's best writers of the time achieved careers for themselves by publishing abroad. If William Briggs were a modern Canadian publisher, why did ambitious Canadian authors such L.M. Montgomery refuse to approach him with their manuscripts? 'I wouldn't give my MS. to a Canadian firm,' Montgomery wrote in a letter about her draft of *Anne of Green Gables*. 'It is much better financially to have it published in the United States.'[23] Before looking for Canadian literature in books with Canadian imprints, it is crucial to grasp that the imprint is not proof of publication; it may name only the printer or bookseller. It may be merely a shell encasing what is in substance a foreign book. To determine whether a book with William Briggs's imprint was in fact an independent edition, it is necessary to reconstruct the process that produced it and theorize or create a model of the larger trade patterns that influenced it. Analytical bibliography is one method by which to approach this goal; examining publishers' papers is another. The model resulting from this study is that copyright law, and in particular the friction between the British and American regimes, coerced expanding Canadian book suppliers into the subordinate role of distributing to Canadian readers books published abroad in the United States, Britain, and Europe. Chapter 4 presents this model through a case study of William Briggs.

The instability in publishing following Confederation led to the establishment of the *agency system*, the structure that would govern the Canadian book trade for most of the twentieth century. In industry jargon, an *agency* was a book – a foreign edition – exclusively distributed to the national market by a local company, the (publisher-) *agent*. The agency system took its shape from the Canadian Copyright Amendment of 1900,[24] a short act that spelled out a process by which one Canadian wholesaler could prevent another from dealing in the same British copyright work. It addressed the problem of multiple foreign editions of the same work undercutting each other in the Canadian market. By complying with the 1900 amendment, the wholesaler became the sole Canadian importer of the work; all copies sold in Canada had to come through him or her. (The one exception was that libraries were allowed to import two copies directly from the foreign publisher if they so desired.) The first publisher-agent was George N. Morang, who was instrumental in the passing of the 1900 amendment, and his issue of Rudyard Kipling's *Kim* is perhaps the first instance of one bookseller supplying the whole Canadian market and effectively preventing all rival importation. It took some time for the trade, both local and foreign, to get used to the Canadian agency system – Toronto wholesalers continued cunningly to undercut one another for a time by importing illegal American editions, and one of the objects of Macmillan and Company, the British publisher, in establishing its Canadian branch in 1905 was to stamp out competition from successful publisher-agents like Morang – but in time it established itself. Chapter 5 examines in detail the transition to the new order.

We must not assume that the creation of the Canadian state led to the birth of a national literature. Canadian reading and writing were and remain inextricable from the international book trade, a field that from before the advent of the printed book has witnessed powerful business interests striving to centralize their property while expanding their reach into new markets. The *dominion* and the *agency* were both distinctly Canadian formations when they arose in the later-nineteenth and the early-twentieth century, respectively, but the power that coursed through both came largely from abroad. The result was that in the case of Canada the communications circuit, Robert Darnton's rough but memorable diagram of the life cycle of books,[25] was not to any important extent nationally contained. There were writers in Canada and there were readers, but the one who generally connected them was based elsewhere. The structural hindrances to Canadian publishing drove the most ambitious writers to leave home in order to be closer to the people who successfully published books.

Sara Jeannette Duncan, looking back at her native country after more than a decade abroad, summed up the Canadian book trade with this miniature portrait (from chapter 21 of *The Imperialist*):

> He [Dr Drummond, the Presbyterian minister] and Hugh Finlay were sitting in the Doctor's study, the pleasantest room in the house. It was lined with standard religious philosophy, standard poets, standard fiction, all that was standard, and nothing that was not; and the shelves included several volumes of the Doctor's own sermons, published in black morocco through a local firm that did business by the subscription method, with 'Drummond' in gold letters on the back. There were more copies of these, perhaps, than it would be quite thoughtful to count, though a good many were annually disposed of at the church bazaar, where the Doctor presented them with a generous hand.

The principle behind Duncan's realism is that profound truths are manifest in commonplace things. Given this charging of detail, it is reasonable to interpret this passage as an overall judgment of the Dominion of Canada as a whole. It was a place where the canonical authors of the English-speaking world dominated the shelves in the uniform series of large international publishers, and the only locally published books were ones printed and bound at self-sacrificial expense by the author and his or her friends.

1 Conceiving the 1875 Act, 1868–72: The Principles of Copyright

The Canadian Copyright Act of 1875 promised literary nationhood. What it delivered, however, was a perplexing complication of literary property. It did not encourage the independent publishing industry or the national literature that many Canadians expected as the corollary of Confederation; instead, it amounted to a minor tool with which London publishers might increase their control over the circulation of books in a place that remained, in this respect, a mere colony, albeit a contested one. Its local proponents initially hoped that it would position Canada to produce cheap books for the vast anglophone markets of North America and the British Empire, thereby founding a profitable book manufacturing industry that in due course would naturally take on original publishing. However, along the way it was diverted towards a quite different goal – consolidating the existing publishing centre in London – and although it failed to encourage Canadian industry, it remained in force for fifty years. Its long obsolescence marked the Dominion of Canada as a place where, despite ardent desires to the contrary, original book publishing would not take root.

The origin of this ambivalent act is anything but bland. Its tortuous legislative history reveals a host of compelling perspectives on the vexed issue of property in language, each activated by a different principle. The property and livelihood of authors, the unrestrictive social essence of language, the education of the populace, and the development of regional industry all exerted magnetic influence on the evolution of Canada's first federal copyright law. But the issue inevitably boiled down to one question, which remains at the heart of the intellectual property debate today: is it justifiable to reproduce a text without the permission of its author? Depending on the circumstances of the case and the principles invoked, the answer varies, and it is instructive to observe how legislators and businesses have dealt with it in the past. In this case, the clash of interests eventuated in a subtle if not deceptive statute that paraded as a compromise but in fact served one party (the London publishers) under whose influence the act took its final form, while disappointing another (the Canadian printers) at whose instance the reform was begun.

The nineteenth-century Canadian book trade evolved under peculiar circumstances. As part of the British Empire, the colonies that would become Canada were implicitly subject to British copyright law, which prohibited the unauthorized reprinting of British works. However, those colonies were also uniquely close to the United States, where printers and booksellers had been free to ignore British copyright since the American Revolution. This proximity was geographic: most Canadians of European descent lived in a thin strip of settlement stretched out along the American border, their cities often lying closer to it than to each other. The proximity was also cultural: Canadian anglophones spoke the language of their neighbours, oriented themselves equally towards Protestantism, shared their pioneer history, their democratic spirit, and in many cases their ancestry, and in the realm of modern literature both Americans and Canadians overwhelmingly acknowledged the pre-eminence of British authors past and present. Combined, these conditions made British North America a ready market for American books, especially American editions of British authors. The printing industry flourished in the United States in the early nineteenth century, and a mass reading public emerged. At the heart of these twin developments lay the cheap, unauthorized reprint, which from the beginning spread north to the loyal colonies, such that already by the 1830s American imports and the popular literacy they entailed were so common that colonial bookselling had more or less organized itself around them.[1] So the chief peculiarity was this: from its origin Canada did not print unauthorized copies of British authors' works, but it did import and sell them. It was, and it was not, under the thumb of British copyright.

This importation became unequivocally illegal after the passage of the imperial Copyright Act of 1842, which explicitly extended British copyright through all the colonies, banning the printing, commercial importation, and sale of unauthorized copies of works first published in the United Kingdom.[2] However, the practice was so widespread and the social benefits of cheap editions so palpable that the colonies, led by

Nova Scotia in 1845, petitioned the British government to change the new law. One argument that hit home was that, new books from London being as expensive as they were, British North Americans would absorb the moral and political values of the contemporary British author through the cheap reprint or not at all. In other words, if the 1842 act were enforced, it would prevent the colonists from reading American editions of British authors, leaving them only American editions of American authors, along with the seditious anti-monarchism that these might contain, while British editions of British authors would remain out of reach because of price. The London publisher John Murray did launch a cheap series for the colonies in the wake of the 1842 act at the urging of William Ewart Gladstone, then vice-president of the Board of Trade, but the initiative failed to oust the American reprint from its niche because of Murray's obligation to authors, his higher (transatlantic) shipping costs, his ignorance of the colonial market, and the lack of incentives for colonies to enforce the ban on reprints. Not long after its inception Murray abandoned this attempt to retake the overseas market and reoriented the series toward readers in the United Kingdom instead.[3] It was also a plain fact that the northern American states were ahead of the British North American colonies economically, and the freer circulation of knowledge seemed largely responsible for their obvious superiority in education, industry, and commerce.[4]

In 1847, under pressure from the colonies, the British government passed the Foreign Reprints Act,[5] which legalized the importation of unauthorized reprints of a British author's work into a British colony as long as that colony instituted some measure to protect the copyright owner. In 1848, Nova Scotia, New Brunswick, and Prince Edward Island each created an import duty of 20 per cent; it was to be levied on reprints of British copyright works entering the colony and then transferred to the British government, who would see that it be paid to the copyright owner. When the British government had approved this measure by Order in Council (a necessary procedure spelled out by the act), the flow of American reprints into those colonies resumed with new legality. Newfoundland followed suit in 1849. As for the Province of Canada, it initially tried the bolder move of legitimating local reprinting instead, but the Foreign Reprints Act had specifically allowed only for 'importing, selling, letting out to hire, exposing for Sale or Hire, or possessing Foreign Reprints' – not making them – and this audacious attempt at reform failed. In 1850 the Province of Canada settled for a duty ('not exceeding twenty per centum' but soon set at 12.5 per cent), and importing unauthorized reprints became legal there too.[6] Now the peculiarity was enshrined in legislation.

On the one hand, the Foreign Reprints Act was a blessing for colonial readers. It gave them access to the best literature of Europe at low prices. From the novels of Dickens and Thackeray to the discoveries of German biblical criticism, the latest developments in European thought rapidly communicated themselves to British North America thanks to the cheap American reprint. If there was any obstacle to their absorption into colonial society (Canadians were not quick to embrace Darwinism, for example), it was not economic. Affordable American editions of British, French, and German authors were omnipresent. Reviews in periodicals, advertisements by booksellers, library catalogues of literary societies and colleges, and auction lists of private collections all bear witness to the overwhelming presence of American books in the colonies from the 1850s on.[7] That British North America prospered to the extent that it did must in part be ascribed to the availability of books – and not merely the classics but also the latest advances in learning and culture. Even when, in the 1870s, Canada was striving to reform copyright in the interest of its publishing sector, it could not bring itself to deactivate the Foreign Reprints Act, so obvious were the advantages of cheap access to new works.

On the other hand, major problems attended the operation of the act. As before, it was up to individual customs officers to sort through small, frequent shipments in order to identify reprints of British copyright works, but the lists they had to work from were only published at intervals, and many imports could slip through before the officers were aware of a copyright. Even if reprints were detected, the importer often chose to abandon that particular shipment rather than pay the duty, expecting that the next shipment would slip through unnoticed.[8] The amount of foreign-reprint duty actually collected never amounted to much. Between 1851 and 1855, the Province of Canada imported £390,470 worth of books from the United States but collected only £456 14s. in duty. The duty did not apply to all American books, of course; some were not reprints. Nevertheless, the amount collected was an absurd sliver of what it should have been – it was nothing near 12.5 per cent – and it shrank even further after the Canadian customs had subtracted its administrative expenses.[9] The British Treasury then had the tedious task of distributing this pittance proportionally among the myriad copyright owners, a task rendered more difficult by the lack in some cases of sufficiently detailed records of whose work had been imported.[10] If the colonies were remiss in enforcing the duty, they also had little incentive to do so. Unlike other duties, it was not revenue for the colonial government and did not protect colonial industry. Of all the problems associated with the act, however, the one that would prove most aggravating was its delivering of the colonial market to the American publisher. Among British publishers interested in imperial sales and among colonial printers desirous of becoming publishers dissatisfaction smouldered.

The formation of the Dominion of Canada in 1867 reignited the issue. The British North America Act listed copyright among the items falling under the jurisdiction of the new federal parliament. This inclusion initially excited little interest; it merely continued the power previously enjoyed by each colony to govern the printing of works first published there, classifying this copyright in local works henceforth as a federal rather than a provincial concern. Still, in not differentiating between works first published in Canada and those first published in Britain, the 1867 act exposed itself to another interpretation, which would increasingly take hold – that Canada was free to set its own policy touching copyright in all works, regardless of the place of first publication:

> It shall be lawful for the Queen, by and with the Advice and Consent of the Senate and House of Commons, to make Laws for the Peace, Order, and good Government of *Canada*, in relation to all Matters not coming within the Classes of Subjects by this Act assigned exclusively to the Legislatures of the Provinces; and for greater Certainty, but not so as to restrict the Generality of the foregoing Terms of this Section, it is hereby declared that (notwithstanding anything in this Act) the exclusive Legislative Authority of the Parliament of *Canada* extends to all Matters coming within the Classes of Subjects next herein-after enumerated; that is to say, – . . . 23. Copyrights.[11]

The precise meaning of this clause would be much debated. Although those who passed the 1867 act could hardly have contemplated an abrupt break from imperial copyright, the notion among Canadians that their country ought to be as self-governing in copyright as it was in tariffs, taxation, and patents would increasingly solidify around this strongly worded passage of the constitution.

Desire for sovereignty fuelled the legislative struggle that would follow. What immediately sparked it, however, was the mundane matter of reactivating the Foreign Reprints Act. Much of the work of the first parliament consisted in updating and harmonizing for the Dominion the several old laws of the colonies, and in April 1868 the government turned to copyright. Two bills were introduced. The first, identical to that passed by the Province of Canada in 1850, imposed a duty on foreign reprints; the second, the proposed Canadian Copyright Act, defined copyright for the Dominion of Canada and set up a structure to administer it. Both would pass and receive royal assent on 22 May.[12]

This legislative housekeeping, however routine, was enough to provoke a re-examination of the peculiarity of copyright in Canada. In the Senate, the first bill caught the attention of Thomas Ryan, vice-president of the Bank of Montreal and a future director of the Dominion Type Foundry, who as the Member for Montreal represented Canada's leading literary printer of the day, John Lovell.[13] With acuity Ryan explained the drawback of letting foreign reprints into Canada under a duty now that the domestic printing industry was flourishing: doing so alienated Canadian printers from the substantial profits to be made on the sale of British literature in Canada, diverting those profits instead through Canadian booksellers to American publishers. He therefore moved that the Senate address the Governor General 'to impress upon Her Majesty's Government the justice and expediency of extending the privileges granted by the above cited Act [the Foreign Reprints Act], so that whenever reasonable provision and protection shall, in Her Majesty's opinion, be secured to the authors, colonial reprints of British copyright works shall be placed on the same footing as foreign reprints in Canada, by which means British authors will be more effectually protected in their rights, and a material benefit will be conferred on the printing industry of the Dominion.'[14] In other words, the address requested that the British government allow Canadians not only to import and sell but also to produce unauthorized reprints of British copyright works.

Ryan was well informed. He understood that the prohibition against reprinting stemmed from an imperial statute and that the shortest route forward therefore lay through the imperial parliament; any Canadian bill attempting to legitimate reprinting would run afoul of the 1842 act. He did not propose an abolition of British copyright. What he hoped to implement was a duty on reprinting to match the current duty on importing. Under this scheme Canadian printers would reprint British copyright works without permission but pay a royalty to the author. This would at last liberate them to supply the domestic demand for books of general literature. The costs of production being cheaper in

Canada than in the post-bellum United States, it would also enable them to export their reprints to the American market. Since these copies would be taxed at the point of production (within the empire) rather than at the point of sale, British authors stood to gain substantial new revenue on the American sales of their work, in addition to the ad hoc courtesy payments that some of them currently received from American publishers in exchange for advance sheets.[15] The scheme was cleverly devised to encourage Canadian printing and publishing while remunerating the British author, and it realistically envisioned industrial development in the context of continental competition; after all, those in the business knew that when it came to general literature, anglophone North America was essentially one book market.

Debate flared up on the necessity of an address. On one side, Alexander Campbell and Jonathan McCully approved of Ryan's circumspect approach, agreeing that the Dominion probably had no power to alter the nature of British copyright in Canada. On the other, John Sewell Sanborn, Ulric-Joseph Tessier, and Robert Duncan Wilmot argued that Confederation had rendered Canada sovereign in all matters of copyright and that unilateral legislation was therefore preferable. Nationalist independence waxed strongest in the words of the Liberal, American-born Sanborn, the Member for Wellington and a former annexationist: 'Are we to minimise our powers into a mere municipality having only the powers delegated to us by the strict terms of the Union Act, or are we to be considered as something almost approaching to a nation, having power to legislate upon whatever would benefit our people if not adverse to the sovereignty of Great Britain ... We have full powers given us in the 91st Section of the Union Act to legislate upon this subject, direct and specific, but we have approached it from a wrong stand point.'[16] Rashness and passion are at play here. Sanborn did not comprehend the issue in its details. He was animated by a simple indignation that a law might be tolerated that sacrificed Canadian industry to protect British authors, not to mention foreign publishers. In this he was essentially in agreement with Ryan. His speech bears citing as a raw manifestation of what persistently drove Canadian efforts at nineteenth-century copyright reform, namely, the inextinguishable interest in a national publishing industry. However negligible to those elsewhere, the prospect of Canadian publishing was indispensable to Canadians.

The Senate endorsed Ryan's address, and the Governor General, Charles Stanley Monck, wrote to the British government accordingly, enclosing the new acts. The Colonial Office issued the requisite Order in Council, reapproving the 12.5 per cent duty. At the Board of Trade (the department responsible for overseeing copyright policy) the undersecretary, Thomas Henry Farrer, grumbled at this rubber-stamping, doubting Canada's sincerity in enforcing the duty, and questioning its rate: 'But assuming that the power to do a thing coupled with a promise to do it are sufficient, the question of substance remains, viz. whether 12 ½ per cent duty upon Foreign reprints of English books is sufficient to protect the copyright.' He did not obstruct the process nor did he speed it, and as for the address from the Senate, it made hardly a ripple. The Board's letter to the Colonial Office merely remarked that more information was necessary before the question of copyright in Canada could be dealt with properly.[17]

Meanwhile, John Lovell wrote to the Canadian minister of finance, John Rose, urging him to press for the desired reform. His arguments were essentially those presented by Ryan in the Senate, but the letter to Rose sheds more light on the situation. The newly amalgamated Canadian market, suddenly comprising 'nearly three millions of English-speaking people,' was significant and would only grow as the Dominion expanded from one sea to the other. Given this size, Lovell asked 'whether it is not now desirable for the English publishers to produce copyrights in this country independent of the editions emanating from home presses.' This was the perspective of a printer, not a rival publisher. Canada being big enough to support a domestic book manufacturing industry, Lovell hoped that British publishers would begin to engage Canadian printers like himself to supply the Canadian public non-competitively with respect to each text. He did not wish for a legal hiatus in which anyone might steal a British author's work; what he wanted was reasonable industrial growth. The problem was that Canadian printing was haemorrhaging. Lifting the prohibition against reprinting 'would have the happy effect of bringing back a large number of our skilled workmen who have been forced to leave the Dominion to find a remunerative field of labour. Indeed it is not too much to say, that as things are at present, our very best compositors are constantly leaving with a view to improving their condition on the other side of the line. This is a most serious evil, which can only be remedied by a removal of the disabilities under which the Dominion publishing interest languishes.'[18] This revelation touched a nerve. The constant loss of skilled labour to the United States was a grave matter, one that threatened the very future of Canada.

In John Rose, the Canadian movement for copyright reform acquired its best ally. Besides being a member of John A. Macdonald's Cabinet and a seasoned man of business, he was a gifted consensus-builder who approached opponents with grace, spoke to the point, and eschewed polemic. In June 1868 he sailed for London, his chief business being the settlement of claims related to the transfer of Oregon to the United States, but Lovell's letter was in his pocket. At the Colonial Office he left a memorandum entitled 'Canadian Copyright,' in which he explained the address from the Senate and proposed a system of licensed Canadian reprinting. In its first breath the memorandum anticipates the objection that Canada would oversee the licensing as negligently as it had the import duty. Rose specified that 'effectual practical checks should be interposed, so that the duty on the number of copies actually issued from the press should be paid into the Canadian Government by such publishers for the benefit of the author.'[19] Here was an invitation to govern. A policy that effectively channelled American money through Canadian books to British authors would go a long way in solving the problems of the Foreign Reprints Act.

Forwarded to the Board of Trade, Rose's memorandum touched off a serious discussion. The secretary, Louis Mallet, immediately saw a full-blown conflict; unauthorized reproduction, whether licensed or not, was at odds with the old principle of copyright as a form of property. Quite apart from the theory behind it, the principle was functional: like other matters of property, copyright disputes were settled through private action in a civil court, the onus of prosecution lying with the aggrieved individual, not the government. This was the principle that Britain was pursuing in its international copyright treaties, and it could not well abandon property in texts in the empire while insisting on it in foreign countries.

However, Mallet knew that this principle was far from immanent. The Foreign Reprints Act had 'seriously compromised' it: 'it may be argued that it is too late to assert this principle in its integrity + that it is better to correct an undoubted anomaly which springs from that arrangement, viz. that the U.S. publishers are protected against those of the N.A. Provinces.' He disliked the contingency of Rose's proposal – if American reprints were the true problem, the solution was not to adapt to them but to sweep them away with a copyright treaty – but he was sensitive to Canada's plight. Moreover, Mallet was not sure that the unauthorized reprint was a problem. After all, the high price of books in Britain was deplorable: 'It seems to me a great injustice to the British Public to give a sanction to any arrangement which places the reading public in a foreign country, or in a British Possession in a better position than the countrymen of the author. – If we cannot enforce an equal protection it is a subject of regret, but if we allow (in cases where it can be prevented) the publication of British works on payment of 12 ½ p. cent, or any other small sum, surely it is time to revise our domestic Copyright Laws – + this is the result to which, I think, the question now raised directly points.'[20]

What is striking here is Mallet's willingness to entertain a new basis for copyright. A proponent of free trade, he was not sure that society benefited from treating texts as property, even for a limited time. If the price of new books was highest where that sense of property was most entrenched, surely the public would prosper if the author's control over publication were reduced. Perhaps it was time to reconceive of copyright in its entirety, establishing it on more liberal grounds and steering the force of British policy, weighted though it was with foreign, imperial, and domestic ramifications, towards better promoting the circulation of literature through all classes. Perceiving a fundamental conflict between the principles of property and productivity in literature, Mallet suggested that a parliamentary committee be struck to evaluate the matter. The seeds of the Royal Commission on Copyright, which would take place in the following decade, are visible here, and the fact that it was soon struck indicates that Mallet was not the only one willing to cut to the bone. Indeed, his reflections on the principles of copyright were connected to a larger debate in mid-Victorian Britain over patents. Inspired by laissez-faire economics, a movement to abolish property altogether in inventions had been gathering momentum since the 1850s, and it hit its zenith in 1868 when Gladstone and the Liberals swept to power. Many in the new parliament, such as the Scottish industrialist Robert A. Macfie, were eager to dismantle what they regarded as bureaucratic obstacles to discovery and commerce, and they might have succeeded were it not for the defeat of the Liberals in 1874.[21] Mallet's comments on Rose's memorandum thus drew strength from what was by then a crescendo of opposition against proprietary restrictions in science.

In response, Undersecretary Farrer cautioned, 'It may be a very good thing to substitute for the present system of Copyright, a sort of Royalty payable to the Author. But this would be a great change in the practice of the whole civilized world + would require much ventilation + discussion.' For the time being, then, it was agreed that pursuing a treaty with the United States was the best way forward. In its official reply to the Senate address, dated 22 July, the Board of Trade rejected the proposal of licensed Canadian reprinting.[22]

Seven months elapsed. A new Governor General, John Young, Baron Lisgar, was installed in February 1869, and the Montreal Typographical Union lost no time in alerting him to the problems of the Foreign Reprints Act. On 25 February, Lisgar's office forwarded the Board's letter to the Canadian government, and John Rose promptly gave it his attention. His reply took the form of a second memorandum, entitled 'Copyright Law in Canada.'[23] It was a piercing analysis that met the Board's concerns point for point and added information that had not yet been considered. The Board feared that sanctioning the exportation of cheap Canadian reprints to the United States would provoke the Americans, cancelling all hope for a copyright treaty. Rose replied that, on the contrary, Canadian reprints would powerfully induce the Americans to come to terms. If they not only lost the Canadian market but also felt the threat of being undersold at home, they would rapidly move to embrace international copyright. As for the central objection, that unauthorized reprinting represented a serious departure from the principle of property in texts, Rose admitted it. The measure that he was proposing was a necessary corrective to the Foreign Reprints Act, which was itself a departure from that principle, and it should last no longer than the act itself: 'The exceptional legislation, it is to be observed, is only meant to be temporary and provisional, in other words, to be in force so long, and only so long, as the exceptional legislation which gives rise to it.' The conclusion of a treaty with the United States would dispel Canada's need to combat the unauthorized American reprint, and Rose joined the British government in looking forward to that eventuality.

The sale of American reprints in Canada was not the only problem, however. Rose's second memorandum bored deeper into imperial copyright, discovering profound flaws and biases. One, clarified by the recent ruling of the House of Lords in *Routledge v. Low*,[24] was the granting of imperial copyright to the American author. By virtue of publishing first in the United Kingdom, any author, regardless of nationality, could obtain the protection of the 1842 act. American law, of course, did not reciprocate. The result was that, while the United States could reprint Canadian editions with impunity, imperial copyright prevented Canada from retaliating. Given this unrequited generosity to the American author, Rose could not help but wonder whether any inducement remained to draw the United States into an international copyright treaty.

Yet another problem, also brought into relief by *Routledge v. Low,* was that Canadian editions did not qualify for imperial copyright. The 1842 act, informed by mercantilism, was designed to concentrate book production in Britain and to make the rest of the empire a vast export market. To this end, it withheld imperial copyright from works originally published in a British possession overseas. First publication had to occur in the United Kingdom. Original Canadian editions were thus exposed to unauthorized reprinting not only in the United States but also in Britain and the other colonies. Joseph Howe of Halifax, Nova Scotia, had discovered the lack of imperial protection for colonial editions as early as 1837, when he published *The Clockmaker* by Thomas Chandler Haliburton and then looked on as the London publisher, Richard Bentley, reprinted it without permission.[25] Rather than redress such injustice, the 1842 act had entrenched it.

In pointing out these problems, Rose moved past the principle of property and touched the rationale of copyright: 'If the policy of England, in relation to copyright, is to stimulate, by means of the protection secured to literary labour, the composition of works of learning and utility, that policy is not incompatible with such a modification of law as will place the colonial publisher on a footing of equality not only with the publisher in the United States, but even with the publisher of the United Kingdom.' In other words, if the ultimate purpose of copyright was not to engender property but to reward intellectual achievement and creativity, Britain ought to let Canadian publishing develop on a fair and level basis; as things stood, the law left it at a fatal disadvantage in both the North American context and within the empire. Regional development called for better governance than this. With a mastery of the details and a moderate tone, Rose succeeded in fleshing out the importance of the possibility of Canadian literature: 'But while the present copyright law thus operates in effect as a tax upon the reading public in Canada, without securing any countervailing advantage to the British author, it is felt, by those directly interested, to bear with especial severity on the printing and publishing interests here – interests not only large and in themselves important, but equally so perhaps in their connection with the development and growth of literary talent and pursuits in the Dominion.' Beginning with the Foreign Reprints Act (a 'tax' in the sense that it protected American reprints in Canada when Canadian books could have been produced more cheaply), the government would have to lift the impediments to local publishing in order for invention, discovery, community, and self-knowledge to flourish in the Dominion. Canada needed to be more than a market; it needed the material infrastructure for producing literature.

Rose's second memorandum stirred the Board of Trade to action. Mallet and Farrer continued to disapprove of the 'temporizing expedient' of licensed reprinting – in Mallet's words, 'a thing cannot be right in Canada + wrong in England' – and insisted that a treaty with the United States was the best solution. Moreover, the necessity of coordinating imperial and foreign policy remained plain. Mallet reiterated the 'rank absurdity of claiming protection for our authors in the U. States + other Foreign countries, when we at the same time throw them over in our own Colonies.'[26] Farrer also thoroughly researched the origin of the Foreign Reprints Act in order to exonerate the Board of Trade. The colonies, not the British government, were responsible for the departure from principle in 1847. However, Rose's criticism of the mercantilism of imperial copyright was unanswerable, and Mallet and Farrer agreed that this injustice should be remedied at once: 'we ought to remove everything which can be complained of as a relic of the unjust system under which England formerly imposed restrictions on the Colonies in the protective spirit + for the benefit of her own producers. That the refusal to allow the Colonial publisher to enter the List against the London publisher is a restriction of this kind can hardly be doubted. It is a restriction which does no good either to British authors or to British readers + it ought to be removed.'[27] In a long letter to the Colonial Office, the Board explained its reasons for rejecting licensed Canadian reprinting but recommended that the Foreign Office promptly reopen negotiations with the United States; it also recommended that the government immediately draft legislation to grant imperial copyright to colonial publications, a purpose that was soon embodied in the 1870 bill.[28]

The Board presented a united front, but in fact it was in turmoil. Rose's exposure of vestigial protectionism in British colonial policy deeply unsettled Mallet, and he saw the conferring of imperial copyright on colonial books as an opportunity to advance a more liberal imperial system, one aimed at free trade and unrestricted competition among producers throughout the empire. Opening the imperial market to Canadian printers and publishers would extend a benefit to them – not the one they were intent on, but a benefit nonetheless – and this overture might be enough to appease them; more important, it would bring cheap Canadian editions to Britain.[29] In its first draft the Board's letter to the Colonial Office outlined Mallet's plan to make new books more accessible to the British public. Granting imperial copyright to Canadian editions 'might considerably reduce the price of books in the U.K.':

> It is stated, in the Memo. of the Canadian Minister of Finance, that a Canadian publisher could undersell the piratical reprints of English copyrighted works, even if he were obliged to pay 12 ½ p.c. to the author. As above stated my Lords think this to be doubtful. But it is the case [that] it is probable that the Canadian publisher if he had the right of publishing works entitled to copyright in the U.K. + in all the British Possessions, would be able to give more than 12 ½ % to the author + yet undersell the London publisher. In any case the competition of the publishers in the colonies would have a salutary effect on the publishers in the United Kingdom, and both the authors + publishers of the United Kingdom might be compensated to a certain extent for any diminution in their present profits, by securing in Canada + other colonies, a powerful producing class interested in the due enforcement of the Copyright Laws, where they are now a dead letter. But the really essential question is the interest of the public, i.e. the consumer, and this my Lords think would probably be promoted by the proposed change.

To provide British readers with cheaper books was Mallet's goal, but exposing the London publisher to greater competition appeared too bold a means to another secretary at the Board, George John Shaw-Lefevre. Shaw-Lefevre struck the above sentences from the draft, objecting, 'I do not myself believe that the Canadian publisher will undersell the English publisher on any terms which he can arrange with the author.' Mallet retorted that indeed he would and by 'a fortune': 'if the extension of the area of competition does not cheapen the price, it will be contrary to all experience.' He excoriated Shaw-Lefevre's automatic defence of the British publisher: 'Why did the British Publishers who have made our Copyright Laws, reserve the role of Publication to themselves? Clearly because they thought it was their interest – + for the same reason, it is the interest of the Public that they should not retain it.'[30] Yet prudence advised against rousing the lion, and the final draft of the letter, signed by Shaw-Lefevre, omitted all reference to Mallet's plan.

The lion, however, was already awake. The London publishers had learned that Canadian copyright reform was afoot and had chosen one among them, Frederic Richard Daldy, to keep an eye on it. In late spring of 1869 Daldy travelled to Ottawa, where he enquired into Canada's intentions and was directed to Rose. On 23 June, in a circular addressed to the Canadian finance minister, Daldy aired his views on the printing of British copyright works in Canada.[31] The document appears to begin practically, spelling out the conditions on which a new Canadian copyright act could be acceptable. The 12.5 per cent import duty would have to be abolished, which would deactivate the Foreign Reprints Act; every copy of a Canadian edition of a British copyright work would have to bear a government stamp and include the words *Colonial Edition* on the title page; the licensed Canadian printer would have to pay 10 per cent on every copy produced before any left his shop; and so forth. Partway through, it becomes clear that Daldy is not discussing unauthorized reprinting at all. One of the conditions is 'that nothing in this Act be held to modify the duration of Copyright, which a British Author possesses in the Colonies under Imperial Act or Acts.' In other words, imperial copyright would continue in Canada with unmitigated force, and a ponderous licensing scheme for authorized Canadian editions would be heaped on top of it so that, if an author did allow a Canadian printer to produce cheap copies, they could effectively be kept out of the United Kingdom. The London publishers had no interest in countenancing a more liberal book trade, whether that entailed reprinting as Rose wished or free markets as Mallet envisioned; indeed, the first condition in Daldy's list reveals that their abiding motive was to find a way of cancelling the Foreign Reprints Act. When at last the Canadian Copyright Act of 1875 passed, it would deliver precisely this.

In the winter of 1869–70, the British government acted on the two recommendations of the Board of Trade. Edward Thornton, the British minister in Washington, drafted a copyright convention and submitted it to Hamilton Fish, the American secretary of state. Fish's response was discouraging. While American authors approved of the draft, leading publishers such as Appleton and the Harpers vigorously opposed it, predicting that it would deliver the American market into the hands of the London publisher and raise the price of books.[32]

The other recommendation, the extension of imperial copyright to original colonial editions, was uncontroversial in itself but fell prey to extraneous complications. By March 1870 the Board of Trade had drawn up a concise bill centred on this reform, the key clause stating simply that books first published in a British possession would now enjoy the same protection under the 1842 act as those first published in the United Kingdom. The Colonial Office approved, adding that the colonial publication should be registered at Stationers' Hall.[33] However, a letter from the London publishers Thomas Longman and John Murray to the prime minister, William Gladstone, derailed the bill. Proceeding from a meeting of authors and publishers that had taken place at Murray's office at 50 Albemarle Street on 16 March, the letter rehearsed the 'excessive' injury inflicted on British copyright owners by the Foreign Reprints Act; in reaction to *Routledge v. Low* the letter also criticized the lack of imperial copyright for British authors who first published their work in a colony. Charles Dickens, Anthony Trollope, F.R. Daldy, D. Roberton Blaine, Murray, Longman, and seven others present at the meeting put their names to two resolutions – that the act be repealed and that original colonial editions be granted imperial copyright.[34] The second, of course, coincided perfectly with the 1870 bill, and when Gladstone forwarded the letter to the Board of Trade, Farrer expressed satisfaction on this point. The first, however, was a separate and much more tangled issue. Nevertheless, at the beginning of April the Board changed course, deciding to yoke the two issues together. Farrer perceived that 'the concurrence of the British publishers + authors greatly facilitates the passing of our Bill. But their concurrence is no doubt conditional on the repeal of the Act of 1847.'[35] The Board thus adopted the strategy of achieving one reform through another: 'it is proposed by the Bill now under consideration to place the Colonies on the same footing as the United Kingdom with respect to publication, and as Canada will therefore obtain all the advantages of Imperial copyright, it is only right that she should accept its restrictions.'[36] What began as a straightforward matter of justice to the colonies was diverted down a different path.

This episode reveals an underlying problem in the structure of governance through which the matter had to pass. Although the British government genuinely wrestled with the justice of copyright, finally it was not equally responsible to all interested parties. One constituency, the London publishers, was represented in the parliament at Westminster and therefore exercised electoral power over the government; another, the Canadian printers, was not. At the end of the day, the former possessed a disproportionate influence in determining legislation that thoroughly affected both. Mallet, believing in Britain's ability to govern an empire, saw intelligent policy as the solution and fretted at its absence. 'Our relations with our Colonies are in a very confused state,' he lamented from the beginning. 'No attempt seems to have been made in endowing them generally speaking, with what is called "self-government," to define in a consistent + intelligible principle the limits of Imperial + Provincial power.'[37] He desired transparent rules and fair play for the whole empire; otherwise, the British parliament, representing only the United Kingdom, could not justifiably retain authority over the matter. The fundamental problem was one of sovereignty and governance.

The 1870 bill ended in a stalemate. In June the colonial secretary, Earl Granville, sent out two circulars to the governors of the colonies, soliciting views on the contemplated reforms.[38] Francis Hincks, the new Canadian finance minister, embraced the 1870 bill but immediately objected to repealing the Foreign Reprints Act: if the two were coupled, Canada would prefer no legislation at all. The other colonies replied variously, most, including Prince Edward Island and Newfoundland, offering little substantial comment. British Columbia observed that registration and deposit in the United Kingdom would be onerous given the distant location of some colonies. Ceylon, having no local copyright law, desired a uniform one for the whole empire. Bermuda, benefiting from the books it had from New York, protested that 'theoretical or legal protection to the British copyright owner in Bermuda implies little short of the exclusion of modern English literature from these islands.'[39] As late as May of the following year the Board of Trade was still considering the 1870 bill. 'I am satisfied that the only course to take under present circum[stance]s, is to submit the Bill which has been prepared to Parliament + repeal the Act of 1847 – leaving Canada to deal as she pleases with pirated editions – + those who deal in them to the legal consequences,' wrote Mallet with evident fatigue.[40] But the bill never escaped the toxic debate over the act, and it was never introduced.

During its terminal suspension, a new idea sprang up – concurrent publication. In November 1870, Hincks and Christopher Dunkin, the Canadian agriculture minister, expatiated on Hincks's reply to the circulars in a full memorandum. It began with a memorable summary of the impasse: 'The important point at issue, and on which the views of the London publishers, and of the people, both of Canada and the United States are irreconcileable [sic], is that the former insist upon the extension of copyright without local publication, and to this the latter will never consent.'[41] The memorandum then sketched out a solution that comprehended the sundry interests at play. One measure, in view of the unlikelihood of a copyright treaty with the United States, proposed noticeably raising the import duty on foreign reprints of British copyright works. Another addressed the British publisher's discontent with the Foreign Reprints Act by proposing that Canadian booksellers be obliged to declare the imperial-copyright status of all imports. The third and fourth proposals sought to encourage Canadian printing by absolutely prohibiting the importation of reprints of Canadian copyright works and, most interestingly, by allowing unauthorized reprinting if, and only if, a British author failed to publish concurrently in Canada. In their words, 'any author publishing in Canada should be, as at present, protected in his copyright, but . . . unless British copyright works should be published concurrently in Canada, licensed Canadian publishers should be allowed to publish, paying, for the benefit of the author or owner of the English copyright, an Excise duty, which could be collected by means of stamps as easily as other duties of a similar kind.' Hincks and Dunkin thus crafted a solution that recognized authorial property to some extent but insisted on local development. They were careful to distinguish between the British author, who deserved a profit from Canadian sales, and the British publisher, whose interest must come second to that of the local publisher. They hoped that the plan would yield 'great advantage to the English authors' but concluded, 'It is true that British publishers would not gain that Colonial circulation which they have long tried to obtain without success; but it is vain for them to expect that the expensive editions published in England can meet a sale in any part of the American continent.' Hincks and Dunkin's memorandum, particularly the suggestion of concurrent publication, would considerably influence the British government's next attempt at legislation.

The idea intrigued the Board of Trade. Although Mallet wondered whether it would be practical or applicable to the whole empire, he was open to it: 'I do not know what may be the force of the practical objection to the plan of simultaneous publication, but I do not see any serious infringement of principle involved − + I should prefer it to the alternative [unauthorized reprinting] proposed by Canada.'[42] He therefore turned to the London publishers for their opinion of its feasibility, forwarding Hincks and Dunkin's memorandum.

The publishers evidently consulted, for John Murray's long and measured reply, dated 8 March, spoke on behalf of Thomas Longman. Murray rehearsed his dissatisfaction with the Foreign Reprints Act and objected to Hincks and Dunkin's disregard for the sanctity of property, but expressed willingness to consider Canadian editions of British copyright works. They would have to be authorized, and they would have to be kept out of the United Kingdom: 'As we have to pay large sums for the

Copyright and production of our books, we are obliged to publish here at such prices as will reimburse us. It is therefore of the deepest importance to the preservation of our property from utter ruin that we should continue to retain the entire dominion over it, + especially to prevent Colonial or other cheap *reprints* from being imported to the ruin of the original editions.'[43] If British publishing in its present form would not be ruffled by new competition in the home market, Murray had no objection to concurrent publication in Canada or elsewhere. He appended to his letter a proposed amendment to the 1842 act – a single clause that would have classified colonial editions as foreign reprints in order to ban them from the United Kingdom. The same amendment arrived in a letter from Roberton Blaine the next day.[44] Mallet, of course, opposed such protectionism. When he pressed Longman on whether concurrent publication might be made obligatory for a British author desiring copyright in Canada, Longman answered with some irritation that this would amount to a 'confiscation,' a 'grievous injustice,' and a 'most dangerous precedent of national wrong.' Mandatory concurrent publication would not work, according to Longman, because printing a Canadian edition at the same time as the original would be cumbersome, and only very popular works would be worth this effort. Other works would lose their copyright in Canada before their value could be known, and unauthorized Canadian reprints would flood the United Kingdom, destroying the copyright there too.

Longman went on to vent his frustration, lashing out at Canadians who criticized the mercantilism of imperial copyright. The existing rules were not biased in favour of the London publisher, he claimed. All a Canadian publisher had to do was offer an author the best price for his or her manuscript and then publish it first in the United Kingdom. 'In the mean time,' Longman continued, sardonically quoting the French anarchists, 'permit me to observe I am at a loss to see how a Canadian, or any other British publisher, can justly be said to be at an "unfair advantage [i.e., disadvantage] as compared with the English publisher" unless the maxim is to be adopted, that *"toute propriété est le vol."*'[45] Given his own unwillingness to produce books on the other side of the Atlantic, this defence of the status quo is questionable. For a time, however, the publishers' forceful objections swayed the Board to shelve the idea of concurrent publication. 'This is a case in which compromise is very difficult,' Mallet despaired, falling back to half-hearted support for the 1870 bill.[46]

By now the various parties in the struggle for imperial copyright reform had expressed themselves fully, and their positions were entrenched. In Canada, Thomas Ryan continued to pressure the government from his seat in the Senate. In April 1869 he demanded that all government correspondence on the issue since his address of the previous year be made public. This request could not pry internal documents out of the British government, but it did lead to the printing of letters received by the Canadian government, including Lovell's letter and Rose's two memoranda. The next month he presented two more petitions (in addition to that of the Montreal Typographical Union to the Governor General) asking for the legalization of Canadian reprinting – one from William Workman and 2,400 citizens of Montreal and the other from James Thompson and the Typographical Union of Saint John, New Brunswick.[47] A new request to see correspondence in March 1870 brought to light the British government's promise to grant imperial copyright to colonial publications, and Ryan asked after the 1870 bill in May.[48] In February 1871 he rehearsed the issue again from the beginning, laying particular emphasis on one point: although the Foreign Reprints Act had been 'a great boon,' it was now badly out of date because the Canadian printing industry had developed rapidly and – if permitted – could now print British literature more cheaply than it could be imported: 'Our progress in that particular industry forced upon us the anomaly of a foreign country being permitted to supply us with a class of literature which we could produce more cheaply ourselves, and with greater advantage to the British author whose works were so unjustifiably pirated in the United States.' A third request for correspondence brought forth only Hincks and Dunkin's memorandum, and a fourth a year later yielded nothing at all, official correspondence with Canada having ground to a halt.[49] Each time Ryan spoke, Alexander Campbell, the postmaster general and the leader of the government in the Senate, assured him that something was being done, but the dwindling correspondence suggested the opposite. While the Board of Trade was searching for a solution that the London publishers would accept, the Canadian government was increasingly at a loss to answer the senator from Montreal.

The tension built. The existing order threatened to buckle when Canadian printers took matters into their own hands. In 1871 the Canadian News and Publishing Company of Toronto reprinted without permission John Edward Jenkins's *Ginx's Baby: His Birth and Other Misfortunes.* The event appeared to be brazen piracy and caused a furore in the English press.[50] The London publishers scrambled to determine their rights. *Ginx's Baby* was a British copyright work, but Canada was now a self-governing dominion with a constitution giving it 'exclusive legislative authority' over copyright. Was the 1842 act still in force there? At the request of the London publishers, two eminent lawyers, Roundell Palmer and Farrer Herschell, studied the question and found that it was; in their view, section 91 of the British North America Act was intended to divest the Canadian provinces of all authority over local copyright and gave the Dominion parliament no power over imperial copyright. So the reprinting of *Ginx's Baby*, if it had occurred in Canada, was illegal, they counselled, and the next instance of unauthorized reprinting could be decisively punished. F.R. Daldy cleverly pursued the matter with another question. If copyright in Canada flowed from two statutes – the imperial act of 1842 as modified by the Foreign Reprints Act, and the Canadian Copyright Act of 1868, which totally prohibited the importation of foreign reprints – could British books be registered under the Canadian act? If so, the London publishers could exploit it to defeat the Foreign Reprints Act. However, Palmer and Herschell judged that the 1868 act applied only to works first published in Canada; British publications, already enjoying imperial copyright in Canada, were not eligible for it. (If they had been, they reasoned, an owner could have excessively prolonged the term of protection by registering his or her work under the 1868 act on the eve of its expiry under the 1842 act.) Nevertheless, like a parent scolding a child for what has not yet occurred, this negative answer planted an interesting idea in Daldy's mind – to claw back the Canadian market by means of a Canadian statute.[51]

Then came a spectacular protest by John Lovell. 'The peculiar unfairness to this country of the law regulating British Copyrights is about to receive a rather striking illustration,' announced the *Montreal Gazette* in January 1872.[52] In a letter to the newspaper Lovell unveiled that he had recently typeset and stereotyped two British copyright works in his office in Montreal – Macaulay's *Lays of Ancient Rome* (London: Longman, 1842) and William Edmondstoune Aytoun's *Lays of the Scottish Cavaliers* (Edinburgh: Blackwood, 1849) – and then taken the plates and sufficient paper fifty miles south to Rouses Point, New York, where under the imprint of the International Printing and Publishing Company he had printed an unauthorized edition that combined them. He had brought the sheets back to Montreal, paying the 12.5 per cent import duty, and bound them there. Unlike *Ginx's Baby*, the copies that Lovell was now offering for sale to his regular Canadian customers were legal. 'It is perfectly clear that a law which will justify a proceeding of this kind cannot be a just law,' stormed the editorial, playing into Lovell's hand. 'Whatever may be the rights or interests of English authors the industrial interests of Canadians are of infinitely greater importance to this country.' By ostentatiously printing on American soil, Lovell emphasized his old contention with startling clarity: the priority for copyright law in Canada must be the development of a local publishing industry, not the preservation of British property.

A week later he expatiated on the stunt in his own paper, the *Montreal Daily News,* declaring in an open letter to Canadians that he was the one who had counselled the Province of Canada to legitimate reprinting in 1850. He also explained the origin of the Rouses Point manoeuvre. During the American Civil War the costs of labour and material had risen in the United States, and a number of American publishers had escaped this inflation by having their books typeset, but not printed, in Lovell's Montreal office: 'Canadian compositors were kept constantly employed in my own establishment setting up type, from which stereotype plates of English Copyright books were made for American publishing houses; many of which, after being printed in the United States, were imported and sold in Canada.' The war had revealed the feasibility of half-producing a reprint in Canada, and rather than quietly exploiting the loophole, Lovell now argued that the whole cycle of production should be repatriated: 'Let British publishers establish branches in Canada. Let the printing, &c., of their books for this market be executed here, and we shall not only enjoy the fruits of home industry, but the foundation of a great publishing business will be laid in this country.'[53]

Lovell's 1872 campaign is noteworthy for another idea, which was thrown in at the end of the *Gazette* editorial in a gesture of compromise. Under the existing rules, even if a British publisher did permit a Canadian edition of a new work, the Canadian printer was defenceless against the American edition, which could well flood his market before his edition was ready. Lovell therefore called for a system of interim copyright to reserve the local market while the Canadian edition was in preparation: 'All that is needed is that the publisher shall have a right to copyright protection by depositing notice of intention to publish, provided the book itself be deposited within a short time, say three or four weeks, of such notice.' He assumed that an authorized Canadian edition of a British book could be registered under the Canadian Copyright Act of 1868; the London publishers were in the midst of learning that this was doubtful. Nevertheless, it is important to note this early surfacing of the idea of interim copyright in Canada because it would find its way into the 1875 act, where it would console Canadian printers for that act's otherwise intolerable shortcomings.

Lovell's activity in Rouses Point began as a mere threat. The following year he would follow through by building a five-storey printing office and bindery on the shore of Lake Champlain, with estimated costs of $60,000 in construction and $100,000 in equipment.[54] At its peak the factory would employ 800 people, possess an electrotype machine, and boast an auditorium and a running track; Lovell's son, John Wurtele Lovell, would manage it before going on to his own meteoric career in New York City as a cheap-book publisher.[55] In 1872, however, the little edition of Macaulay and Aytoun sufficed to raise alarm in the corridors of power and renew efforts at legislation.

John Rose had moved to London in the autumn of 1869. He had returned to a private career in transatlantic banking and finance, becoming a partner in a firm that would help fund the building of the Canadian Pacific Railway. Although he had resigned from government, he continued to act as Canada's representative in the United Kingdom. (The office of high commissioner would not be created until 1880.) At the end of January 1872 he clipped out the articles on Lovell in the Montreal press and handed them to Thomas Farrer at the Board of Trade (Louis Mallet having departed for the India Office). The information touched off a profound debate between the two men, a frank, private correspondence in the heat of which the undersecretary of the Board of Trade would have his mind changed and would forge a bold new plan for reform.

Farrer, frustrated by the impasse to which the 1870 bill had led, delivered the opening salvo, characterizing American publishers and readers as thieves who 'steal unconditionally, being out of reach of the policeman,' and dismissing Lovell's grievance in the same blunt terms: 'In the paper you gave me, the plea that the Canadian publisher cannot afford to pay the English author is the common thief's usual plea.' He granted the exorbitance of English book prices and the injustice of the lack of imperial copyright for colonial publications and then tersely sketched the solution: uniformity of copyright throughout the empire, a total ban on unauthorized reprints whether domestic or foreign, and liberalization of the book trade such that British and colonial publishers would compete to attract the world's best authors and produce affordable editions for the whole empire. He was under no illusions as to the likelihood of this reform, however, given the recalcitrance of the parties involved, and added blackly, 'If this is impracticable, I see little use in stirring in the matter, and certainly feel no inclination, unless pressed by British authors, to extend licenses to steal to Canadian publishers.'[56]

Rose bristled at Farrer's reductive terms. His reply of 11 March acknowledged the maturity, if not overripeness, of the debate by now – 'the subject has, doubtless, already been before you in all its aspects' – but took issue with describing the problem merely as one of thief and policeman. The challenge was to devise an effective measure to control the flux of books across a long land border: 'Canada has a frontier of many thousand miles and I think between 200 + 300 ports of entry (many of them little more than preventive stations) and to give the Officers the requisite information, you have to send periodical lists of English Copyrights to every one of these places. You must bear in mind that the American reprints often differ *in name* from the original book, and ordinary intelligence cannot, in many cases, detect what is copyright and what is not.' Whereas a restrictive approach to trade across this border was not practical, a competitive one was: a Canadian reprint would beat the American out of the local market and probably capture a portion of the foreign market too. Addressing the flagrant lack of revenue for the author from present Canadian sales, Rose embraced the solution that would attract the support of an industrializing, increasingly self-governing state: 'What is the remedy? To repeal the permissive [Foreign Reprints] Act and prohibit the importation into Canada of everything except what is printed in England? or to provide for the *real* collection of a just amount of tribute from any publisher who wishes to use the property?' He emphasized Canada's loyalty – as yet all of the proposals had paid heed to British authors' rights – and approvingly quoted the four measures proposed by Hincks and Dunkin. Finally, he observed that what Canada was asking for, that copyright be conditional upon local printing, was gaining favour in the United States too. This was only logical: 'You need not expect a concession of International Copyright, *pur et simple,* from a young Country where authors are few and readers many and poor.' The social and economic position of both North American countries in relation to the world's production of literature called for legislation that would spread literary wealth, not siphon it away.[57]

'She [Canada] has failed to collect a Customs duty, and an Excise duty will be more obnoxious, if not more difficult, of collection,' answered Farrer on 26 March. As he saw it, the fundamental problem remained the erosion of the principle of the author's property. Hincks and Dunkin's suggestions of a higher import duty and a declaration by the importer were fine, but if Canada were truly committed to authorial property, they would already be in place. Farrer professed great disappointment that Canada's defence of the principle depended on narrow prospects of immediate gain. He would be 'sorry' to learn 'that Canada has no interest in enforcing the present law, but that she will, when the arrangement is to have the effect of protecting Canadian publishers as well as British Authors, have an interest in enforcing it, + that she will do then, what she can, but will not do now!' The 'want of good faith + honest effort' shown by the Canadian government to date argued against any more temporizing measures: 'Let us rather try to return to the true principle, and see if we cannot reconcile it with Canadian as well as English interests.' Simply put, the solution would be 'to let the author, whatever his nationality, publish either in Great Britain or in Canada, and then to give the books so published Copyright throughout both countries, with absolute prohibition of all piracies + Foreign reprints in both countries.' Not only would this lower prices by increasing competition among publishers, but anything less would be an affront to the author's title to property in his work – Farrer had in mind Dickens's notorious bitterness at the reprinting of his work in the United States.[58]

However, authorial property was not the only principle involved, nor was it an uncomplicated one in itself. With evident knowledge of the philosophy and history of copyright, Rose stepped into a theoretical discourse of the subject, invoking its other great principle, the public nature of language:

> An Author's thought is absolutely his own property until he utters it; but the property is peculiar. If he once part with it, he cannot by his own act prevent the whole world using it. He cannot reclaim it, like any other property; but he must invoke the machinery of exceptional legislation, specially designed to give him protection, and insure the fulfilment to him, of the conditions on which he is willing the world shall have it. Here the consideration of the general good comes in. Have not the public the right to say we will protect your thoughts so far as to secure you what you considered the money value of them when you agreed to part with them? but the bargain you make must, like every other sanctioned by Parliament, be reasonable; capable of being carried out without the violation of other principles which the Legislature is bound to guard; and not be clogged by arrangements unsuited to the progress of events throughout the Empire, and the condition of its rising communities. I might take some exception

to the argument that securing the money value of an author's thoughts is the only thing we have to look to. Reputation, fame, and the desire for a wide dissemination of, and for the impress of their thoughts on the world, are often considerations which, even with authors themselves, are perhaps hardly secondary. And may it not be said that the national good requires, that while valuable thought shall be encouraged by according ample protection to it; yet that as wide and rapid a permeation of it as possible shall also be secured? . . . I say then that Justice to the Author and usefulness to the community are both principles which should form the basis of copyright Legislation.[59]

In short, Rose described the two magnetic poles between which a fair law of copyright must hover (poles that commentators today capture with the paired terms *owners' rights* and *users' rights*).[60] He pressed Farrer on the absurdity of boiling text down to property: 'If a man tells, or reads to you, the contents of any copyright work, will you refuse, under any circumstances whatever, to listen? If you see it reproduced in a magazine or newspaper, will you prefer remaining ignorant of it, lest you should commit a breach of the Eighth Commandment?' Surely the reader's moral obligation to pay ceased at some point. On the one hand, authors deserved to benefit from the circulation of their work; on the other, society deserved to develop without undue barriers to education and industrialization.

Rose's letter of 9 April made another astute observation. The conflation of the author's and the publisher's interests was an age-old rhetorical trick of the trade; in fact, the two were quite separable: 'what the *author* wants is the widest possible dissemination of his thoughts, combined with the best money return for them; what the *English publisher* wants, and has tried to secure is the monopoly of printing *here* [in Britain], and selling everywhere what he so prints! It is not unfair to say that in this he has an interest apart from the author.' The proposal of licensed Canadian reprinting, an abomination in the view of the London publishers, was not unattractive to British authors, and Charles Edward Trevelyan, Macaulay's heir, had confirmed this in a series of open letters to Longman in February. If a royalty on unauthorized Canadian editions were in place, he and other copyright owners would now be enjoying 'a real 12 ½ per cent' on Canadian sales.[61] As far as Trevelyan was concerned, it was perfectly understandable that proprietary control lessen the farther a text travelled from its author: 'an absolute monopoly is only possible under the protection of the municipal law of the countries in which the books were originally produced. As regards other countries, the owners of the copyrights must be content with some more general acknowledgement, which, like a circle in the water, would increase in diffusion as it diminished in intensity.'[62] Given the distinction between the interests of British authors and publishers, Rose urged Farrer to adopt a policy for Canada that would benefit the former and exclude the latter, for 'is not the combination of these two interests – the attempt in fact to serve two masters – the real lion in our path?' Given the disadvantages to British authors and Canadian printers, there was little justification in the London publishers' continuing to interfere in the moulding of the law for Canada.

Finally, Farrer's recourse to uniform and absolute copyright throughout the empire might be sound, but it was not equitable. Canadian society was as removed from that of England as the pioneer farm was from the office of the imperial financier, and these vast material discrepancies would make utterly different things of the same law. Rose, who had lived in both countries, knew how implausible it was to expect an accomplished British author to send his or her manuscript first to an untried Canadian publisher: 'If the condition of things in both countries were the same as to the number of authors or the class of readers, and there was equality generally, the regulations might suit, and we might hope for their acceptance. But, as you know, there are few authors in Canada; the readers have yet to become thinkers or writers. The English authors would have no motive for going beyond the English publishers; and would not the system of dear editions for the richer class practically continue as before?' The argument to property was tempting for its offer of simplicity amidst the welter of opinions, but a uniform copyright law would only perpetuate the disparity that currently marked the publishing industry. A more complex, more attentive policy was necessary to counteract the inertia of capital and stimulate Canadian literature.

These arguments persuaded Farrer. 'It is not easy, without care and thought, to write a worthy answer to a letter like yours, which goes so thoroughly into the subject,' he began.[63] He had theoretical reservations. If copyright was different from other forms of property, that difference was already manifest in its limited term, and during its term the analogy to real property let it function very well, not least in leaving it to the individual owner rather than the state to assert the title. He warned Rose that a royalty system would not be easy to install: 'if you attempt to qualify an author's ownership, you have to devise new and comparatively artificial forms of property hitherto unknown to the law, and consequently difficult to administer, and sure, if operative at all, to give rise to much litigation before they are understood.' This being said, however, he admitted Rose's basic point that copyright law must balance the claims of the author with the needs of the community. He was also convinced by Rose's suggestion that the London publisher, though the most vocal party in the debate, was not the most important: 'One of the great practical difficulties in dealing with the question of copyright is that of getting at the real parties, viz., the author and the public, who are imperfectly represented, whilst the publisher, who is the man of business, has perhaps too much to say.' At root what mattered was stimulating creation on the one hand and facilitating access on the other.

Orienting himself afresh to writer and reader, Farrer now boldly laid hold of the cause that Louis Mallet had envisioned as early as July 1868, over which the row with Shaw-Lefevre had occurred in 1869 – cheaper books for the whole empire, including Britain:

> I think that the evil of dear books is an evil for this country as well as for Canada; and that if it is our duty to see that colonial readers get books at a fair price, it is no less our duty, in examining the existing law, to see whether arrangements, fair to all parties, cannot be made, by which the same benefit may be conferred on the English reader. This is a point, the importance of which has grown upon me since we began our correspondence. If good books are the best means of education, what an evil must it be for such a community as ours, if they cannot be procured in such a form and at such a price (being of course remunerative) as to be accessible to poor as well as rich.

Rose's eloquent exhortation to look beyond the proprietor to the wider public overcame Farrer's reluctance and convinced him to don the mantle that Mallet had left behind. The public he perceived was not identical to Rose's – for Farrer, the readers in the United Kingdom came first – but he agreed with Rose that luxurious book publishing must be pried from its hereditary seat, and he welcomed Canadian publishing as the instrument. Dusting off the idea of concurrent publication and applying the opinions of Palmer and Herschell, he outlined a new proposal, in which the seeds of the 1873 bill are easily discerned:

> It seems that under the present law Canada has a copyright law of her own, similar to the imperial law, that under it books published in Canada

are protected within the limits of Canadian jurisdiction. But a book first published in England cannot be again published in Canada, so as to obtain Canadian copyright. Now, suppose that this were altered, and that a book published in England, so as to obtain imperial copyright, might also be published in Canada, so as to obtain Canadian copyright; and suppose further that whilst books so published in England were, as at present, admitted into Canada, books published in Canada were allowed to enter the English market; would not such an arrangement effect all the objects we have in view?

The core of this proposal was that copyright in each part of the empire be contingent on local publication. Authors would arrange to have their work concurrently published in the other country or accept the loss of that market to a reprint, and readers in both places would be assured access to the cheapest edition. Farrer would work out the details over the next year, but the essence was here at the moment of insight: the author had a right to arrange publication as he or she wished but also a duty with respect to the public not to withhold a popular edition, and if the author failed in this responsibility, it was acceptable that the work be exposed to a free play of supply and demand. What Farrer had dismissed as thievery a few months earlier he now conceived to be public access; what in all cases he had called property was now in some cases a questionable restriction on the intellect and the economy. This transformation is remarkable. He acknowledged it in his closing words: 'although I may have used positive language, I feel that I am not so much expressing opinions as endeavouring, by means of discussion with one much more competent than myself, to form them.'

2 Achieving the 1875 Act, 1872–5: The London Publishers Prevail

John Lovell's reprinting at Rouses Point, the incident that caused the transformative correspondence between John Rose and Thomas Farrer, also prompted the London publishers to organize. On 5 February 1872, a week or so after the news had reached England, John Murray held a meeting at his office at which it was resolved to form the Copyright Association, a coalition of British publishers and authors interested in defending and extending the principle of property in texts. At the first general meeting on 19 March, Thomas Longman was appointed treasurer and F.R. Daldy honorary secretary. The association soon printed a pamphlet, 'Memoranda on International and Colonial Copyright,' which surveyed the prospects for a treaty with the United States and attacked the 'pernicious Act of 1847' from several angles. Roundell Palmer and Farrer Herschell had been sounded out again, this time on Lovell's stunt, and their grim response was that it was technically legal, thanks to the Foreign Reprints Act. The pamphlet also printed some of the recent letters of Murray and Longman demanding the repeal of the act, imputing sluggish neglect to the government.[1] Longman carried the battle to the press in an impatient letter to the *Times,* in which he mocked Canada's excuses regarding the difficulty of controlling imports along its long border: 'We must suppose that the Government of that Dominion has, since the passing of the Act, become acquainted with the peculiarities of their geographical position.' He also accused his own government of surreptitiously betraying British authors and publishers at the act's origin: 'This Act appears to have passed through Parliament without observation and without debate. There is no record of a remark in "Hansard," and no writer or publisher heard of it until it had become law.'[2] Farrer responded by suggesting that Longman have his Member of Parliament move for copies of all official correspondence relative to the act. The result was the monumental 'Colonial Copyright: Copies or Extracts of Correspondence Between the Colonial Office, the Board of Trade, and the Government of Canada' (1872), an eighty-page parliamentary paper that in its bulk alone revealed the enormous activity of the government on the issue since 1845 and, by extension, the foolishness of Longman's accusations.[3]

If Lovell's adroit move raised eyebrows in Britain, it caused consternation in Canada. It impelled the government there to the grave step of introducing the Copyright Bill of 1872. The Dominion's foremost literary printer was gravitating to the great republic to the south, and the force of the example attached new gravity to the issue. In the Senate, Thomas Ryan captured its national significance: 'We should certainly endeavour to encourage Canadian publishers and keep them in the country, instead of forcing them across the border.'[4] He drew great support from Trevelyan's letters, which Charles Belford had reprinted in the *Toronto Mail*.[5] Still ultimately aiming at a settlement of the problem by Britain, Ryan called for Canadian legislation that would make a system of licensed reprinting ready for immediate implementation should the imperial government approve it. He asked Alexander Campbell, leader of the Senate, 'whether, in expectation of, and preparatory to such Imperial Legislation, it is the intention of Government to introduce during the present Session any measure whereby authority may be conditionally obtained to levy a suitable excise duty on all reprints of British Copyright books in Canada.' The issue had more urgency than before, however, and patience with the imperial process was wearing thin. John Sewell Sanborn now importuned the government at last to legislate on the question directly. Speaking more wisely than before, he recognized the scope of the 1842 act but pointed out that Canada was sovereign in the cognate matter of patents precisely because it had asserted its sovereignty. 'Will we not give equitable justice to authors, by dealing directly with this subject?' Sanborn demanded. 'Where is the impropriety of asking what Colonial Parliaments have done in several instances, legislating upon matters where there was, to a certain extent, an infringement of Imperial Legislation, but where, at the same time the spirit of our constitution, gave us this power of acting.' Shaken by the force of these speeches, Campbell agreed to consult John A. Macdonald and draw up a bill.[6]

The Canadian Copyright Bill of 1872 spelled out a system of licensed Canadian reprinting. Campbell introduced it in the Senate on

31 May; it encountered some qualms about Canada's sovereignty in the matter, underwent minor amendments, and passed through both chambers within two weeks. Tactically it hovered between Sanborn's nationalist and Ryan's imperialist legislative route. On one hand, the preamble asserted the 'express power' over copyright that the British North America Act had conferred on the Dominion; on the other, the tenth and last clause stated that the bill could not become law until specially proclaimed by the Governor General – an unusual stipulation that pointedly left ultimate responsibility with the British government. The first clause cut straight to the reprinting of British copyright works: 'Works of which the copyright has been granted and is subsisting in the United Kingdom, and copyright of which is not secured and subsisting in Canada, under any Canadian or Provincial Act, or which have not been bona fide printed and published in Canada, under the copyright so subsisting there, within one month from the time at which copyright may have been secured in Canada, may be reprinted, published, and sold in Canada, but only on the conditions and under the restrictions hereinafter contained.' In other words, for an author publishing in Britain to enjoy copyright in Canada, he or she would have to print and publish an edition of the work in Canada too; if there was no Canadian edition (or if the author declared one but failed to produce it promptly), unauthorized reprinting of the work could commence. However, the reprinting would not be a free-for-all. A licence from the Governor General would be necessary, and the unauthorized edition would have to be entered in a reprints register kept by the agriculture minister. The reprinter would have to pay an excise duty of 12.5 per cent (of the wholesale price) for the benefit of the British copyright owner, entering into bonds to do so before receiving the licence. Once a Canadian reprint was underway, no foreign reprints of the work could be imported. Finally, in the case of works not reprinted in Canada, the bill offered to improve the operation of the Foreign Reprints Act by doing away with the cumbersome lists of British copyrights that Canadian customs officers had to consult; henceforth, importers would have to pay the 12.5 per cent duty on all suspect books from the United States or else swear that they were not reprints of British copyright works.[7] This clause, a conciliatory gesture to British interests, was a late amendment by the House of Commons.[8]

Canada had thrown down the gauntlet. As soon as word of the bill reached Britain, it was clear that a decisive confrontation was at hand. Rose scribbled Farrer a note on the day he learned of the bill: 'As I feared the Canadian Government have taken the matter into their own hands and asserted their right to deal with the question of Copyright . . . My friends write that it [the bill] may probably be reserved for the Royal Assent as they do not wish to precipitate any issue of a Constitutional kind at the present moment.'[9] The mere mention of a *constitutional* issue, even in Rose's delicate negative, was unsettling. On 14 June the Governor General, Lisgar, did withhold royal assent. The Canadian Privy Council had advised that the bill clashed with the 1842 act and therefore could not be proclaimed without the special sanction of the British government.[10] However, this was only part of Canada's plan. Britain was now under intense pressure to settle the issue, either by assenting to the bill or by speedily delivering another. Rose articulated this pressure eloquently in a final missive to Farrer, in which he argued that if Britain disallowed the 1872 bill, 'such disallowance must be sustained by arguments of no ordinary cogency,' arguments that rested on the magnificence of the empire or the advancement of human thought and progress – not on the narrow, technical ground that the British North America Act had failed to confer adequate power. If only this superficial reason were cited, Canada's next move, consistent with the great decentralization of imperial governance that had otherwise commenced, would be to take this power, for '[was] it a matter of Imperial concern, or in the interest of intellectual progress that mental product should be disseminated throughout the empire only through English presses?'[11]

Once again, the vision of a Canadian publishing industry had arisen and uncovered a wide gulf between Canadian and British estimations of its importance. In an auxiliary memorandum Campbell explained the purpose of his bill in plain terms, referring to the imperial copyright acts as 'encroachments' on what since 1867 had been a Canadian jurisdiction. Someone at the Board of Trade underlined this word in pencil and put a question mark beside it. In the same way the annotator questioned Campbell's closing sentence: 'Should it be allowed to take its course, the Bill will be a reasonably fair adjustment of the question, and will prevent a serious inroad upon one of the industries of the Country, which the anomaly produced by Imperial legislation has rendered imminent.' Here the annotator objected to the phrases *serious inroad* and *one of the industries of the Country*.[12] The pencil marks record doubt as to whether Canada had a publishing industry to damage – doubt that is both accurate and callous. Statistically insignificant from afar, the development of local publishing was paramount to Canadians, who could not know themselves, navigate their immediate environment, or well posit the existence of their country without it.

Pricked on by Rose, Farrer now set his hand to the task of giving shape to the ideas engendered by their correspondence in order to provide an alternative to the 1872 bill. He began by calling meetings with the men from whom he expected the most trouble. John Lovell had come to England along with another hopeful Canadian publisher, Graeme Mercer Adam, to lobby for the 1872 bill, and on 7 August Farrer received them at his office and heard their view. They did not manage to win any promises from him. 'There is as much feeling as interest in it,' wrote Farrer in his minute; 'Canada feels degraded by not being a place of publication.' He remained unconvinced that, burdened with an excise duty as well as American import duties, they would be able to undersell American reprints in the United States. Farrer was equally unmoved after listening to F.R. Daldy the same day: 'I suggested that Colonial Editions should be allowed to come back into this country – at any rate after the lapse of, say, a year. Mr. Daldy did not like this, but did not I think give any good reason.'[13] In hopes of persuading Daldy of the justice to the public of furnishing cheap editions in a timely manner, Farrer gave him a printed copy of his correspondence with Rose. In the margin beside Farrer's statement 'if cheap books are a good in Canada they would be a good here,' Daldy retorted, 'To attempt to produce them by act of Parliament would lead to killing the fowl that lays the golden eggs.'[14]

In response to the 1872 bill the Copyright Association produced a document, the 'Scheme of Compromise of the English Copyright-Owners,' which proposed an avenue of reform consisting of two points: that Canada enact a law allowing future and existing British books to be registered for Canadian copyright upon republication there, and that Canada promise not to tax or prohibit the importation of any British edition (even if there was an authorized Canadian edition of the same work). A footnote added that Britain, however, should totally ban the importation of Canadian editions.[15] Slanted though this approach was towards preserving the pre-eminence of the London publishers, it is precisely what the Canadian Copyright Act of 1875 would ultimately deliver. Lovell and Adam struck back in mid-August with a pamphlet that perceptively exposed the 'compromise' as a stratagem to nullify the Foreign Reprints Act and reclaim the Canadian market. Echoing Farrer, they criticized the lavish books of London, urging the publishers instead, 'in the interest of the reading masses at their doors, as well as in the interest of their own pockets, to try the experiment of large, moderate-priced, popular editions.' The age had witnessed a marvel in the United States – book sales and literacy rates that towered over those of Britain – and Lovell and Adam knew that cheap books were the cause.[16] Daldy indignantly rejected this pamphlet as a selfish plea for 'a vicious form of protective class legislation at the expense of another class (Copyright owners) of the community,' obstinately calling through the autumn for further meetings with Farrer, which the latter, already more than acquainted with his views, declined.[17]

Farrer also sought out his former colleague, Louis Mallet, at the India Office, and Mallet encouraged him to strive on behalf of the reader and the colonial publisher. 'The ultimate object of copyright law,' wrote Mallet, 'I presume to be the interest of the reading public as the recognition of all private property rests upon considerations of the public good.' In other words, he agreed with Rose that the end of copyright was the spread of learning and intellectual achievement through society; the private gain of the author was only a means. Mallet also echoed Trevelyan somewhat in arguing that the strength of copyright should be inversely proportional to its geographical scope: 'Now surely every arrangement which extends a new field of protection to copyright disturbs the calculation on which the amount of that protection was originally fixed + ought to be followed by a reduction of that protection in the inverse ratio of the extended area of monopoly.' If, for example, the copyright term of twenty-eight years had been judged fair for remunerating the author a century earlier, when royalties came mostly from Britain, would not half or less than half of that term suffice for the present author, now that royalties flowed in from a number of countries at once? Lastly, Mallet approved of any reform that would recognize the Canadian publisher as naturally the ablest person to supply books to the Canadian market.[18]

Over the winter Henry Ludlow laboured on the bill under Farrer's supervision, and in March a preliminary draft was ready for internal comment.[19] The British Copyright Bill of 1873 was a full, well-considered answer to the whole problem to date. At its heart was the idea that local publication function as the condition and guarantee of imperial copyright. Under the plan of the bill a British author wanting copyright in a colony would have to arrange for the concurrent publication of his or her work there 'in such number and manner as are suitable for general circulation'; failing this, a local printer could obtain a licence to reprint it and pay the author a royalty. By making the local printer in effect the sole copyright holder for that colony, the licence would prevent a melee. If after six months there were still no local edition, or if the colony was not sufficiently industrialized to produce one, the importation of foreign reprints could commence. The converse would also hold: a colonial author wishing copyright in the United Kingdom would have to publish an edition there or be content with licensed or imported reprints. Keeping the whole empire with its variously industrialized regions in view, the bill carefully balanced the claims of all parties. The author would have the option of actively controlling imperial publication or passively collecting revenue from it; publishers in every part of the empire would be involved in bringing the work to their respective market; and the reader ultimately could not be deprived of an accessible edition. Farrer cherished this last object most and reinforced it in the fifteenth clause, which provided that licensed reprints produced in one jurisdiction (for example, Canada) could be imported into another (for example, the United Kingdom) one year after the original publication of the work.

These were significant reforms. In order to smooth their presentation Farrer had Ludlow draw up a synopsis of the bill.[20] His cogent memorandum listed the numerous grievances to the existing law, including one that Rose had overlooked, namely, that although a book first published in a colony received no imperial copyright, the colonial publisher still had to deposit a copy of it at the British Museum and, if requested, at four other libraries in the United Kingdom, under penalty of fine.[21] The list concluded with the judgment that, apart from the latitude granted by the Foreign Reprints Act, 'India and the colonies are subject to all the burdens, but enjoy none of the benefits, of imperial copyright legislation as to books.' The memorandum made another key observation. Licensed reprinting was not the novelty that it seemed. A precedent existed in the 1842 act, which empowered the judicial committee of the Privy Council to license a person to reprint a work without authorization if the original publisher refused to keep it in print.[22] The reprinting contemplated by the 1873 bill was thus an extension of a mechanism, approved by a previous generation, not to withhold books from the public. Graced with such preventive explanations, the 1873 bill proceeded to circulate confidentially among the stakeholders.

Rose saw an early draft. Apart from some minor queries he gave it a thorough welcome and was soon working with Farrer to promote it.[23] Trevelyan approved of everything but the allowance of Canadian reprints into the United Kingdom: 'The 15th clause of the Copyright Bill is the one which seems to me to be open to objection for the reasons I mentioned to you. With this exception it is an excellent Bill, and I hope it will be speedily introduced in order that it may become publicly known and may obtain the support it deserves.' Henry Reeve, clerk to the Privy Council, protested that the administration of licences would be overwhelming: 'I also think that the Privy Council (or as you term it the Jud[icial] C[ommit]tee) would be wholly incapable of discharging the duties your bill would lay upon it. I sincerely hope that you + Ch[ichester] Fortescue will not press this measure.' Farrer patiently replied that, while increased paperwork was not attractive, imperial copyright was at stake: 'it will be out of the question to attempt to continue to prevent their publication of English books in the Colonies. The question is whether this can be done in such a manner as to preserve anything to the English Author.'[24] Mallet generally supported cheaper books for Britain but was non-committal regarding the fifteenth clause, wondering whether a radically new copyright act that allowed reprinting everywhere at once subject to a royalty might not be preferable.[25]

As for the London publishers, they were astonished at the bill. The legalization of reprinting was bewildering enough, but the fifteenth clause would in their estimation annihilate them. Farrer tried to point out that by concurrently publishing in Canada they could prevent reprints,[26] but they were too alarmed to trust him. At his suggestion, then, they drew up their own scheme for concurrent publication and licensed reprinting in Canada.[27] Although they proposed stricter regulations for the latter, such as the stamping of each copy and the advance payment of the royalty, it is remarkable that they countenanced it at all. Farrer used the scheme to improve his bill, incorporating for example the suggestions that all reprints be made from the latest authorized edition and that the original publisher receive notice of the granting of a licence. His annotations also record a major compromise on his part in his reluctant agreement to abandon the controversial fifteenth clause.

By now Farrer's patience was wearing thin, and when public criticism of the confidential draft was threatened, he rounded on Daldy:

It can, I am sure, not be true, that any one to whom the Draft Bill on Colonial Copyright has been shewn should think of making any sort of attack on the Govt. about it. Such a rumour has reached my ears + I therefore write to you at once.

It is needless to say that any such action would amount to a gross breach of confidence, and would be grounded on a misapprehension of facts, since the very purpose of giving the Bill to Mr. Murray, Mr. Longman + yourself was to elicit opinion before the Govt. had made up their own minds.

May I add that the impression left on my mind by what you stated to me last year – viz. that English publishers always do give the English public cheap editions of books which will sell, within a certain time of first publication, is very much weakened, to use a mild term, by the reception which English authors + publishers have given to the suggested Draft.[28]

To this Longman replied coolly that 'several Authors + publishers have called upon me expressing hostile intentions, but I have had sufficient influence to stop them, on the assurance that I knew the Government were anxious to give ear to the views of those who were interested in the question,' implying that the government could well expect trouble if it ignored them.

The deterioration of relations between the Board of Trade and the Copyright Association drove the latter to the aggressive alternative that Daldy had hit upon two years earlier, at the time of Palmer and Herschell's opinion on *Ginx's Baby* – swaying Canadian legislators instead. In July 1873 Daldy sailed for Canada, taking with him a rival draft bill, into which the publishers' scheme had evolved. On the whole, the Anglo-Canadian Copyright Bill was a complicated concoction that mostly addressed a non-issue, 'British Royalty editions' (the licensed reprinting of Canadian books in Britain); as Farrer and Rose saw at once, nowhere did it explicitly address the real mess of Canadians reprinting British books, although it did refer to 'Canadian Royalty editions' in passing. However, as an overture to Canada it had a certain charm, suggesting that Britain would give copyright to Canadian books if Canada returned the favour. At several points its real goal can be descried – to annul the Foreign Reprints Act. It approached this both indirectly, proposing that British books be eligible for registration under the Canadian act of 1868 (s. 2), and directly, stipulating that all Orders in Council, existing or future, allowing the importation of foreign reprints into Canada would henceforth be void (s. 14).[29] Daldy succeeded in meeting with several prominent Canadians during his trip and at every opportunity promoted his bill. He met with John Lovell, who appears to have rebuffed him. According to Daldy's report, Lovell no longer cared about reform, because of the success of his factory in Rouses Point. By contrast, Daldy built a firm ally in another Montreal printer, Samuel

Dawson, who liked the idea of securing a local monopoly on the authorized republication of British books under the 1868 act. Francis Hincks was under the impression that this was already possible; learning that it was not, he thought that 'alteration giving such right could easily be made,' but warily noted that Rose preferred the government bill. Alexander Campbell likewise saw no problem with giving Canadian copyright to British books republished in Canada if the British government approved of this route. What is most remarkable is the positive civility of Daldy's meeting with his great opponent, Thomas Ryan: 'he cordially approved of our scheme, said it was all they wanted and that he much preferred the Copyright Bill to the Government Bill as being plainer and more easily understood ... He offered if we wished it to bring in a Canadian Bill to help us in bringing the question to a practical issue.'[30] How sincere Ryan's approval really was is difficult to gauge, the only surviving account of the meeting being Daldy's.

Like the 1870 bill, neither the 1873 bill nor the Copyright Association's rival bill reached first reading in the British parliament. At the end of July the colonial secretary, John Wodehouse, the Earl of Kimberley, sent the revised government bill to Canada and all of the other colonies for comment. Gone was the contentious fifteenth clause. In his letter, Kimberley underlined what made the government bill superior to the publishers': it was applicable to the whole empire. Rather than treating Canada as a unique problem, it framed a policy suitable for all of the colonies, with particular regard not only to their different stages of development but also to the increasing industrialization and self-government of many of them. Given this imperial scope and the concessions already made to the London publishers in the revision, Kimberley expected that the government bill would be introduced into the House of Commons early the following year.[31] But in the fall of 1873 the Canadian government fell. The Pacific Scandal knocked John A. Macdonald's Conservatives from power and ushered in a Liberal government. Neither the new prime minister, Alexander Mackenzie, nor any of his Cabinet brought to the copyright issue anything like the expertise that Rose, Hincks, Dunkin, Campbell, and others had acquired over the course of the struggle since 1868. In January 1874 Mackenzie dealt with Kimberley's dispatch. The complexity of the 1873 bill baffled him, and he was blind to the unprecedented boon offered in the plan for unauthorized reprinting. A brief round of consultations with Canadian printers, booksellers, and authors was of little help. Samuel Dawson, for example, warned that any sort of reprinting would lead to internecine competition, resulting in 'mutilated or abridged editions' of the author's work.[32] He evidently had not read the 1873 bill very closely. Without a consensus to guide him, Mackenzie judged 'that any change beyond the extending of the privileges of copyright to Canadian authors is not urgent, and that a postponement of the final solution of this complicated question would not be likely to cause detriment to the public interest.'[33] With this discouraging official reply from Canada, the pressure to introduce the provocative bill in the British House of Commons vanished. A monumental opportunity, to temper afresh the principle of property in texts with that of regional development in publishing and public access, passed unseized. This was the closest Canada would come to the copyright reform that it needed. Britain would never again bend so far towards relaxing the status quo to accommodate rising colonial printers. The 1873 bill was dead.

Irrespective of colossal effort and the best intentions, the original problem of American books dominating the English-Canadian market thus continued to fester. 'Bills will come, and bills will go,' observed Thomas Ryan dryly, 'but the disability remains, I am afraid forever.' In April 1874, for the seventh straight year, he raised the issue in the Senate, this time demanding that the new government press for royal assent to the 1872 bill. If assent did not come before 14 June, two years after the bill had been reserved, it would expire, and Canada would be as far from a solution as ever. He knew his opponents – a 'very powerful combination of publishers in England' – and he knew that other bills had come into play, but this did not deter him from once more protesting that 'American publishers can continue to send in works without any, or small remuneration to British authors, and can put upon the Canadian market articles which our own people are prevented from producing.'[34] He therefore turned to the measure that had got furthest and moved an address to the Governor General not to allow it to lapse, which the Senate endorsed on 28 April.

The address reverberated in the House of Commons. A robust authority on the copyright issue arose in Alfred Hutchison Dymond, the newly elected Liberal Member for North York, who was not however in Mackenzie's Cabinet. Born in London, England, Dymond had managed a radical newspaper and authored a book on the abolition of capital punishment; in 1869 he had come to Canada to take up a position at the *Toronto Globe*. His expertise in copyright appears to date from 1872, when he analysed a debate in the English press over international copyright for Graeme Mercer Adam's *Canadian Monthly and National Review*.

In that article Dymond advocated American copyright for British authors (but not for British publishers) and aligned himself with the call for licensed Canadian reprinting.[35] His experience as author and editor on both sides of the Atlantic gave his opinions on copyright peculiar weight. On 13 May he explained the reasons for the Senate address and asked the House of Commons to endorse it too. His lengthy speech was an illuminating contribution. Dymond grasped how, despite imperial loyalties and the absence of international copyright, an American publisher could in practice completely shut a Canadian rival out of the publication of a British work for the North American market: the publisher paid the author for advance sheets, invariably outbidding the Canadian publisher (his domestic market being larger), and his edition enjoyed security because of the courtesy of trade in the United States and imperial copyright in Canada. This practice was the wall that Lovell had run into.

> A few years ago Mr. Charles Reade's work 'Foul Play' was published by an American firm. It did not enter Canada as an English reprint, but as an American copyright work. To test the state of the law, Mr. Lovell printed and published about 3,000 copies of that work at 25 cents, the American edition being sold in Canada at 75 cents. This left an admirable profit both for himself and the retail dealer. He was, however, threatened by Mr. Reade with an action at law, and although the action was never tried, he thought it better to place the profits to the credit of those who might be declared legally entitled to them, and there the money remained to this day. Mr. Lovell desired to publish another work of Mr. Reade's, 'Put Yourself in his Place,' but on applying to Sheldon & Co. of New York for permission to publish it in Canada, he was told that he might do so for the trifling sum of twenty thousand dollars.[36]

In another case, Lovell had approached the English publisher first, 'but Mr. Longman adhered to the determination that none of his copyright works should be published, as he said, by a colonist, and ended by the exclamation, "Thank God, we have got the power and we intend to keep it."' Dymond granted that some Canadian houses, such as Hunter, Rose of Toronto, had fared better in arranging Canadian editions of British authors' works, but these were fragile experiments, and in fact the 1868 act offered them no protection against foreign reprints. Dymond concluded with the case of a mathematics textbook by Isaac Todhunter, which someone in Canada had recently reprinted under a false name, adapting the content to suit Canadian schools. This sort of piracy could be expected if Britain did not quickly redress the injustices of imperial copyright. To this arresting speech from the backbench, Mackenzie replied weakly that he hoped the address would be successful.[37]

The Governor General, the Earl of Dufferin, immediately telegraphed the twin addresses of the Canadian parliament to the Colonial Office. The Conservatives, led by Benjamin Disraeli, had defeated Gladstone's Liberals in the general election of 1874, and the new colonial secretary was the Earl of Carnarvon. Carnarvon turned for advice to the law officers of the Crown, who counselled him not to allow the 1872 bill, because it contradicted the prohibition against unauthorized reprinting contained in the 1842 act, which, in their opinion, the Dominion of Canada had no constitutional authority to alter.[38] As for the Board of Trade, it could only concur. Carnarvon now had the unenviable task of terminating the Canadian legislation on the narrow, technical ground that Rose had warned against, without being able to offer an alternative. He waited until 15 June – one day after the automatic lapse of the bill – before replying. Reluctantly but firmly he relayed the law officers' reasoning, pointing out that the Canadian Privy Council had itself admitted that the bill clashed with the 1842 act. He added that not even royal assent could have helped, because the Colonial Laws Validity Act of 1865 stated that any colonial act that was 'repugnant' to an imperial one must be construed as 'absolutely void and inoperative.'[39]

In the meantime, word of the addresses reached the English press, and the Copyright Association sprang into action. 'This particular measure has been looked upon as dead,' wrote Daldy to Carnarvon in surprise. He then hammered home all the reasons for refusing it with a veteran's familiarity with the issue. His final reason, that the 1872 bill should be rejected because 'it interferes with the natural law between vendor and purchaser,' was a significant refinement. It challenged the very definition of copyright as statutory. However, Daldy's letter went beyond mere objections. He was in fact about to depart for Canada in order 'to make another effort to bring the matter to a conclusion.' In his view, all that Canada 'can reasonably ask' could be obtained in two 'very simple steps': '1. By the Canadian Government enacting that a Book etc. possessing Imperial Copyright shall if *republished* in Canada be treated as if originally published there, and thereby obtain Copyright under the Local Act . . . 2. An Imperial Act prohibiting the importation of Colonial editions into other parts of the British Dominions.' In other words, he proposed a Canadian act giving copyright to British books republished there, and a British act banning the Canadian issue from the rest of the empire. His purpose, as ever, was to protect the London publishers' traditional market while giving them a means of blasting foreign reprints from Canada. The strategy was clever – to layer Canadian copyright on top of imperial copyright. It is crucial, however, to understand that Daldy's final plan gave no quarter to independence in Canadian publishing; it would not remove the imperial copyright of any British book *not* republished in Canada. The emergency that the London publishers had faced in the 1873 bill had passed, and the Copyright Association was no longer inclined to grant unauthorized Canadian reprinting on any terms. In fairness, Daldy did acknowledge Canadians' desire for a local publishing industry and a national literature: 'This arrangement would satisfy the Canadian Privy Council Report [i.e., Hincks and Dunkin's memorandum] by ensuring *Local republication.* It would not violate the rights of property or conflict with the Imperial Act and it would produce a Local Literature as fast as the Canadian market is capable of consuming it.' However, these rhetorical afterthoughts are not what motivated him. As for granting imperial copyright to books first published in Canada, it did not figure in the plan at all. All in all, it is fair to state that Daldy set forth to influence the Canadian government to legislate in the interest of the London publishers.[40] Carrying an introduction from Carnarvon, he obtained a meeting with Mackenzie while in Canada, at which, according to his own report, he persuaded the latter to accept the Copyright Association's suggestions.[41]

The endgame commenced with the introduction of the Canadian Copyright Act of 1875 the following winter. Mackenzie's agriculture minister, Luc Letellier de Saint-Just, presented it for first reading in the Senate on 12 February. It did not entirely correspond to Daldy's plan. Letellier had studied the matter seriously, and in its original form his bill completely redefined copyright in Canada, answering to local interests very well. The main thrust came in the fourth clause: works were eligible for Canadian copyright upon being 'published or produced in Canada, whether they be so published or produced for the first time, or contemporaneously with or subsequently to publication or production elsewhere.' (The final text would substitute *printed and published or reprinted and republished* for *published or produced*.) Existing British books, therefore, were eligible if the author came to terms with a Canadian publisher. The Ministry of Agriculture remained responsible for registration and legal deposit. The ninth clause laid out the declaration that every copy of a registered book had to include: 'Entered according to

Act of Parliament of Canada, in the year _____ by A. B., in the Office of
the Minister of Agriculture.' The third clause made explicit an author's
perpetual ownership of an unpublished manuscript, regardless of nationality, residence, or citizenship. As for published works, the term of
copyright was twenty-eight years, renewable by the author or an heir
for a further fourteen years, provided, however, that in any case it did
not last longer in Canada than elsewhere. This harmonization of term
with that of British copyright removed the difficulty that Palmer and
Herschell had pointed out previously with respect to registering British
books in Canada. The interim copyright that Lovell had outlined in
1872 was also realized here. An author republishing his or her work
in Canada could register the title with the agriculture minister and so
receive the full protection of the act while the Canadian edition was
in preparation. The eleventh clause delivered the longed-for strictures
against American editions by stipulating that no one could import foreign reprints of a Canadian-copyright work without the owner's consent; in other words, by complying with the Canadian act, a British
author could possess the Canadian market and render nugatory the
Foreign Reprints Act.

The pivotal clause, however, was the fifteenth, which attempted to
make the Canadian act the full and sufficient basis for copyright in
Canada:

> If, through the neglect or unwillingness of an author to obtain in the man-
> ner herein prescribed, the Copyright of his work, or through the want of
> republishing and registering in Canada, within the three months, a work
> having been the subject of an Interim Copyright, any person has under-
> taken the republication of such work, or has imported foreign reprints of
> such works after paying the Royalty prescribed in virtue of any Imperial
> law on the subject, such person shall have acquired the privilege of dis-
> posing by sale or otherwise of the number of copies thus actually repro-
> duced or in process of being reproduced, or thus imported.

That is, an author (even a British author) who did not publish or republish his or her work in Canada would have no copyright there (not even
imperial copyright). In germ, then, the 1875 act was no different than its
predecessor, the 1872 bill. While according opportunities to the British
author, the default was freedom for the Canadian printer. Once again,
a Canadian had gone through the problem thoroughly and concluded
that industrial independence was the solution. The complex desire for

sovereignty that had coursed through Ryan's speeches and informed Campbell's bill – desire not for a global rupture from Britain but for true responsibility in this one matter, namely, of producing and consuming literature – manifested itself equally in Letellier's initiative. Had this section of the original draft stood, the Canadian Copyright Act of 1875 would have liberated the Dominion from the debilitating rule of imperial copyright.[42]

What happened next, however, was a perplexing amendment that twisted the act away from this purpose. The motivation for it is difficult to trace. Instead of praising the new bill, Ryan asked for the latest government correspondence on the issue in order to ascertain exactly why the last bill had been rejected, and Letellier handed him Carnarvon's letter.[43] It seems to have affected him. Without a doubt, the law officers' unwavering assertion of British supremacy in the matter was persuasive; whether or not it persuaded Ryan to cease striving for the unauthorized local reprinting of imperial-copyright works is impossible to know. He was inclined to favour the imperial bond. He was also by now a seventy-year-old man. Perhaps he was growing weary with the struggle. On the other hand, his pursuit of the ideal of unfettered Canadian publishing had been so resolute that it is difficult to believe that he suddenly sacrificed it for a plan that would leave executive control in London. Whatever his motive, Ryan decided to emasculate the fifteenth clause in order that the 1875 act not meet the same fate as the 1872 bill.

In this he did not act alone. Before the bill went to second reading, a 'delegation of gentlemen' arrived in Ottawa in order to ensure that it conformed to their desires. The identity of these men remains unknown, and the mystery is compounded by conflicting accounts of the second reading of the bill. A newspaper report printed the day after the second reading portrays Letellier presenting a bill for the benefit of Canadian printers and warily noticing the arrival of this delegation, which represents the rights of authors, including British authors:

> Hon. Mr. LETELLIER moved the second reading of the Copyrights bill. This bill was for the protection of the printing and publishing interest. The question had been brought to the notice of the Senate by the member for Montreal [i.e., Ryan], who had taken so much interest in the matter. A delegation of gentlemen interested in the question had come to Ottawa for the purpose of conferring with the Senate as to the best way of protecting their own rights and those of their fellow authors, either from the authors

of Great Britain or elsewhere. He hoped, therefore, that when the bill was examined and referred back to a Select Committee it would come back to the House so amended as to be acceptable to the printing and publishing interest generally. The main features of the bill, in which it resembled the protection afforded to patents for invention, was the extension of the privilege of copyright, and it also extended to the profession an interim copyright. Next the free republication of those works was allowed, which the author did not choose to copyright. They thus offered to publishers a chance of publishing first-class books; there was another provision which enacted that in case anyone who had a copyright did not choose to supply the market with a sufficient quantity of books so copyrighted, the Department, under whose control this act was to be placed, might give a license to publish. The general features of the bill were similar to those of the act of 1868, and the changes would be easily understood. He intended to refer it to a special committee, and therefore he would not speak further on the subject.[44]

Of particular note is the comparison to patents, which repeated the logic of the 1872 bill and amounted to a clear argument for Canadian sovereignty.

By contrast, the official record of this speech has Letellier presenting a tough compromise between authors and Canadian printers. There is no claim that the bill will allow the unauthorized reprinting of unregistered works. As for the 'gentlemen,' they are not attached to any cause, there appears to be no danger that they will wrench the bill from its intended path, and their presence merely indicates public interest in the legislation:

> Hon. Mr. LETELLIER moved the second reading of the Copyrights bill. This bill was for the settlement of a long debated conflict between various interested parties – settlement in which the general public is also very much concerned. At the same time that the interests of the authors are recognized and respected by this measure, it also protects the interests of the public and provides for the encouragement of our printers and publishers. The subject was brought on a former occasion, (in 1872) to the notice of the Senate by the member for Montreal, who had taken a great deal of pains in trying to arrive at a satisfactory conclusion. The importance of the bill is such that a delegation of gentlemen had come to Ottawa to follow the proceedings in regard to this bill. It is intended to refer the measure to a Select Committee, and he hoped that when it is brought back to the House, with

or without amendments, it will meet with general approbation. The general features of this bill are, while keeping the beneficial provisions of the Copyright Act of 1868, and of the application of the Imperial Legislation as regards the importation of reprints of books not patented in Canada, it does away with the difficulties and obscurities heretofore encountered in the practical working of the previous laws. The bill provides for the registration of Interim Copyrights, pending the preliminary proceedings for the publication in Canada of a reprint of English copyrighted books. That part of the measure which relates to what may be called the administrative of [sic] or office provisions, will be found a marked progress, and a great improvement on what existed before. He intended as already expressed, to refer the bill to a Select Committee, and therefore would not speak any further on the subject.[45]

The discrepancies between these two versions go far beyond the kind of error that might accidentally creep into a journalist's transcription. Furthermore, the next speech, in which Ryan declared that the present bill 'did not go into the reserved point of 1872,' is the same, word for word, in both sources. There is no explanation but that the official record of Letellier's speech was sanitized after the fact to accord with the revised shape of the bill and to downplay the influence of the unnamed 'gentlemen' upon it.

The bill proceeded to committee, and the six members – Hector Fabre, George Brown, Edward Goff Penny, Campbell, Letellier, and Ryan – carefully changed the bill the following day. One alteration was the exclusion of the American author. To register a work in Canada, the author would have to be a 'person domiciled in Canada, or in any part of the British Possessions, or . . . a citizen of any country having an International Copyright Treaty with the United Kingdom.' Another key change was the substitution of a new fifteenth clause:

Works of which the copyright has been granted and is subsisting in the United Kingdom, and copyright of which is not secured or subsisting in Canada under any Canadian or Provincial Act, shall, upon being printed and published, or re-printed and re-published, in Canada, be entitled to copyright under this Act; but nothing in this Act shall be held to prohibit the importation from the United Kingdom of copies of such works legally printed there.

2. In the case of the re-printing of any such copyright work subsequent to its publication in the United Kingdom, any person who may

have, previous to the date of entry of such work upon the Registers of Copyright, imported any foreign reprints, shall have the privilege of disposing of such reprints by sale or otherwise; the burden of proof, however, in such a case will be with such person to establish the regularity of the transaction.[46]

This change was momentous but subtle. Whereas the previous clause had permitted the unauthorized reprinting of British books if there was no authorized Canadian edition, this one did not. Rather, it reinforced that imperial copyright works were also eligible to be registered for Canadian copyright, upon which the importation of foreign reprints into Canada must cease. In other words, a British book could be protected in Canada by virtue of imperial copyright alone, or by virtue of Canadian and imperial copyright; a lack of *Canadian copyright* did not necessarily mean a lack of *copyright in Canada.* If this was the true construction of the clause, and it was, its subtlety is preposterous. The passive voice ('works ... being ... re-printed') invites the mistake that someone other than the imperial copyright owner may reprint the work in Canada. The opening phrases are too susceptible to the idea that British copyright does not automatically extend through Canada ('copyright ... is subsisting in the United Kingdom, and ... not ... subsisting in Canada'). Most curiously of all, the wording bears an uncanny resemblance to the first clause of the 1872 bill. The opening phrases are virtually identical to it, although the overall meaning is opposite. If the intent was to communicate that a British author could enjoy copyright in Canada with or without conforming to the local act, surely this might have been put more clearly; if however the purpose was to craft deliberately ambiguous language that appeared to satisfy opposite interests at once and so smooth the passage of a controversial bill, the revised clause was a fine piece of work indeed.

Ryan delivered a lengthy speech that attempted to please everyone when the bill returned to the Senate a few days later. He referred to the committee's having been 'assisted ... with the views of those gentlemen most interested in the bill in this country,' without specifying who they were; he also thanked Canadian printers and publishers for supplying 'a vast deal of information' and added that the committee had been 'anxious to regard in the fullest way and the strongest manner, the rights of the English author and the English publishers.' This last point was an innovation for him. He had not previously recognized that English publishers had rights in Canada. Then came an equivocation that would cause mischief. Ryan stated that the bill protected the English author, 'but as a condition of obtaining copyright in Canada, his work must be printed and published here'; he continued, 'On the other hand, the bill provides that if, through neglect of the author to take out his copyright here, or if he is unwilling to do so, then individuals in this country may take out a copyright for such works.'[47] He thus implied that the fifteenth clause legitimated unauthorized reprinting. Whether this was an outright deception of his constituency or a sliver of a hope on his part that Canadian courts might construe the clause in this way is impossible to tell from the words of the official record. His motivation is scrupulously indeterminate.

Notwithstanding Ryan's equivocation, the bill could not satisfy both those who desired unauthorized reprinting and those who did not. The Senate passed it and referred it to the House of Commons, but when Mackenzie moved the second reading in that chamber on 11 March, Dymond requested more time to examine it. A week later he delivered a piercing critique, accurately construing the fifteenth clause:

> In more or less express terms the Bill assents by section 15 the validity of the Act of 1842. If it did contravene that Act we knew it would be invalid; if not, then it practically failed to touch the one question at issue. If the British publisher or author chooses to disregard our law he falls back on the Act of 1842. A British author might make his bargain with an American publisher to take out no copyright in Canada, and his reprints would come in here while our publishers were bound by their allegiance to the law, and the right to sell reprints was expressly recognized by subsection 2 of clause 15. The old sore thus remained, and the Bill altogether failed to heal it.

The fifteenth clause thus left the Canadian publisher pinioned. The 1842 act bound him to the rock while the foreign reprint pecked at his entrails. Worse, by admitting the Dominion's submission to imperial copyright, the act would release the British government from the pressure it was currently under to reform the law. It would be better not to legislate at all, Dymond reasoned, than to pass an act that so compromised Canada's aspect towards sovereignty: 'in a question so purely domestic in its character as the publication and circulation of literature, the people of Canada ought to be able to legislate exclusively in their own interests.' Given the intransigence of the United States in the realm of international copyright, the necessary course was to amend the British North America Act in order to give Canada the power to beat the Americans at their own game. The policy that would achieve this would be one that gave copyright to authors who printed and published in Canada – who 'contribute[d] to the wealth and taxation of the country by encouraging that branch of industry with which copyright was connected' – and one that refused copyright to those who did not. Regrettably, the present bill did not embody this policy. Moreover, Canadian printers had been sufficiently lured by the offer of interim copyright to disregard the bill's central flaw. Without the undivided support of the local industry, Dymond's resistance to the legislation was a mere point of honour. He voiced his objections but could not hope to defeat the legislation. Mackenzie then defended the bill as 'the result of deliberations held with Canadian publishers, English authors, and other persons who had taken an interest in the subject of copyright' and admitted its expediency: 'the Government had to deal with circumstances as they existed.' After the second reading, Dymond was put in charge of the committee to examine the bill; he reported it without amendment, and it passed on third reading.[48]

What was a failure in Dymond's eyes was a victory for the Copyright Association. The passing of the transformed bill through the Canadian parliament achieved the first part of Daldy's plan (the granting of Canadian copyright to British books). Dufferin promptly reserved the bill for scrutiny by the British government, and when Mackenzie wrote to him soon after to justify it, he assured him that it fulfilled the demands of the Copyright Association impeccably: 'Mr. Daldy has written me suggesting certain verbal alterations which might or might not be improvements, do not in any way affect the principle of the Bill, but which reached me too late to consider . . . I have only to say in conclusion that we endeavoured as far as possible to mould this Bill in the interests of the English author which the proximity of the United States makes it exceedingly difficult to protect, and I cannot see how it is possible for me to make any further attempt to settle this vexed question if this Bill is unsatisfactory.'[49] Even if Daldy's final suggestions to the prime minister were not incorporated, it is clear that deference to the British copyright owner shaped the legislation.

The next step was for the law officers of the Crown to go over the bill. Daldy confidently predicted that they would not object to it and wrote to the Colonial Office outlining all that remained to be done to achieve his plan (the banning of Canadian editions of British copyright works from the United Kingdom and from the rest of the empire). No doubt pleased with the progress of events thus far, he was nevertheless anxious that his full plan be realized quickly. It was now clear that the British parliament intended to strike a commission on copyright, as Louis Mallet had long advised, and this might not only imperil the present measure but shake the very concepts upon which it rested. 'It is particularly desirable that these steps should be taken before Parliament is prorogued,' urged Daldy, 'because the settling of the question will remove a cause for grumbling from the Canadian mind and set the whole question at rest before any Commission meets to consider the general subject.' He therefore enclosed a draft clause to outlaw imperial traffic in colonial editions.[50] This urgency left a mark on Carnarvon, who was, however, far less sure about what exactly the fifteenth clause meant. Emphasizing 'that nothing should occur to prevent Her Majesty's assent being given,' the Colonial Office put the question to the law officers: would the fifteenth clause let Canadians pirate British copyright works? Carnarvon also had doubts regarding the eleventh clause. If the Foreign Reprints Act permitted the importation of foreign reprints of a British copyright work into Canada, was not the current bill, which would prohibit such importation, repugnant to it?[51] The answer was negative to the first enquiry but positive to the second.

In response, Carnarvon leaped to give special sanction to the Canadian bill. In order to confirm the latter notwithstanding the Colonial Laws Validity Act, an act of the British parliament was necessary, and Carnarvon catered to the Copyright Association to make its passage as straightforward as possible. His measure, known as the Canada Copyright Act,[52] did more than merely confirm the Dominion's legislation; it also included a clause modelled on Daldy's draft. This occurred over the fervent protests of the Board of Trade. As soon as he learned what was afoot, Farrer exposed Carnarvon's bill for the protectionist measure it was. How could the Canadian edition be declared illegal, he asked, if it could not be produced without the author's consent? On what grounds could the British public be denied the cheap edition if the rightful copyright owner was reaping a fair profit from it? 'Can anything be more artificial than a law emanating from one + the same Nation, + Government, saying that a book published in one part of its dominions shall not be allowed to enter another part, the same language prevailing in both[?]'[53] Robert George Wyndham Herbert, an undersecretary at the Colonial Office and Farrer's former colleague, replied apologetically that Daldy was in the ascendant: 'One reason for proposing this clause, (which *in principle* we join you in disliking,) is the political + practical one that unless it is in the Bill the English Copyright owners will prevent our legislating, as we desire to do, this session; we cannot at this period, if we could at any time, carry a strongly opposed Colonial Copyright Bill.'[54] The Copyright Association exercised a formidable influence over the whole process.

Carnarvon introduced his bill into the House of Lords on 17 June 1875. Upon the second reading a week later, a perceptive but inconsequential debate occurred – perceptive because some of the Lords had seen the issue from different angles, but inconsequential because none of them rated colonial publishing above the British author's property. In explaining the situation, Carnarvon himself admitted the necessity of adapting copyright to the colonies, although he did so mainly for reasons of imperial progress and cultural hegemony: 'The necessity for the Colonies of cheaper editions of new works than those published in England must be admitted. He believed that long ago Lord Macaulay and Sir Charles Trevelyan thought it necessary to sanction the introduction of these reprints into India.' His commentary confirms that the Foreign Reprints Act was never merely a stopgap for Canada; rather, it was consonant with the wider policy, championed by Macaulay, to educate the empire in English. Philip Henry Stanhope, who had introduced the bill that had become the 1842 act, granted that a growing colony needed cheap books and that the practice of selling advance sheets to the American publisher put the Canadian at a fatal disadvantage; however, he was also a committee member of the Copyright Association and therefore praised and thanked the government for the present bill. Lisgar, who had not only lived in Canada but as Governor General had received Rose's second memorandum and reserved the 1872 bill, offered the only penetrating criticism. If the pair of bills now before them (Carnarvon's and the Canadian one) did not allow unauthorized reprinting in some form, he doubted that they would have any practical effect. He 'thought the success of the Bill depended on the single question whether the publishers of Canada would be able to reprint editions of English works as cheap as the United States publishers could print pirated editions of these works. He was afraid they would not find it worth their while to enter into the competition.' Richard Monckton Milnes, Baron Houghton, another committee member of the Copyright Association, failed to answer Lisgar but nevertheless stoutly praised the bill. Kimberley feared that Lisgar was correct, adding his doubts whether Canada, not having been able to tax imported foreign reprints, would be able to prohibit them. All agreed, however, that the present legislation posed no threat to the English author, and on the strength of this it passed through the House of Lords, with an amendment allowing Canadian editions into the rest of the colonies (but still not into Britain).[55]

As it became clearer that the Board of Trade would be sidelined in order to ram the bill through, Thomas Farrer intensified his dissent: 'We here object in toto to sacrificing the interests of the British public in this country to the passing of your Bill this Session. The step is really a most important one + once taken can never be recalled.' He broached the matter with Stafford Henry Northcote, the Chancellor of the Exchequer and a former president of the Board of Trade, hoping to divide the Cabinet. As for the amendment, it only made the bill worse: 'England is to be the only English speaking country which is not to have cheap books.'[56] But Carnarvon was moving fast, and there were limits on what a civil servant could do to stop him. Despite further remonstrations from Farrer, the bill passed through the House of Commons in July without debate, a lone observation being raised by John Edward Jenkins, the agent-general for Canada (and the author of *Ginx's Baby*), who stated that Parliament ought to wait for the report of the Royal Commission on Copyright before legislating.[57] On 2 August, the Canada Copyright Act became law. This removed the last obstacle to the Canadian bill. The Canadian Copyright Act of 1875[58] now took its last steps down the long, transatlantic legislative path. It received royal assent on 26 October, was proclaimed on 3 December, and entered into force eight days later. It would remain in effect for a half-century, until 1 January 1924.

In its ambiguity the Canadian Copyright Act of 1875 bore the trace of the irresolvable conflict of principle that it had suffered in its genesis. On the surface it appeared to establish local manufacture as the basis for copyright in Canada, following the logic that repatriating the production of literature would lay the ground from which a national literature could rise. In one clause it enshrined the principle of authorial property regardless of nationality; in another it pointedly excluded the authors of the nearest neighbouring state. Finally, read in the context of imperial law, it bowed to the outmoded principle of English protectionism, consolidating the power of the London publishers – shoring up both their control over Canadian editions and their ability, notwithstanding these, to continue to send British products into the Canadian market. Three principal parties had a hand in its creation. Canadian legislators, at the urging of Canadian printers, initiated the reform. They advanced moderate arguments that insisted on local industry without repudiating authorial property, but ultimately their hands were scorched by the explosive constitutional potential of the issue, and they backed away from sundering Canada from imperial rule. The British Board of Trade, the government department responsible for copyright, dutifully attempted to guide the process towards a just and consistent outcome for the whole empire. The group that ultimately prevailed, however, was the third, the London publishers, who although not initially superior in energy and organization were nevertheless best positioned to lever the British parliament, the body in which final authority over the matter was vested. The result was a thoroughly compromised measure that in its substance primarily served the third group. Equivocating between Canadian copyright and copyright in Canada, the Canadian Copyright Act of 1875 seemed to satisfy all demands at once, but no statute so moulded by opposite intentions could function smoothly without severe judicial correction. Given the farraginous interpretations of it that coexisted, that clarification could not come without a shock.

3 Clarifying the 1875 Act, 1876–7: The Stunting of Belford Brothers

The key to independence in publishing is independence in copyright. For about a year after its passage, it appeared that the Canadian Copyright Act of 1875 had fulfilled this logic, making the statute of the Canadian parliament and its attendant regulations the sole basis for any claim to textual property among the rising printers and booksellers of the Dominion. Were Canadian firms now free to produce the books that anglophone North American readers generally wanted, developing their industrial capacity subject only to the rules of their own elected representatives? Was the promise of Confederation – a new nation with its own literature – now at hand in the independence of the book, literature's material base? These were real questions in the public mind in the wake of the 1875 act, and from the summer of 1875 until the winter of 1877 it appeared that the answers to them were positive. A general reprint industry began to establish itself, centred in Toronto and oriented to the continental market. But it was terminated by the case of *Smiles v. Belford* (1876–7), which clarified and publicized the meaning of the 1875 act to be that an imperial copyright and a Canadian copyright could co-subsist in a single literary work: a *copyright in Canada* could consist of the first, the second, or both. Although Canada had the power to enact its own copyright statute, it did not have the power to repeal an imperial one. The British act of 1842 (as amended by the Foreign Reprints Act) and the Canadian act of 1875 therefore overlapped in the Dominion, and 'the old sore' that Alfred Dymond had diagnosed continued to fester. Unlike their American rivals, Canadians still could not without permission reprint works first published in the United Kingdom. This clarification renewed the subordination of Canadian publishers to their counterparts in London and New York, confirming a colonial dependence in copyright that would define modern Canada. It had a sharp impact on the nascent Toronto reprint industry and set a precedent for the rest of the empire.

The constraints re-imposed on the Canadian book trade by *Smiles v. Belford* drew Canadian firms away from independent book production and specialist publishing and channelled them into various forms of bookselling, especially the distribution of American editions to the local market. As far as general literature was concerned, 'publishing' in Canada became essentially the wholesale supply of imported products. Much of what Canadian readers paid for a book went to the foreign publisher. In the absence of local publishers, Canadian authors turned to foreign houses, primarily to those in New York, and the result was an anti-nationalization of the communications circuit. Newspapers and government documents aside, the social process of writing, publishing, and reading a text was not nationally contained. Most of what has since been recuperated as Canadian literature was first published abroad. *Smiles v. Belford* maintained Canada's status as a net importer of books – a captive market – perpetuating the patterns of Canadian writers emigrating and of Canadian readers using American editions. The case was highly significant in arresting the possibility of national literary publishing.

The case of *Smiles v. Belford* has not yet received due scholarly attention. The main obstacle, perhaps, is that the story of the Belford brothers themselves is hard to tell. Most of their business papers, if they survive at all, have not come to light, and apart from Charles Belford, who was only tangentially involved in the book business, the brothers seem to have shunned the public eye. The short accounts that have come to be accepted of their lives rest on sources that are scanty and in some cases dubious. The sympathetic memorial to Alexander Belford printed in *Publishers' Weekly* shortly after his death, for example, is a cordial tribute; as such, it captures the shape of a life and is not concerned with verifying details. The Belfords, especially Alexander and Robert, were men of business, always focused on the next undertaking, rarely given to chronicling the last. Writing their biographies remains a challenge. The purpose of this chapter, then, is to reconstruct the Belfords' activity in the book trade, particularly the Canadian phase of it, from what evidence does survive in order to demonstrate the impact of the trial on their mode of business and on Canadian bookselling in the post-Confederation era more generally. The Belfords began as unauthorized reprinters, independently producing Canadian editions according to what they understood the law to permit, but after learning the true meaning of the 1875 act at great personal cost, they gravitated towards distributing American or British editions. The trial was a major disappointment. It prompted their short-lived merger with George Maclean Rose in 1878 and ultimately drove them to the United States, where they threw themselves with a vengeance into the cheap-book boom of the 1880s. Ultimately they defied all literary property and combusted in the inferno of reprinting that led up to the U.S. Copyright Act of 1891. Their example indicated that cooperatively distributing imports was the safer course for a Canadian firm.

By examining contemporary advertisements and surviving books, one may observe the evolution of the Belfords' mode of business. From 1870, when their first books appeared, until February 1878, when the merger occurred, they brought out over a hundred books under their imprint as well as two magazines. Before September 1876 their production appears to have been more or less autonomous. They originated their own editions, paying for local typesetting and disregarding imperial copyright. Their reprinting of the works of popular British and American authors allowed them to expand rapidly. However, in 1877 their mode turned increasingly to mere distribution. More of their books were issues of a foreign edition. Having been forced to recognize the validity of imperial copyright in Canada, they began to cooperate with the publishers who owned it, dealing with them to obtain printed sheets of the foreign edition or a duplicate set of stereotype plates. These dealings must have involved costs that the Belfords had previously escaped, and in the end they opted to elude them by migrating beyond the bounds of imperial copyright. While in Canada, however, the Belfords changed from an initiator of new editions to a distributor of imported ones, establishing the pattern that successive Canadian booksellers would follow until the 1960s.

The Belford family took part in the mid-nineteenth-century British wave of immigration to Canada. The father, William Belford, had been a constable in charge of the small police force on Valentia Island, County Kerry, off the west coast of Ireland. Standing but not wealth had attached to his position. He was a member of the Church of England and enjoyed the trust of the local landlord, Peter George Fitzgerald, the nineteenth Knight of Kerry, but in 1856 illness obliged him to retire prematurely.[1] He and his wife had several children – William ('Billy'), Rebecca, Charles (1843?–80), Alexander Beaty (1854–1906), Robert James, and another girl whose name has been lost[2] – and the growing family, combined with poor health and a small pension, forced them to emigrate in 1857. 'I have known Sergeant Belford for over 17 years during which time he has been in charge of the small Police Force in this Island,' wrote Fitzgerald in glowing tribute; 'I do not think I have ever known a man in a similar position so generally respected, + regarded by persons of every rank. I cannot bring to my mind that during my acquaintance with him I have heard of a single complaint of him whether as regards his Police duties or his general conduct + I find it hard to say how much I regret the withdrawal of him + his family from this place.'[3] Thomas Bentley, the local doctor, also lamented the Belfords' departure from Valentia, supplying an equally positive testimonial to the father's integrity 'with the hope that it may be conducive to your making up elsewhere for the years which in a pecuniary sense you have sacrificed to the good of this Island.'[4] Charles was fourteen and would keep his ties to the old country, having been educated with Fitzgerald's own sons, in whom, as in the Blackburns (another prominent Valentia family), he found lasting friends.[5] However, Alexander and Robert had no memory of Ireland and would grow up wholly oriented to the new world.

The Belfords chose to settle in Upper Canada. One reason was that a relation, James Beaty (1798–1892), had gone there years before and thrived.[6] The Belfords first appear in Toronto city directories in 1859. In that year William Belford Sr was listed as a 'clerk' living at 146 George Street.[7] The single listing implies that the elder sons had almost but not yet reached the age of majority, for by 1862 he reappears alongside William Belford Jr and Charles Belford, all three residing at 262 Parliament Street. Father and son were now partners in a soap and candle factory at the corner of Beech and Parliament streets. As for Charles, he had trained as a mechanical draftsman but went into journalism when Beaty, his great uncle, took him under his wing and hired him on at the *Leader*.

An appreciation for literature is evident in Charles's involvement in the Ontario Literary Society. In 1860 he took over the role of correspondence secretary from William Alexander Foster, and from then until 1861 he contacted a number of prominent American and Canadian authors on behalf of the society. Those who accepted Charles's invitation to give a lecture in Toronto included George William Curtis and Joshua R. Giddings, Republicans and outspoken opponents of slavery; the Irish essayist Henry Giles; Grace Greenwood (Sara Jane Lippincott), American journalist and poet; and Thomas D'Arcy McGee.[8] The honoraria that the society offered the speakers ranged from fifty to one hundred dollars. Charles's involvement attests to a respect for authors, an appetite for reading and discussion, and an interest in the cultural 'improvement' of his adoptive country.[9]

By 1862 Charles had risen to the rank of assistant editor. On 11 November 1864 he married Jennie Thomas, whose family was established in Toronto and Hamilton. Their first child was born two years later, and together they would have a total of six children – four daughters and two sons. Yet, as Charles and Jennie were establishing a new household, death was ravaging the old. William Belford Sr died in 1865. The Belfords' mother and their sister Rebecca had preceded him. 'How many of your family have passed away since we last saw you all at Valencia [*sic*] now 10 years ago,' exclaimed Isabella Blackburn in sympathy to Charles. 'You have indeed had much sorrow + I trust also rich consolation, for both your parents + Rebecca were among the faithful servants of God I am well persuaded. You will long mourn their loss, + will feel the charge which now devolves upon you of taking care of your little brothers + sister.' Alexander was eleven, Robert younger, when they lost both their parents and were taken in by Charles. Not long afterwards, William Jr vanished too. 'Is Billy now at Toronto?' asked Isabella anxiously, hoping that 'his health is improved.' He moved to 33 Duchess Street and continued as a 'soap boiler' for a time, but his name disappears from the Toronto directories after 1866.[10]

When the editor of the *Leader* retired in 1867, Charles replaced him, holding the position for the next four years. He supported the Canada First movement when Foster and others founded it in 1868.[11] Charles's rise appears to have led his younger brothers to the newspaper business. By the age of sixteen Alexander was a 'clerk' in the office of the *Daily Telegraph* (1866–72), which was owned by John Ross Robertson and James B. Cook.[12] In the fall of 1871, Charles broke with Beaty and decided to launch a new newspaper. John A. Macdonald, whose loyal supporter Charles had become, questioned the move: 'The "Telegraph" and "Leader" both support the Government, or profess to do so, and perhaps will do so during the Contest. A third paper started now could get but little circulation so as to affect the public mind in one year from its establishment.'[13] Despite the prime minister's doubts, Charles founded the Toronto *Mail* in March 1872, serving as its first editor. In 1875 he moved his growing family from 4 Carty's Terrace on George Street to 109 Wellesley Street, and Alexander and Robert took up residence together at 503 Sherbourne Street.[14] While editor of the *Mail* Charles did not hesitate to use his influence to promote his younger brothers and their reprint business. He even went so far as to become a partner in their company for a time. Where the *Mail* comments on the book trade, therefore, one may assume that it represents quite directly the views and interests of the firm of Belford Brothers. Unfortunately Charles's health collapsed in 1878. He lived long enough to accept a patronage appointment in Ottawa but died of tuberculosis in 1880.

Change and upheaval thus marked the private lives of Alexander and Robert Belford. They did not enjoy much formal schooling. Immigration and death had ruptured their family by the time they reached adulthood. Further adversity came in the loss of Charles in their mid-twenties. From a young age they were exposed to the pressures of the world, which doubtless encouraged a certain keenness, expediency, and independence. However, if their family circumstances thrust them into self-reliance, they also gave them a sense of the literary, through the books that Charles possessed, in the authors' lectures that he helped organize, and through his exemplary navigation of the journalistic-political field. Alexander and Robert came of age with an interest in the value of books – in their cultural value, their financial potential, and their tempting technological feasibility given the flourishing newspaper industry of Canada's fastest growing city.

Alexander Belford's career as a reprinter of books began circumspectly in 1870. Without identifying himself on the title page, he produced unauthorized editions of popular American works for various Ontario booksellers. His obituary claims that his 'first venture in book publishing was in 1866 or '67, and either the "Hans Breitmann Ballads" or Joaquin Miller's poems was his first publication.'[15] The recollection of specific works is illuminating, but the date cannot be correct. Charles Godfrey Leland's dialect ballads about the fictional German-American rogue Hans Breitmann circulated in American periodicals beginning in May 1857, but it was not until 1868 that they started to appear in book form, in the editions of T.B. Peterson of Philadelphia.[16] All surviving Canadian copies of the Breitmann ballads mimic Peterson's in appearance and are dated 1870 or later. Likewise, Joaquin Miller's first books of poetry, *Specimens* (1868) and *Joaquin et al.* (1869), were small editions printed in Oregon. His international fame did not begin until 1871, when the English press hailed him as the quintessential poet of the American frontier and showered its adulations upon *Pacific Poems* (London: Whittingham and Wilkins, 1871) and *Songs of the Sierras* (London: Longmans, Green, Reader, and Dyer, 1871).[17] Thus the 1870 Toronto edition of *Hans Breitmann's Barty [sic] and Other Ballads* is the first reprint that can be attributed to Alexander with some certainty. Two more that can be inferred were *The Celebrated Jumping Frog of Calaveras County and Other Sketches* and *The Innocents Abroad,* both by Mark Twain. The various issues of *The Innocents Abroad* that were sold in Toronto, Hamilton, and Montreal in 1870 all derive from one edition printed at the Daily Telegraph Printing House in Toronto.[18] In limiting himself to American authors, Alexander may have assumed that his undertaking was within the bounds of copyright law, and indeed if first publication had occurred outside of Britain (as it had in the case of *Hans Breitmann's Barty*), his was no more an act of piracy than was the American reprinting of British authors. *Routledge v. Low* (1868) held that first publication had to occur in Britain for an imperial copyright to be secured. Nor was the Canadian the first or only unauthorized edition of Leland. *Hans Breitmann's Barty* had been reprinted in London in 1869. Alexander Belford's inconspicuous and law-abiding entry into the business of reprinting should therefore be understood as one case in the wider friction between the copyright regimes of Britain and the United States – tit for tat in the game of international reprinting.

Emboldened by these experiments, Alexander organized the Canadian News and Publishing Company in the fall of 1870. Its advertised location was, briefly, 35 King Street West; by 1871 this had changed to 25 Colborne Street, the address of the printing office of Dudley and Burns.[19] Over the course of the next year, the Canadian News and Publishing Company reprinted at least a dozen popular American books, including Miller's *Songs of the Sierras,* Leland's *Hans Breitmann as an Uhlan, with Other New Ballads,* Bret Harte's *The Heathen Chinee,* and two more works by Mark Twain. Another work, *The Political State and Condition of Her Majesty's Protestant Subjects in the Province of Quebec since Confederation* by Adolpus M. Hart, appears to be an original publication, perhaps paid for by the author. About May 1872, however, the company ceased, and its stock was sold off to the booksellers it had supplied.

Why did the Canadian News and Publishing Company expire? Various hypotheses have been offered, but none has yet taken account of the fact that Alexander Belford was the one who reprinted *Ginx's Baby,* causing furore among the London publishers in the summer of 1871 and prompting them to clarify their rights in Canada. Whether or not he intended to transgress imperial copyright in this case, it nevertheless became obvious that he had, and at eighteen years of age he was probably sufficiently intimidated to close shop.

Ginx's Baby is a blistering satire of England's institutional neglect of its poor. It poses a question – what happens to one who has the bad luck to be born to penury in London? – and lists the dire alternatives as suicide, revolution, or emigration to Canada. Owing to its radical thrust, it was published anonymously in 1870, a move that protected the author, John Edward Jenkins, but simultaneously disowned the text. Unauthorized and competing American editions of *Ginx's Baby* soon appeared under the imprints of J.R. Osgood (Boston, 1871) and G. Routledge (New York, 1871). With the American editions of a popular anonymous text before him, Alexander proceeded to reprint *Ginx's Baby* in at least two editions. One, bearing his company's usual Toronto imprint, was a book of five gatherings with twenty-eight lines of type per page:

Ginx's Baby: Canadian News and Publishing (Toronto) Edition[20]

GINX'S BABY; | HIS BIRTH AND OTHER MISFORTUNES | [rule, 2.1 cm] | [*long serifs*:] *A SATIRE.* | [rule, 2.1 cm] | TORONTO: | The Canadian News and Publishing Company, | 25 Colborne Street. | [rule, 0.4 cm] | 1871.
COLLATION 1^{16} 2–5^{16} [$ 1 signed]. 80 leaves. Pages *ix–xv* xvi *17* 18–168 [=160].
TYPOGRAPHY 28 lines, 113 (122) × 71 mm; 10 lines = 41 mm; capital 2.4 (x 1.6) mm. *On p.* 41: 'e' (line 1) is slanted; 'f' (line 11) hangs below line.

Another comprised six gatherings (five plus an unnumbered preliminary) with twenty-nine lines of type per page through most of the book but with a varying number on the final pages. This one had a unique double imprint that also located the company in Buffalo, New York:

Ginx's Baby: Canadian News and Publishing (Buffalo-Toronto) Edition[21]

GINX'S BABY; | HIS BIRTH AND OTHER MISFORTUNES | [rule, 2.1 cm] | [*long serifs*:] *A SATIRE.* | [rule, 2.1 cm] | BUFFALO: | The Canadian News and Publishing Company, | 198 & 200 Maine Street. | TORONTO: | 25 Colborne Street. | [rule, 0.4 cm] | 1871.
COLLATION ^{4} 1^{16} 2^{16}–4^{16} 5^{12} [$ 1 signed]. 80 leaves. Pages *ix–xv* xvi *17* 18–*45 46–47* 48–168 [=160].

TYPOGRAPHY *Pages 17 to* 163: 29 lines, 117 (113 on pp. 49, 81) (124 [122 on pp. 49, 81]) × 71 mm; 10 lines = 40 mm; capital 2.3 (x 1.4) mm. *Pages* 164 *to end:* 35 lines (33 on p. 164, 34 on p. 165, 32 on p. 166), 118 (113 on p. 164, 117 on p. 165, 110 on p. 166) (125 [120 on p. 164, 124 on p. 165, 117 on p. 166]) × 71 mm.

By ambiguously straddling the Canada–United States border, the double imprint suggests that this edition might have been printed outside of the empire and then imported – the procedure that Lovell would sensationalize a few months later with his Rouses Point edition of Macaulay and Aytoun. Whether or not this in fact occurred, the unusual change of imprint suggests an understanding and an evasion of imperial copyright. Then, in March 1872, the newly formed Copyright Association published its first pamphlet, 'Memoranda on International and Colonial Copyright,' including the grave opinion of Palmer and Herschell that the reprinting of *Ginx's Baby* was strictly illegal. Finally, an editorial published in the *Toronto Mail* in May indicates that Charles Belford had thoroughly grasped the current state of the law: 'During a whole generation this country has been supplied by American reprints, and that practice can be changed only by allowing republication to take place here on the terms offered by our Government. It is idle to suppose that American reprints can be kept out of Canada, and Canadian publishers be prevented from supplying the void.'[22] This protest recognizes the liability to which a 'publisher' like Alexander had exposed himself in 'supplying the void' before reform had occurred. In short, the Canadian News and Publishing Company seems to have met its demise because the Belfords had a run-in with imperial copyright.

For the next two years, while reform hung suspended in the unachieved bills of 1872 and 1873, the Belfords refrained from reprinting or publishing books. In the summer of 1875, when it became clear that the Canadian Copyright Act of 1875 would receive royal assent, Alexander, now aged twenty-one, returned to the reprint business, this time founding a company in his own name. Its first incarnation was Belford and Company.[23] Under this imprint, Alexander reprinted William Robert Ancketill's *The Adventures of Mick Callighin, M.P., a Story of Home Rule,* which Samuel Tinsley had originally published in London in 1874. Like his edition of *Ginx's Baby,* the title page of *The Adventures of Mick Callighin* bears a double imprint, this time giving Detroit as the American location.[24] Again, the double imprint implies technical compliance with the law by suggesting that this edition might have been printed in the United States and then imported.

Robert joined his older brother in July, and the firm became Belford Brothers. They registered their partnership on 4 December 1875, attesting that they had been in business together since 19 October of that year, but their books had been appearing under this version of the company name months prior. Their reprint of *Bluebell* by Mrs George Croft Huddleston, for example, originally published by Tinsley earlier that year, appeared in July under the imprint 'Toronto: Belford Brothers,' the straightforward self-identification that they would employ for the next two-and-a-half years.[25] Thus, as Carnarvon's bill (the Canada Copyright Act) was passing through the British House of Commons, nudging the Canadian Act of 1875 ever closer to the statute book, the Belfords were positioning themselves to be Canadian reprinters of British copyright works, a role they believed the imminent and long-awaited reform would permit. In other words, the firm of Belford Brothers originated on the understanding that a new sovereignty in copyright and hence a new era in Canadian book publishing were at hand.

The Belford edition of *Norine's Revenge,* a romance by the expatriate Canadian author May Agnes Fleming, illustrates the independent mode of production upon which Alexander and Robert founded their enterprise. Sometime in October they picked up a copy of *Norine's Revenge,* first published by G.W. Carleton of New York in an edition running over four hundred pages. The Belfords handed the text to the Toronto printers Bell and Company at 13 Adelaide Street East. Bell not only managed to condense the text to 264 pages but also imposed it so that it might be bound more cheaply, in gatherings of sixteen leaves rather than eight. But his work was also sloppy. Some of the designs decorating the chapters were printed upside down. The sheets then went a few blocks over to Hunter, Rose and Company at 23 and 25 Wellington Street West to be bound:

Norine's Revenge: Belford Edition[26]

NORINE'S REVENGE | BY | MAY AGNES FLEMING |
AUTHOR OF | "Guy Earlscourt's Wife," "A Wonderful
Woman," | "A Terrible Secret," "A Mad | Marriage," Etc. |
[rule, 4.2 cm] | TORONTO: | BELFORD BROS. | 1875.
collation ² 1–8¹⁶ 9² [$ 1 signed (–1₁; +1₂ signed '1*')]. 132 leaves.
Pages *1–5* 6–237 *238–239* 240–252 *253* 254–262 *263–264.*

CONTENTS *1* title. *2* imprint: 'TORONTO: | PRINTED BY BELL & CO. | 13 ADELAIDE ST. EAST.' *3* contents. *4* blank. *5* head title: 'NORINE'S REVENGE.' *5–237* text of *Norine's Revenge. 238* blank. *239* head title: 'A DARK CONSPIRACY.' *239–252* text of 'A Dark Conspiracy.' *253* head title: 'FOR BETTER FOR WORSE.' *253–262* text of 'For Better For Worse.' *263–264* blank.

TYPOGRAPHY 31 lines, 128 (138 [137 on p. 37]) × 85 mm; 10 lines = 42 mm; capital 2.4 (x 1.5) mm.

ILLUSTRATIONS Woodcut banners at the head of each chapter, printed upside down on 92, 183, and 223.

BINDING *Material.* Green cloth. *Front.* '[double frame, black, 17.3 × 10.6 cm] [design, black, 14.9 × 9.0 cm: gate] [design, gold, 3.4 × 6.6 cm: curved banner enclosing title and author] NORINE'S REVENGE | BY | MAY AGNES FLEMING.' *Spine.* '[gold:] [at head:] [triple rule] | [ornament, 0.6 × 2.5 cm: banner with diamonds within circles] NORINE'S | REVENGE. | [rule, 1.0 cm] | FLEMING | [ornament, 0.8 × 1.1 cm: three leaves] | [at foot:] *TORONTO:* | BELFORD BROS | PUBLISHERS | [ornament, 0.6 × 2.5 cm: banner with diamonds within circles] | [triple rule]'. *Back.* '[blind:] [triple frame, 17.8 × 11.5 cm] [inner frame with ornate wheels at corners, 15.4 × 9.2 cm] [3 lilies at centre, 3.8 × 3.9 cm] | HUNTER, ROSE & Cᵒ'.

MARGINALIA University of Toronto, front binder's leaf, black ink: 'Nettie B. Davis | Burlington | Ontario.'; title page, bookseller's ticket: '1,00 | R.R. NEWS | CO.'

The books were bound in both cloth and paper, and by Saturday, 30 October, they were ready. They went to the shop of the Clougher Brothers, retail booksellers located at 25 King Street West, and sold there for $1 (cloth) or 75¢ (paper). They were also sold on trains. One of the copies naturally found its way to a reviewer at the Toronto *Mail,* who read it within a few days and then praised it as 'one of the cleverest novels of the season,' adding that it 'should be in the hands of all lovers of really good fictitious literature.' The geographical dissemination of the Belford edition extended beyond the city of Toronto. A female reader from Burlington, Ontario, purchased one of the copies bound in cloth at the advertised price. The edition did not sell out immediately. Ten months later, the Belfords still had copies for sale.[27]

In this or similar manner the Belford Brothers reprinted some fourteen works in 1875. In general, they selected a text, contracted a local printer to set and print it as cheaply as possible, arranged for the sheets to be bound, and placed the finished product with a local bookseller. They invested little in publicity or overhead, having neither regular advertisements in the newspapers nor a substantial office. They saved money wherever possible in production, shifting their orders to the local printer who offered them the best price: Samuel Bell printed some of their early books, while Hunter, Rose printed others. Their connection with the bookseller John Balfe Clougher and his brothers was more constant. Advertisements in the *Mail* indicate that the Clougher Brothers regularly sold Belford publications until at least the summer of 1877. In all of these aspects – text selection, financing and contracting out of production, and wholesale distribution – their activity as reprinters overlapped with that of a specialist publisher. The one difference, of course, was that Alexander and Robert did not pay the (foreign) author. Like their American counterparts decades earlier, they were able to enter the international fray of English-language literary publishing successfully by spending nothing on (or not being delayed in any way by) permissions or royalties involving distant parties. Their misconstruction of the 1875 act thus made them into the embryo of a Canadian literary publisher.

Competition was always present in the form of the American reprint, and the Belfords tapped into a rhetoric of nationalism in an attempt to beat it. In December, Samuel Richmond Hart and Thomas Wilby Rawlinson, located at 5 King Street West in Toronto, began selling *Farm Legends* by the popular American poet Will Carleton.[28] The work had originally been published by Harper and Brothers of New York. The *Mail* favourably reviewed the volume on 10 December. Within two weeks, Belford Brothers brought out their own edition of the work, and in order to prefer it over the edition praised earlier, the *Mail* focused on its more thoroughly Canadian substance:

> This handsome volume is essentially a Canadian production, save as to authorship. The paper, print, binding, and illustrations are all Canadian, and as pretty as could be turned out in English or American cities claiming a high reputation for the style of their publications. The ballads are charming – full of the atmosphere of home and country life, and human thoughts and affections. Nor is the element of true humour and satire wanting. The volume is eminently suitable for a Christmas offering, chiming in as it does with the amenities of the season. The publishers are to be congratulated upon the good taste and enterprise displayed in bringing out the book.[29]

Reprinters are not encumbered by permissions or royalties, but they also have no assurance that readers will buy their edition over another. If the Belfords took their cue from an American edition, they nevertheless had to struggle to get ahead of it in the domestic market, and Canadian booksellers had long since become expert in the business of importing. Manipulating the ideology of nationalist protectionism was one means that Belford Brothers used to combat the American reprint and promote their own editions in the absence of copyright.

In 1876 Belford Brothers expanded on the reprint formula that they had tested the previous year. In March they compiled *Old Times on the Mississippi* from pieces that Mark Twain had published in the *Atlantic Monthly* – chapters 4 through 17 of what Twain eventually published as *Life on the Mississippi*.[30] *Old Times on the Mississippi* was ready by the end of the month. On Saturday, 25 March, the Clougher Brothers were selling it at the price of 75¢ (cloth) or 50¢ (paper).[31] In April, Alexander and Robert hit a particularly rich vein in Norman Macleod, the Scottish minister and journalist. Donald Macleod's biography, *Memoir of Norman Macleod,* was first published in 1876 by Daldy, Isbister of London and by Charles Scribner of New York. The Belfords soon brought out their own edition. It sold rapidly, and they adapted to the demand by offering more lavishly bound copies. By early May the Clougher Brothers were selling the edition at $2.50 (cloth extra), $4 (half calf), and $6 (morocco).[32] From then until May of the following year Alexander and Robert both fed off and fed Norman Macleod's popularity by reprinting five of his works. The diversification of the bindings and the multiplication of offered titles show them aggressively pursuing what had proved to be a lucrative opportunity. When they reprinted Anthony Trollope's *The Prime Minister* in June, squeezing the four volumes of the authorized edition published by Chapman and Hall of London into a single 547-page tome, they began to advertise directly. Under their own name and address, they publicized *The Prime Minister* at the price of $1.25 (cloth) or $1 (paper), although the Clougher Brothers continued to sell this and other Belford books at equal prices.[33]

With successful reprinting as their base, Alexander and Robert ventured into original publishing. Six of the over forty books they brought out under their imprint in 1876 were new works by Canadian authors. These included *Life and Letters of Richard Cartwright* by Conway Edward Cartwright, *The Fair Grit* and *The Earl of Beaconsfield* by Nicholas Flood Davin, *The Prairie Province* by James Cleland Hamilton, *The Grand Trunk Railway of Canada* by M. Butt Hewson, and *History of the Grange in Canada* by the 'Patrons of Husbandry.' The financial arrangements behind each of these editions are unknown, and it may be that the authors were made to shoulder the bulk of the risk. However, it is clear that these publications were authorized. How else but through dealing with the author would the Belfords have obtained an unpublished text? The possibility of original Canadian publishing, involving local authors and backed by solid profits in reprints, is discernible in these examples.

The most palpable effect of the Belfords' interpretation of the recent copyright reform, however, was their turning to supply the wider North American market. In expanding their Toronto operations to ship books south, Belford Brothers dazzlingly realized the theory articulated in John Rose's second memorandum on copyright, namely, that Canada could compete in what was in many ways a single continental arena. As Rose had predicted, Americans sat up and took notice when Canadian reprints began appearing in the United States. No case achieved greater notoriety than did the Belford edition of *The Adventures of Tom Sawyer*. Expecting great profit from the work, Mark Twain had made careful arrangements for its publication. Chatto and Windus were to publish it first in London in order to secure British copyright, and the American Publishing Company of Hartford, Connecticut, would follow with a high-priced edition for the United States that was available only by subscription. The London edition duly appeared on 9 June 1876. Disastrously for Twain, the American edition was beset with delays and would not be ready until December. In the interval, Alexander and Robert acquired a copy of the Chatto and Windus edition (selling in Toronto at $2.25), had it reprinted, and by the beginning of August were offering an edition at $1 (cloth) or 75¢ (paper).[34] By November, Twain had discovered that the Belford edition had pre-empted his in his own country. He vented his frustration in a letter to his friend Moncure Daniel Conway, who represented his interests in London: 'Belford Bros., Canadian thieves, are flooding America with a cheap pirated edition of Tom Sawyer. I have just telegraphed Chatto to assign Canadian copyright to me, but I suppose it is too late to do any good. We cannot issue for 6 weeks yet, and by that time Belford will have sold 100,000 over the frontier and killed my book dead. This piracy will cost me $10,000, and I will spend as much more to choke off those pirates, if the thing can be done. Ask Chatto if he gave Belford Bros permission to publish.'[35] Conway duly alerted Chatto and Windus, and on 15 November they telegraphed the Belfords that *The Adventures of Tom Sawyer* was protected by imperial copyright. The Belfords' reply (transcribed by Conway in his next letter to Twain) clearly indicates that they held the Canadian Copyright Act of 1875 to be the sole basis for any claim to copyright in Canada: ' "We today recd your telegram in reference to Tom Sawyer. We should be very sorry to conflict with your interest in any way in Canada. We know Americans are in the habit of taking out copyright in England, but we doubt if it would hold there: we are well advised that it gives no right in Canada. We shall be glad, however, to hear further from you on the subject." '[36] The matter ended there. The unauthorized Belford edition was being sold at news-stands or through the mail across Canada and the United States, but neither the American author nor his English publisher could stop it, because Canada had apparently become a sovereign copyright zone. Twain's next letter to Conway indicates acceptance of the Belfords' position. Chatto and Windus had even gone so far as to request a legal opinion of the 1875 act: 'The Publishers say that as near as their lawyers can make it out, English copyright is not worth anything in Canada, unless it be recorded in Canada, within sixty days after publication in England.'[37] (The 1875 act was indeed subtle if even an English publisher urgently searching for a confirmation of imperial copyright could not find this in it.)

Besides the ambiguity of the 1875 act and Mark Twain's vexation, the case shows the Belfords realizing the full potential of Canadian reprinting as Rose and others had imagined it. They had expanded prodigiously, reconfiguring their business in a way that defined the Canadian book as a North American commodity, a definition that the American book had been enjoying for decades. A Canadian edition had been showered with outstanding North American sales. Succeeding generations of Canadian publishers would dream of but not again achieve this until the late twentieth century. The Belfords' *Adventures of Tom Sawyer* channelled money from across the continent into profits concentrated in Toronto. It must have been a powerful inducement for Americans to reconsider the idea of international copyright. In his final remonstration over the 1875 act, Alfred Dymond had urged, 'we should seek to place our publishers on such a footing as regards our American rivals that they might be able to enter the market with the possibility of successfully competing with them.'[38] Under a genuine misconstruction of the 1875 act, Belford Brothers had achieved this footing, but they would not hold it long.

Precisely because it was so successful, the bold new independence in Canadian book production could not escape international attention. Twain was not the first to feel the impact of Canadian reprinting. When they wrote to Chatto and Windus in November, Alexander and Robert had already been ensnared in the lawsuit that would ultimately undo their Canadian success.

Thrift was the third in a series of didactic works on social improvement. The author, Samuel Smiles, had been born in Scotland to Calvinist parents. He trained as a physician but abandoned medicine for journalism. Through George Stephenson, he became a secretary in various railway enterprises; when Stephenson died, Smiles wrote his biography, which was published in 1857. It met with great acclaim and set Smiles on the path to becoming a distinguished biographer. In 1859 he persuaded John Murray to publish an expanded lecture on popular education, entitled *Self-Help, with Illustrations of Character and Conduct.* It sold 20,000 copies in its first year, was translated into a dozen languages, and remained in demand for the rest of the century. The other works in the series were *Character* (1871), *Thrift* (1875), *Duty* (1880), and *Life and Labour* (1887). By the 1870s, Smiles was a well-established author with a multifaceted and international fame.[39]

In the fall of 1875 Smiles arranged for the publication of *Thrift* by Murray in London and by Harper and Brothers in New York. No contract of this arrangement has come to light, but the arguments subsequently heard in court, which refer to 'an edition . . . by Messrs. Harper Bros., of New York, being already in the [Canadian] market,' suggest that Smiles followed the usual pattern of ceding Canada to the American publisher.[40] Murray published his edition on 15 November 1875.[41] Printed by Hazell, Watson, and Viney of London and Aylesbury, it was a book of twenty-six gatherings bound in green cloth profusely decorated in black and gold:

Thrift: Murray Edition[42]

COLLATION ⁶ 1–24⁸ 25⁶ [$ 1 signed]. 204 leaves. Pages *i–v* vi *vii* viii–xi *xii* 1 2–378 *379* 380–384 1–12 [= 408].
TYPOGRAPHY 37 lines, 135 (145) × 84 mm; 10 lines = 36 mm; capital 2.5 (x 1.5) mm.

On 3 January 1876 Smiles took the precaution of registering it at Stationers' Hall in London.[43] An important provision of the imperial Copyright Act of 1842 was that one could not litigate in defence of one's copyright without having first registered it.[44] The American edition may have appeared simultaneously with the British or slightly after it; the earliest copy I have examined is dated 1876. Whether working with advance sheets or a published copy from Murray, the Harpers Americanized the spelling, altered the title page, and substituted new advertisements. They typeset the work afresh, devised a more economical imposition, and cast a new set of plates. The American edition ran to the same number of pages but was altogether a different book, consisting of seventeen twelve-leaf gatherings:

Thrift: Harper Edition[45]

COLLATION 1^{12}–17^{12} [$ 1, 5 signed (–1_1)]. 204 leaves. Pages *1–5* 6 7 8–11 *12–13* 14–400 *401* 402–404 *1* 2–4 [= 408].
TYPOGRAPHY 36 lines, 136 (147) × 82 mm; 10 lines = 38 mm; capital 2.4 (x 1.5) mm.

It was bound in a lighter green cloth and had the author's signature stamped in gold on the front. Its retail price was $1.50.

In April 1876 Belford Brothers reprinted *Thrift,* contracting out the production to George Brown's Globe Printing Company, located at 26–28 King Street East in Toronto. Charles later wrote that they had applied to Smiles for permission but that he had not answered[46] – a claim that is impossible to verify. Similarity in spelling suggests that the Belfords modelled their edition on the Harpers'. The employees at the Globe typeset the text, cast stereoplates from them, and printed off sheets that contained the whole work in three hundred pages – a hundred fewer than the original copy:

Thrift: Belford Edition[47]

COLLATION ^{4} 1–18^8 19^4 [$ 1 signed]. 152 leaves. Pages *5–9* 10–307 *308* [= 304].
TYPOGRAPHY 38 lines, 130 (142) × 89 mm; 10 lines = 39 mm; capital 2.3 (x 1.4) mm.

The books were bound in dark green cloth. Imitating the Harper edition, they had the author's signature stamped in gold on the front. The Belford edition was priced below the others and sold in great quantities from April on.[48]

It is not known who was the first to object to the Belford reprint, the American publisher or the British author, but both were interested in arraigning it. The Harpers would have been more aware of being undercut in the North American market and may have complained to the author about the invasion of their territory. However, Smiles was a member of the Copyright Association,[49] and as the party ultimately responsible for the 1875 act the Association would have been all too ready to see it correctly interpreted and enforced. On 21 June the Toronto firm of Beatty, Miller, and Biggar wrote to the Belfords on behalf of Smiles, accusing them of copyright infringement, forbidding their edition, and demanding that they hand over all profits from it as well as any unsold copies.[50]

Faced with a formal charge of infringement, Alexander and Robert appealed for help to their second cousin, James Beaty Jr (1831–99), who was senior partner in the firm of Beaty, Hamilton, and Cassels. On 24 June he responded to Smiles's lawyers: 'Messrs. Belford Bros. hand us your notice concerning this Canadian publication. The persons for whom you act have no interest or right in the matter and you may so inform them.'[51] An application was filed in the Ontario Court of Chancery for an injunction against the reprinters, and the case came before Vice-Chancellor William Proudfoot at Osgoode Hall in Toronto on Tuesday, 1 August 1876. Arguments continued on 5 and 12 September. During this time the motion for an injunction was changed to a motion for decree (a clarification of the law) because the defendants did not dispute the facts of the case. On 25 September, after a period of consideration, the vice-chancellor delivered judgment.[52]

The decision hinged on a simple question: was imperial copyright still in force in Canada?[53] The prosecution argued that it was, relying on the well-researched line of argument that the Copyright Association had obtained from Palmer and Herschell five years earlier during the skirmish over *Ginx's Baby*. Notwithstanding the 'exclusive legislative authority' over copyright granted by section 91 of the British North America Act, section 129 of the same act stated that the Dominion had no power to repeal any act of the British parliament.[54] Hence the 'exclusive' Canadian control over copyright must merely distinguish a federal power from a provincial one. True sovereignty over copyright rested with Britain.

The defence argued that imperial copyright was not in force in Canada, because the 1875 act conflicted with the 1842 act. As the former had received extraordinary confirmation from the British parliament through the Canada Copyright Act, it could not be invalid. The Crown had pored over it and made special allowance for it, and no clause could be deemed repugnant after such a careful process. It must therefore

1 Thomas Ryan (1804–89) (Canadian senator), 1869. Library and Archives Canada.

2 John Rose (1820–88) (Canadian minister of finance), date unknown. Library and Archives Canada.

3 Thomas Henry Farrer (1819–99) (British undersecretary at the Board of Trade), circa 1897. *Notables of Britain: An Album of Portraits and Autographs* (London: Review of Reviews Office, 1897), 196. McGill University Library.

4 Alfred Hutchison Dymond (1827–1903) (Canadian Member of Parliament), 1874. Library and Archives Canada.

THRIFT.

By SAMUEL SMILES,

AUTHOR OF 'CHARACTER,' 'SELF-HELP,' ETC.

" Be thrifty, but not covetous: therefore give
Thy need, thine honour, and thy friend his due.
Never was scraper brave man. Get to *live*,
Then live, and use it : else it is not true
That thou hast gotten. Surely use alone
Makes money not a contemptible stone."
GEORGE HERBERT.

" To catch Dame Fortune's golden smile,
Assiduous wait upon her ;
And gather gear by ev'ry wile
That's justify'd by Honour :
Not for to hide it in a hedge,
Nor for a train attendant ;
But for the glorious privilege
Of being Independent."
ROBERT BURNS.

LONDON:

JOHN MURRAY, ALBEMARLE STREET.

1875.

The right of Translation is reserved.

5 Title page of *Thrift* by Samuel Smiles (London: John Murray, 1875). Thomas Fisher Rare Book Library, University of Toronto.

THRIFT.

By SAMUEL SMILES,

AUTHOR OF "CHARACTER," "SELF-HELP," ETC.

"Be thrifty, but not covetous: therefore give
Thy need, thine honor, and thy friend his due.
Never was scraper brave man. Get to *live*,
Then live, and use it: else it is not true
That thou hast gotten. Surely use alone
Makes money not a contemptible stone."
GEORGE HERBERT.

"To catch Dame Fortune's golden smile,
Assiduous wait upon her;
And gather gear by ev'ry wile
That's justfy'd by Honor:
Not for to hide it in a hedge,
Nor for a train attendant;
But for the glorious privilege
Of being Independent."
ROBERT BURNS.

NEW YORK:

HARPER & BROTHERS, PUBLISHERS,

FRANKLIN SQUARE.

1876.

6 Title page of *Thrift* by Samuel Smiles (New York: Harper & Brothers, 1876).
Author's copy.

THRIFT.

BY SAMUEL SMILES,

AUTHOR OF "CHARACTER," "SELF-HELP," ETC.

" Be thrifty, but not covetous: therefore give
Thy need, thine honor, and thy friend his due.
Never was scraper brave man.   Get to *Live*,
Then live, and use it : else it is not true
That thou hast gotten.   Surely use alone
Makes money not a contemptible stone."
GEORGE HERBERT.

" To catch Dame Fortune's golden smile,
Assiduous wait upon her ;
And gather gear by ev'ry wile
That's justify'd by Honor :
Not for to hide it in a hedge,
Nor for a train attendant ;
But for the glorious privilege
Of being Independent."
ROBERT BURNS.

TORONTO:
BELFORD BROTHERS, PUBLISHERS.
1876.

7 Title page of *Thrift* by Samuel Smiles (Toronto: Belford Brothers, 1876).
Thomas Fisher Rare Book Library, University of Toronto.

DOMINION OF CANADA.

All communications
should be addressed to
The Minister of Agriculture
(Copyright & Trade Mark Branch.)
Ottawa.

Circular No 5.

Department of Agriculture,

(Copyright & Trade Mark Branch.)

Ottawa, Canada, Sept. 29th,1915.

PROHIBITION ORDER.

Whereas by an Act passed in the 63-64 year of the reign of Her Late Majesty, entitled "An Act to Amend the Copyright Act," it **is** provided that if a book as to which there is subsisting copyright under *The Copyright Act* has been first lawfully published in any part of His Majesty's dominions other than Canada, and if it is proved to the satisfaction of the Minister of Agriculture that the owner of the copyright so subsisting and of the copyright acquired by such publication has lawfully granted a license to reproduce in Canada, from movable or other types, or from stereotype plates, or from electro-plates, or from lithograph stones, or by any process for facsimile reproduction, an edition or editions of such book designed for sale only in Canada, the Minister may, notwithstanding anything in *The Copyright Act*, by order under his hand, prohibit the importation, except with the written consent of the licensee, into Canada of any copies of such book printed elsewhere ; provided that two such copies may be specially imported for the *bona fide* use of any public free library or any university or college library, or for the library of any duly incorporated institution or society for the use of the members of such institution or society.

AND WHEREAS there is subsisting copyright under *The Copyright Act*, as to the book the

title of which is " A Far Country," by Winston Churchill,

," which book was

first lawfully published in Great Britain, and whereas it has been proved to my satisfaction

that Winston Churchill,

the owner of the copyright,

so subsisting and of the copyright acquired by such publication, has lawfully granted to

The MacMillan Company of Canada,Limited, of the City of

Toronto, Province of Ontario, a license to reproduce in Canada
editions of such book designed for sale only in Canada.

I do, therefore, order, subject to the proviso contained in the said Act, that the

importation, except with the written consent of the said The MacMillan Company

of Canada, Limited,

into Canada of the said book printed elsewhere, be and the same is hereby prohibited.

Given under my hand and seal on the day and date above written.

Actg. Deputy of the *Minister of Agriculture.*

THE COMMISSIONER OF CUSTOMS,
OTTAWA.

for Registrar of Copyrights, &c.

8 Prohibition order re: *A Far Country* by Winston Churchill, 29 September 1915.
Macmillan Company of Canada Fonds, box 146.

have rescinded the latter. Beaty and Hamilton cited the many particu-
larities of the 1875 act and pointed out that Smiles had not complied
with its conditions; however, in assuming that the two acts clashed, they
failed to grasp the difference between *Canadian copyright* and *copyright
in Canada.* Triumphantly they pointed to the fifteenth clause, believing
it to mean that an author had to print an edition of his or her work in
Canada in order to enjoy any copyright there. They thus fell prey to the
act's subtlety. Where they saw a basic separation between British copyright on the one hand and copyright in Canada on the other, there was
in fact none. Although it got mired in these legal niceties, the defence
nevertheless made a compelling argument on economic and cultural
grounds. The Belfords were attempting to prove the commercial viabil-
ity of the Canadian book. The purpose of the Canadian parliament in
undertaking copyright reform in the first place was precisely this, to
free Canadian printers from imperial copyright so far as to allow them
to compete with American publishers in the field of general literature. If
Canadian copyright were not disentangled from the empire, Beaty and
Hamilton warned, American publishers would continue to possess the
Canadian market while Canadian publishers would be prevented from
competing. American books would for the foreseeable future dominate
Canadian bookstores and Canadian minds: 'Such a state of affairs could
not have been contemplated by our Legislature.'[55]

Vice-Chancellor Proudfoot ruled in favour of the plaintiff, accepting the prosecution's arguments and adding that the defunct Canadian
Copyright Bill of 1872 was proof of Britain's continuing supremacy in
the matter of copyright notwithstanding Confederation. (This was the
point that had so affected Thomas Ryan.) Proudfoot corrected Beaty
and Hamilton's concept of the 1875 act, explaining that it could be read
as merely complementing imperial copyright. Section 15 did not divide
Canadian from British copyright: what it did was prescribe the way in
which imperial copyright in Canada could be reinforced by Canadian
copyright in order to stop the importation of foreign reprints. The two
overlapped and were not mutually exclusive, and Smiles's failure to
secure the latter in no way abrogated the former. But on the economic
and cultural impact of his decision, the vice-chancellor was noticeably
silent. Doubtless he felt that it was not the role of the judiciary to shape
the law with an eye to increasing the monetary or intellectual wealth of
the country, this being the duty of the legislature; as a judge, he could at
best clarify the existing law. Nonetheless, he did show sympathy for the
Belfords' position with a certain clemency in his judgment. Smiles had

demanded that the Belfords hand over their profits. Proudfoot denied this demand on the grounds that it was impossible to know how many expensive, authorized editions would have sold if the inexpensive, unauthorized edition had not been available.[56] He therefore merely ordered that the defendants pay the plaintiff's legal costs.

The reaction to the judgment was twofold. Immediately, the decision provoked disappointment, confusion, and anger in Canada. These feelings culminated in an unsuccessful appeal of the ruling in the winter. In the longer term Canadian firms evolved under the unfavourable decision, adapting their business to its irresistible implications. The Belfords began to distribute foreign editions, negotiating for the right to do so from the foreign publishers who held sway over the imperial copyright, and subsequent Canadian book suppliers followed this path. Alexander and Robert soon abandoned Canada, but the legal conditions that they had illuminated continued to prevail over literary book production there long after their departure.

After the judgment Charles Belford leaped to his younger brothers' aid, formally joining their publishing firm on 2 October 1876, days after the judgment.[57] There is no indication that Robert's involvement ceased, but the name Belford Brothers now designated a partnership between Charles and Alexander. Charles used the columns of the *Mail* to protest the outcome of the trial and drum up support for an appeal. A long editorial on the day after the judgment bristled with frustration and stubbornly repeated the arguments of the defence. He dwelt on the Canada Copyright Act as proof that the intention of the government was to give English authors no copyright in Canada unless it was Canadian copyright: 'But when the Imperial Parliament deliberately set to work to remove whatever repugnancy existed, and agreed that the law passed in Canada should govern in Canada, it is somewhat humiliating and extremely ridiculous to awake to the consciousness that the two Parliaments have been engaged in the broadest farce it is possible to conceive. The Canadian Act is but waste paper, the Imperial Act a delusion and a snare, and the proclamation based thereon a *brutum fulmen* [empty thunder], so far as English authors are concerned!'[58] Charles pleaded for financial assistance for legal costs by presenting the Belford brothers as leaders who battled imperial law on behalf of their fellows. He regretted that the oppressive dictum of the court would now constitute the law of the land, coyly adding, 'unless the defendants ask for a rehearing, which, in their own interest, they may probably not feel disposed to do.' In other words, an appeal was possible and desirable if adequate money flowed in.

Charles's editorial ended with an accurate prediction of the effect of the judgment. Since imperial copyright was enough to suppress a Canadian edition, publishers in Canada would abandon their ambition to print works locally, choosing instead to import American editions. The result, exemplified by Lovell's Rouses Point factory, would be a recession in all industries of the Canadian book trade except import distribution:

> The absurdity of the thing becomes more apparent when we add that the judgment just given, the legality of which we are not questioning, will not materially affect Canadian publishers driven to the extremity of getting around it. There is no publisher in Canada, we feel confident, who would not rather make an arrangement to pay the English author a royalty than to republish his book without his consent. But there are authors and publishers in England who will enter into no arrangements with publishers in this country, for the avowed reason that they have sold their rights in Canada to American publishers! We have been shown a letter from a leading English publisher to a publisher in Canada, which, in reply to a request for an arrangement for re-publication in Canada, says that he has already sold to a publishing house in New York, 'which will no doubt take steps to secure its rights in Canada.' The Canadian Act of 1875 was intended to overcome by force of law such absurd arrangements as these; but as the law, as now interpreted, declares that that Act is of no force or effect, the only recourse left for Canadian publishers is to get such English books as they cannot arrange for, printed in the United States. Mr. Lovell, of Montreal, had to remove his large printing house from that city to Rouse's Point, to get over the absurdities of the copyright law as it affected Canada. The Canadian Parliament was patriotic enough to attempt to remedy the monstrous evil which drove Mr. Lovell out of the country, and the Imperial Parliament and Government were loyal enough to the connection to give effect, as they supposed they were doing, to the Act of our Parliament. But it appears that the legislation of both Parliaments, and the assent given thereto by the Queen, are not of the value of a straw; and the upshot of the whole thing is that a good deal of work which should be done in Canada, thereby giving employment to printers, designers, engravers, and paper makers, must, perforce, be done in the United States. This is indeed a condition of things which ought to cause us to hang our heads in shame.

We have said that the defendants may not think it worth their while to ask for a rehearing. And the reason for this is, that the judgment of Vice-Chancellor Proudfoot is at least quite as advantageous to Canadian

publishers who are anxious to enter into arrangements with British authors and publishers as a reverse judgment would be. Indeed in many
respects it is more advantageous. In some cases it will drive our publishers
to get their printing done in the United States; but this will be more the
country's loss than theirs.[59]

Charles's analysis was prescient. Unable to build up a reprint business, the leading Canadian book suppliers would generally arrange to
import American editions rather than have their own manufactured locally. If a British author such as Samuel Smiles ceded Canadian sales
to an American publisher such as the Harpers, there was no role left
for an aspiring Canadian publisher such as the Belfords besides that of
dealing out the American edition to local retailers. The best-sellers of the
English-speaking world would not nurture a local publishing industry,
though thousands of copies flowed to Canadian readers. Canada was a
captive market.

The next day, Charles reprinted the editorial of an ally at the Hamilton
Spectator. It echoed his disappointment, declaring copyright to be a
'puzzle' and lamenting the ability of the British copyright owner to 'ha-
rass' Canadian book suppliers. It also decried the advantage given to
imported American books, but this was not all: American magazines
also entered Canada, to the detriment of Canadian magazine publishing. Moreover, the writer of this editorial criticized the structural problem of governance that had warped the reform from the beginning,
accurately identifying the London publishers' role in blocking both the
1872 and 1873 bills:

> After years of such agitation as the small number of men interested in
> the trade could raise, the attention of the Canadian Parliament was called
> to the anomalous state of the law, and in 1872 an Act was passed which
> provided that the holder of a copyright for Canada must have the book
> which it protects published in Canada, within a certain time from the reg-
> istration of the copyright. This Act, however, was held to conflict with the
> Imperial Act, and an effort to obtain legislation in the Imperial Parliament
> to harmonize the two Acts was defeated through the influence of British
> publishers.[60]

The Copyright Association, a private British lobby group, was interfer-
ing in the proper government of Canada in a way that the British North
America Act should have precluded. It was exercising undue power

over the legislative process and hence over the economic development of Canada. Louis Mallet had anticipated and attempted to avert this accusation as early as 1869 but had not been successful; it now hit home with some force. Most unsettling of all were the cultural ramifications of sacrificing local publishing:

> If the interests of the publishing trade alone were affected by this decision, the matter involved would still be an important one. The publishing trade is the nursery of literary genius. The gifted mortals whose thoughts thrill mankind, and move our laughter and tears, are rarely endowed with practical business qualities. It is their part to create the splendid thought, but it is the part of the publisher to coin it into money, and without money in some adequate measure even genius cannot display the full grandeur of its power. If Burns' life had not been a fierce struggle with poverty we might have had companion pieces to 'The Cotter's Saturday Night,' and the charms of the 'Vicar of Wakefield' would have been duplicated in other similar works if less of Goldsmith's energies had been directed to the means of paying his rent and purchasing a scuttle of coals. If we are making special arrangements for the suppression of the Canadian publishing trade, as we seem to be doing, we are building to that end much better than most of us are aware of.[61]

It is not true that commercially successful publishing must yield good literature. However, literature *is* a function of authorship combined with reception; creation is dependent on an encouraging audience, and publishing connects the two. Bookselling might continue as before, but distinctively Canadian literature would suffer from the judgment because insecurity in specialist publishing would hinder local authors from connecting with local readers without the mediation of a distant party holding the trump card of capital.

The Toronto *Globe* also expressed surprise. George Brown, the proprietor, had been on the Senate committee that had revised the fifteenth clause of the 1875 act, and still its full import seems to have caught him off guard. An editorial complained that if this was the result of the arduous reform process that had led to the 1875 act and the Canada Copyright Act, then 'the work expended on these two measures has simply been thrown away.'[62] Nevertheless, the criticism of the ruling in the Canadian press was not unanimous. In a moderate editorial the *Montreal Herald* found that, however disappointing to the defendants, the judgment had interpreted the new law as the legislature had intended. The writer granted that copyright remained a 'vexed question' but recommended waiting for the Royal Commission to settle it fairly; in the meantime, reprinting remained 'but another name for thieving the products of the brains of the hardest workers in the world, and selling them at dishonest prices to all who care to buy.'[63]

On 26 September, the day after the judgment, the Belfords circulated a letter to the Canadian book trade soliciting support for an appeal:

> We enclose you leading articles from the Globe and the Mail of this city on the judgment delivered by Vice-Chancellor Proudfoot in the case of Smiles v. Belford. The Judgment is on all hands regarded as so extraordinary that a very general desire has been expressed that we should appeal against it. It is not to our interest to do this. It is better for us to pay royalty on 'Thrift' and the costs of the suit than to obtain a reversal of the present judgment. The issue involved is however an important one: it is whether the Imperial and Canadian Parliaments conjointly have power to change their own laws in favor of Canadian interests: and we should be unwilling to stand in the way of having it fairly tested if the trade desire to have that course taken and are willing to contribute towards the cost of the trial. We leave ourselves wholly in the hands of the trade. We should be therefore glad to hear from you on these two points
> 1. Do you desire to have the Case reheard?
> 2. Are you willing to help in obtaining a Judgment from the full Court?[64]

This statement of the issue identified the Copyright Association's influence over legislation as an unjust obstacle to Canadian sovereignty.

A few days later Joseph-Charles Taché wrote to the *Mail*, having 'seen in a printed circular that it is desired to have opinions obtained on the important subject of copyright previous to entering into further litigation and expense.' Taché was the deputy agriculture minister, the senior civil servant in charge of administering Canadian copyright. He sought to head off the appeal by explaining the current controversy as a misunderstanding arising from the Senate's revision of the fifteenth clause. Taché suspected that the astonishment at Proudfoot's ruling had ensued because 'many have remained under the impression (I know to a certainty that some have) that the 15th section of the bill, introduced in the Senate by the Minister of Agriculture, is identical with the 15th section of "The Copyright Act of 1875."' He went on to demonstrate the change. First he quoted the original fifteenth clause and remarked, 'Were this section of the bill now the law, Messrs. Belford would be quite right in answering Mr. Smiles as they did, and any Canadian publisher could reprint the book entitled "Thrift" as long as Mr. Smiles should decide not to republish and register the said book in Canada. But such is not the law.' Then he quoted the revised fifteenth clause and explained that it did not contain 'any derogation from the general disposition of both the Imperial and Dominion legislation which declare that *he who is the author of a work,* (or his legal representatives), *has the sole and exclusive right and liberty of printing, reprinting, publishing and republishing,* &c., &c.,' concluding that 'Messrs Belford had not the right to republish the book of Mr. Smiles without his agreement and consent.'[65] Taché ended by addressing the hot issue of Canadian sovereignty and defending the value of British supremacy. The United Kingdom was the 'parent state,' and Canada a 'dependency.' The law of copyright might not fulfil all the desires of domestic publishers, but it was not useless, because it allowed for the exclusion of some American books. More generally, it served Canadians well because it bound them to the parent state; the 1875 act embodied 'the recognition of a supremacy which must last as long as colonies are colonies and the United Kingdom their Mother Country: a state of dependence which may occasionally bring its difficulties, but which compensates them many times over, by the advantages derived from the connection.'[66] According to Taché, Canada gained more in imperial protection than it lost in national liberty.

One further reaction is worth noting. When word of the ruling reached him in London, John Rose wrote to Thomas Farrer at the Board of Trade, wondering at the failure of the 1875 act to permit and regulate Canadian reprinting: 'I can not conceive that the Act should be inoperative in principle. I can only imagine that the publisher neglected to comply with some of the formalities, such as notice + registration, required to give them the right to publish. I can not get hold of the text of the judgment, but I think that the case must have gone off on technical grounds. It will be curious if both Parliaments have been so singularly at fault.'[67] Confusion and reproach emanate from Rose's words. Had they spilled so much ink in vain in their 1872 correspondence? He was amazed that the reform over which they had laboured should have led to this – the confounding of a Canadian publisher.

Despite Taché's prediction that the case of *Thrift* 'cannot fail to meet, before any tribunal, the adjustment it has met with in the Court of Chancery of Ontario,' the Belfords went ahead with their appeal, supported by fellow members of the trade. The case came before Chief Justice John Godfrey Spragge and Justices Burton, Patterson, and Moss at the Ontario Court of Appeal on 15 December.[68] Beaty continued to speak for the Belfords, and he enlisted the assistance of the eminent lawyer Christopher Robinson. Miller and Biggar once more represented Smiles. The arguments, somewhat sharpened in their expression, were essentially the same as before. The defence attempted to come at the issue of Canadian sovereignty by insisting that the British North America Act had transferred all responsibility for copyright to the Parliament of Canada and that the complex path of the 1875 act through the Dominion and imperial legislatures implied a repeal of imperial copyright in Canada. The judgment was reserved for several months. When finally delivered on 17 March 1877, it upheld the ruling of the lower court. It spelled out again the compatibility of imperial and Canadian copyright. The appeal was dismissed, and the Belfords were again ordered to pay their opponent's legal costs.[69] The reaction in the *Mail* was muted. Apparently Charles decided that nothing further could be achieved. The Belfords had lost.

Belford Brothers continued energetically through the autumn of 1876 and the winter of 1877, but after the dismissal of the appeal, things began to change. With much fanfare they launched *Belford's Monthly Magazine* on 22 November 1876, following the example of leading American publishers. The declared intentions of the magazine were to reprint the best literature being written in English and so to reach a large audience in Canada, and a large circulation would in turn allow for the publication of local writing: 'The general popularity of the magazine is the prime requisite to a virile Canadian literature.'[70] *Belford's Monthly Magazine* was not unsuccessful. It continued as long as Alexander and Robert were in Toronto and after that was reincarnated for a time in New York. After the unsuccessful appeal, however, the Belfords adopted a new approach to periodical publishing. In April 1877 they announced that they had obtained from Chapman and Hall of London the right to be the Canadian distributor of the English magazine *The Fortnightly Review*. Each month thereafter the Belfords bought a duplicate set of stereotype plates from the English publisher and used them to produce a Canadian issue of the magazine, identical in every respect to the English original except in its imprint and somewhat cheaper price.[71]

The Belford brothers continued to reprint American books as individual cases allowed (that is, if they were not first published in the United Kingdom and therefore had no imperial copyright), but after their defeat in court they began to explore the possibility of collaborating with publishers abroad. In the spring of 1877 they issued Melville D. Landon's *Eli Perkins (at Large): His Sayings and Doings.* J.B. Ford of New York had published this in 1875:

Eli Perkins (at Large): Ford Edition[72]

ELI PERKINS | (*AT LARGE*): | HIS SAYINGS AND DOINGS. | BY | MELVILLE D. LANDON. | WITH MULTIFORM ILLUSTRATIONS BY UNCLE CONSIDER, | *After models by those designing young men, Nast, Darley, Fredericks,* | *Eytinge, White, Stephens, and others.* | [ornament, 1.6 × 1.3 cm: 'J', 'B', 'F', '& CO' intertwined] | NEW YORK: | J. B. FORD & COMPANY. | 1875.
COLLATION A^{12} B^{12}–C^{12} D^{12}–E^{12} F^{12}–G^{12} H^{12} I^{12} K^{12}–L^{12} M^2 [\$ 1 signed; F12 (143) signed 'H']. 134 leaves. Pages *i–iii* iv–viii 9–248 *1* 2–18 *19–20* [= 268]. Plate [1] (facing A1^a [*i*]).
CONTENTS *i* title. *ii* copyright statement: 'Entered, according to Act of Congress, in the year 1875, by | MELVILLE D. LANDON, | in the Office of the Librarian of Congress, at Washington.' *iii–iv* preface. v–viii contents. 9–248 text. *1–18* miscellaneous advertisements (one for J.B. Ford and Company, most for businesses located in New York). *19–20* blank.
TYPOGRAPHY 31 lines, 136 (145) × 84 mm; 10 lines = 44 mm; capital 2.3 (x 1.5) mm.
ILLUSTRATIONS Engraved frontispiece, signed 'A Bobbett': 'UNCLE CONSIDER's ADVICE. | *"Don't you never blow a man's branes out to git his money, Eli;* | *but you jes' sly aroun' an' blow his money out, an' so git his branes."'* Small illustrations on letterpress pages throughout.

The Belfords' book is almost identical to Ford's. The only differences are their name on the title page, the lack of copyright statement or frontispiece, more worn type (note the missing *d* in the title), and two fewer leaves (M^2) at the end of the advertisements. All in all, it is clear that the Belfords sold an issue of the American edition:

Eli Perkins (at Large): Belford Issue (Ford Edition)[73]

ELI PERKINS | (*AT LARGE*): | HIS SAYINGS AND DOINGS. | BY | MELVILLE D. LANDON. | WITH MULTIFORM ILLUSTRATIONS BY UNCLE CONSIDER, | *After mo<d>els by those designing young*

men, Nast, Darley, Fredericks | Eytinge, White, Stephens, and others. |
[rule, 2.4 cm] | TORONTO: | BELFORD BROTHERS, PUBLISHERS, |
MDCCCLXXVII.

COLLATION A^{12} B–C^{12} D–E^{12} F–G^{12} H^{12} I^{12} K–L^{12} [$ 1 signed; F12 (143)
signed 'H']. 132 leaves. Pages *i–iii* iv–viii 9–248 *1* 2–16 [= 264].

CONTENTS *i* title. *ii* blank. *iii*-iv preface. v–viii contents. 9–248
text. *1*–16 miscellaneous advertisements (one for J.B. Ford and
Company, most for businesses located in New York).

TYPOGRAPHY 31 lines, 136 (145) × 84 mm; 10 lines = 44 mm; capital
2.3 (x 1.5) mm.

ILLUSTRATIONS Small illustrations on letterpress pages throughout.

The near identity of physical form reveals the subsuming of the
Canadian production process by the American. Rather than making
their own edition as they had with *Norine's Revenge,* Belford Brothers
purchased part of Ford's for distribution to the Canadian market.

In May, Belford Brothers obtained permission from the popular
English novelist Ouida (Maria Louise Ramé) to issue three of her works
in Canada. In a flowing script on blue paper she wrote from her villa
in Florence in reply to their request: 'Be so good as to specify to me
more in detail what it is you wish + to which works yr. application has
reference. In any event or in any part of the world I could never accept
any arrangement for any royalty or percentage, that being a method
of payment that is most uncertain + undesirable. If y are willing explain y.self more fully by next mail the matter should be immediately
considered by me.'[74] An agreement was soon reached, and Belford
Brothers proceeded to issue at least three of Ramé's works over the
summer, again cooperating with the American publisher. *Ariadne,* for
example, was first published in three volumes in London, thus securing imperial copyright, and then in a single volume by J.B. Lippincott
of Philadelphia:

Ariadne: Lippincott Edition[75]

ARIADNE. | THE STORY OF A DREAM. | BY "OUIDA," |
AUTHOR OF "STRATHMORE," "GRANVILLE DE VIGNE,"
"UNDER TWO | FLAGS," "IDALIA," ETC. | [ornament, 2.8 ×
1.4 cm: book with entwined initials, 'J B L & Co', belt with
motto, 'DROIT•ET•AVANT', lamp] | PHILADELPHIA: | J. B.
LIPPINCOTT & CO. | 1877.

COLLATION Signed A–I^{12} K–Q^{12} [$ 1, 5 signed; A1 unsigned; $ 1, 3, 7, 9 also signed numerically from 1 to 32, for alternate gatherings in sixes: e.g., B1 (25) signed '3', B3 '3*', B7 '4', B9 '4*']. 192 leaves. Pages *1–4* 5–384.
CONTENTS *1* blank. *2* advertisement. *3* title. *4* copyright statement: '[rule, 1.7 cm] | Copyright, 1877, by J. B. LIPPINCOTT & Co. | [rule, 1.7 cm]'. *5* head title: 'ARIADNE: | THE STORY OF A DREAM.' 5–384 text.
TYPOGRAPHY 41 lines, 137 (147) × 82 mm; 10 lines = 33 mm; capital 2.3 (x 1.4) mm.

The Belfords arranged for their own issue of the Lippincott edition, either purchasing sheets printed expressly for them (with their name on the title page) or acquiring a duplicate set of plates and printing the sheets themselves. The books were then bound with their name on the spine and sold through local bookshops such as Willing and Williamson's:

Ariadne: Belford Issue (Lippincott Edition)[76]

ARIADNE. | THE STORY OF A DREAM. | BY "OUIDA," | AUTHOR OF "STRATHMORE," "GRANVILLE DE VIGNE," "UNDER TWO | FLAGS," "IDALIA," ETC. | [ornament, 2.8 × 1.4 cm: book with entwined initials, 'J B L & Co', belt with motto 'DROIT•ET•AVANT', lamp] | TORONTO: | BELFORD BROS. | 1877.
COLLATION A–I^{12} K–Q^{12} [$ 1, 5 signed; A1 unsigned; $ 1, 3, 7, 9 also signed numerically from 1 to 32, for alternate gatherings in sixes: e.g., B1 (25) signed '3', B3 '3*', B7 '4', B9 '4*']. 192 leaves. Pages *1–4* 5–384.
CONTENTS *1–2* blank. *3* title. *4* copyright statement and imprint: '[rule, 1.7 cm] | Copyright, 1877, by J. B. LIPPINCOTT & Co. | [rule, 1.7 cm] | [rule, 1.7 cm] Printed by J. B. LIPPINCOTT & Co., Philadelphia.' *5* head title: 'ARIADNE: | THE STORY OF A DREAM.' 5–384 text.
TYPOGRAPHY 41 lines, 137 (147) × 82 mm; 10 lines = 33 mm; capital 2.3 (x 1.4) mm.
BINDING *Material.* Purple cloth. *Front.* '[design, gold, 3.7 × 9.2 cm: author's signature, 'Yrs. [?] L de la Ramé Ouida']'. *Spine.* '[design, gold and black, from head to foot, including all of following] [at

middle:] OUIDA'S | NOVELS | ARIADNE | [at foot:] BELFORD
BROS.' *Back*. '[ornament, blind, 4.2 × 3.5 cm: entwined Bs, back to
back]'. *Endpapers*. Smooth brown. VARIANT BINDING LAC copy 2:
Material. Green cloth.
MARGINALIA LAC copy 1, front pastedown, ticket: 'Willing &
Williamson 12 King St Toronto'. LAC copy 2, title, black ink: 'Geo.
Stewart'.

The debt to Lippincott's edition is explicit: title page, copyright statement, and imprint all declare it. In producing this authorized Canadian
issue, the Belfords accepted the English author's property and the
American publisher's primacy. Having been chastened for infringement, they genuinely tried to adapt to the rules of imperial copyright.
Judging from their migration to the United States, however, these attempts to collaborate with the foreign publisher were not especially
rewarding.

In the fall of 1877 the Belfords' production entered a steep decline. A
Christmas advertisement lists under the headline 'New Publications' a
number of old titles originally reprinted long before.[77] February 1878 saw
the appearance of the first titles under a new name – the Rose-Belford
Publishing Company.[78] In April the merger was made official with letters patent and by-laws signed by George Maclean Rose, Alexander
and Robert Belford, and others.[79] Less than a year later, the connection
dissolved. Charles had entered his final illness. Alexander departed for
the United States, and Robert, though he remained in Toronto for a
time, soon followed him. The meteoric career of the Belford brothers as
Canadian reprinters was finished, but the structures that their struggle
had illuminated remained in place. For the next four decades aspiring
Canadian publishers of literature would mainly distribute American
and British books, constrained by the definitions of copyright in Canada
that the case of *Smiles v. Belford* had established and publicized.

Resentment and defiance marked Alexander Belford's later career.
He left Canada with the bitter sense that the law of copyright was artificial and unjust in its specific application there, and in the ensuing decade this attitude deteriorated into a reckless disregard for it generally.
Moving beyond the frontier of imperial copyright, he joined other expatriate Canadians such as George Munro and John Wurtele Lovell in
pushing American reprinting to the extreme, upsetting the traditional
courtesy of trade observed by the older American publishing houses.
The ferocious competition in cheap-book production of the 1880s, in

which Alexander took a leading part, was what ultimately inclined the United States to embrace copyright for foreign authors in 1891.[80]

In March 1879 Alexander joined with James Clarke to found Belford, Clarke and Company in Chicago.[81] Clarke had acted as a subscription agent for Belford Brothers in Toronto as early as 1877,[82] and when Alexander moved to Chicago, he followed. The Chicago firm, which both reprinted existing works and published new ones, had a brush with bankruptcy within its first twelve months but incorporated in May 1880 and expanded rapidly over the next few years, establishing 'retail stores, or agencies, in the largest cities of the United States,' including an office in New York in 1883 under the direction of Robert.[83] The aggressive and innovative strategy of placing their products in clothing stores may have given rise to the phenomenon of the selling of books by department stores.[84] At the peak of his success Alexander married Helen McNally, the daughter of the millionaire publisher Andrew McNally, and built a luxurious estate in San Juan Capistrano, California. They had two children, a boy and a girl, born about 1889 and 1891.[85]

Another copyright suit erupted in 1884. Charles Scribner of New York had published a popular cookbook, *Common Sense in the Household*, by Marion Harland (Mary Virginia Terhune) in 1871. When after ten years 100,000 copies had sold and the stereotype plates had worn out, the author revised the text, and Scribner's published a second edition. Alexander Belford appears to have begun reprinting this cookbook as early as 1877, while he was still in Canada, and he continued to do so after the move, contracting Donohue and Henneberry of Chicago to do the printing. Belford, Clarke's edition copied 170 recipes verbatim from Scribner's, rephrased a number more, imitated the arrangement of subjects and the index while altering some of the headings, and buried all of this behind a new preface and thirty pages of original recipes. A variety of title-pages, with different titles and fictitious authors and editors, masked the reprint. One title it sold under was the *Economy Cook Book*; another was *How to Cook*; yet another was the *Home Cook Book*. Between 1882 and 1884, Belford, Clarke sold at least 9,500 cloth-bound and 44,000 paper-bound copies of their edition – half as many again as the authorized edition had sold over the previous decade. On 18 January 1884, Scribner's charged Belford, Clarke with infringement. The defendants stubbornly fought back on a number of technical grounds, and the case dragged on for eight years. At last, in 1892, the Supreme Court of the United States ruled in favour of Scribner's and ordered Belford, Clarke to hand over what profits could be accounted for ($1,092), in addition to covering the prosecution's legal costs.[86] The covert reprinting and the obstinate protraction of the struggle through the maximum channels of appeal show a rabid denial of literary property in every form.

The reversals worsened in 1886. Individual creditors had complained of losses since the beginning, but Belford, Clarke's problems did not break into the open until a fire destroyed the firm's Chicago headquarters at the corner of Congress and Wabash avenues in May of that year. The collapse of an associate in San Francisco shortly thereafter dealt Belford, Clarke a further blow, and they contracted their national network of offices to two branches, one in New York, the other in San Francisco. The last straw may have been Andrew McNally's refusal to take on any more of their debt.[87] In 1889 the First National Bank of Chicago took legal action to recover a loan of $30,000, and sheriffs seized Belford, Clarke's entire property in Chicago and New York. Their liabilities, in the hundreds of thousands of dollars, outstripped their assets by a factor of two.[88] Owing to this enormous gap, Alexander and his partners were able to persuade the creditors most involved, such as the Trow Printing Company, to agree to two desperate proposals: first, to allow the firm to continue operating under a receiver, and second, to accept one-quarter of what they were owed ('twenty-five cents on the dollar'). These major creditors then coerced the minor ones into swallowing the unattractive deal. The previous firm divided into two new corporations – the Belford, Clarke Company in Chicago, which would focus on reprints, and the Belford Company in New York, which would continue to publish new works and issue *Belford's Magazine* – both operating in receivership.[89] By this scheme the Belfords and Clarke seem to have escaped the most crippling of their debts, at least temporarily.

In the early 1890s James Clarke left Alexander and Robert and went on to publish the American edition of the *Encyclopedia Britannica,* and the *Century Dictionary.* The Werner Company subsumed the Belfords' publishing business in the late 1890s, and Alexander may have been a major shareholder, but at the turn of the century it too went into receivership. Shortly thereafter Alexander ceased trying to make money from books and moved to California, where Robert had preceded him.[90]

He did not have a comfortable retirement. His health was failing, and his marriage was in ruins. At some point in the 1890s Alexander and Helen separated, bitterly disputing the division of their property. A sister or sister-in-law, Eleanor Belford, refused to leave the house at San Juan Capistrano. Although the McNallys removed all the furniture

from it, she stubbornly occupied the barren building for months before finally quitting it. Meanwhile Alexander's former creditors turned
to suing Helen, but in 1904 she at last secured a divorce. The terms
granted Alexander little more than the right to see his children occasionally. He was reduced to taking a low-salary job as a clerk at a real
estate company in Los Angeles. In early September 1906 he suffered a
paralysing stroke and was admitted to the Good Samaritan Hospital.
A few days later, on 7 September, he died.[91]

The British government studied the problem of imperial and international copyright exhaustively in the later nineteenth century. When
the Royal Commission on Copyright delivered its report in 1878, one of
the recommendations was for a system of state-licensed, unauthorized
reprinting, with a set rate of royalties to be paid to the author, for developing regions of the empire interested in establishing their own book-
publishing industries. The recommendation was never implemented. If
it had been, reprinters such as the Belfords might have continued on a
moderate course, and Canada would have developed a stronger, better
rooted, and more diversified book trade. As it happened, the inflex-
ibility of imperial copyright stunted and impoverished Canadian publishing, provoking emigration among book producers and wild reprint
practices beyond the empire's frontier, ultimately necessitating stricter
copyright legislation in the American republic too. Ultimately, the story
of the Belford brothers is a fascinating and vivid example of the ways
in which copyright law can impel capital, labour, and creativity to flow
into brilliant centres of cultural production, which tower over the vast
peripheral expanses that must pay them tribute.

4 Living with the 1875 Act: William Briggs, Printer, Binder, and Distributor

After *Smiles v. Belford,* Canadian firms generally turned once more to the subordinate role of distributing American or British editions. The clarification that Canada was not a separate copyright zone limited them from becoming general literary publishers, in that it inevitably stopped the unauthorized reprinting of popular texts, which was the simplest way to enter the game. The elimination of this possibility left the choice of whether or not to print an edition in or for Canada at the disposal of the imperial copyright owner, whose preference was usually to come to terms with an American publisher since the United States constituted the more important market. American publishers could demand that contracts cede them the Canadian market, which they were accustomed to supplying because of the Foreign Reprints Act. Owing to the continuing dominance of imperial copyright in Canada, members of the Canadian trade continued to ask permission to sell an imperial or foreign edition in Canada and to approach American publishers as often as British ones with their request.

Despite this fundamental obstacle, original Canadian publication intermittently occurred during the last quarter of the nineteenth century, and some leading Canadian book suppliers strove to attain the role of literary publishers, implicitly or explicitly presenting themselves as such. William Briggs, book steward (head) of the Methodist Book and Publishing House of Toronto (the forerunner of the Ryerson Press) for forty years, was the most important of these, and any revaluation of the term *publisher* in the period must account for him. Moreover, he exerted a formative influence on the next generation of Canadian book suppliers; George J. McLeod, Thomas Allen, John McClelland, and Frederick D. Goodchild all learned their trade at the Methodist Book and Publishing

House before founding companies of their own.[1] Previous assessments of Briggs's achievement, celebrating the many Canadian-authored editions that appeared under his imprint, have not disturbed his legacy as an important Canadian publisher. This chapter will review what is known about his books and then turn in detail to the case of a foreign publication in order to argue that Briggs's accomplishment as a literary publisher is in fact questionable. While the Methodist Book and Publishing House did indisputably publish religious periodicals throughout the period, it did not generally initiate, organize, and finance the production of original trade literature while William Briggs was at its head. He was a printer, binder, and wholesale distributor of literary books but not finally a specialist publisher.

At first glance, Briggs appears to have been not only a Canadian publisher but a prolific one. W. Stewart Wallace lists over seven hundred books in total that appeared with Briggs's imprint between 1879 (when he was elected book steward) and 1919 (when he officially entered retirement).[2] The annual tally jumps from about a half-dozen titles before 1879 to fifteen or twenty during Briggs's tenure, peaking at thirty-seven in 1897. Of the total, some were pamphlets, but many were full-length books, and while a fair number were religious (sermons, theological works, hymn books, and tracts), an increasing number were historical and literary.[3] Secular works began to dominate the list in 1893.[4] Furthermore, these figures purport to include only the Canadian original editions, not the agencies (foreign editions distributed in Canada). As Wallace explains, to include the latter 'would swell this check-list to an impossible size.'[5] It is the resultant enumeration of Canadian books that lies behind Wallace's judgment that Briggs 'gradually developed from being the publisher of books, pamphlets, and periodicals for the consumption of the members of the Methodist Church in Canada, into a publisher of Canadian literature, without reference to denominational considerations.' Stepping back to put this assessment in context, he goes on to claim that Briggs 'was the first Canadian publisher to undertake, on a large scale, the publication of books by Canadian writers.'[6]

At bottom, however, this celebration of Briggs as a Canadian publisher rests on the deceptive evidence of title-page imprints. An imprint does indicate involvement of some kind in the production or dissemination of a work, but alone it is not proof of a firm's having financed and organized an edition. The imprint may name only the printer or the regional distributor, leaving the real publisher unidentified. To determine whether a book with Briggs's imprint was in fact a Canadian original edition, it is necessary to look beyond the imprint. Business records are the best evidence of the publishing process, but other editions of a work are also illuminating. Despite his stated purpose, Wallace silently includes foreign editions of works by Canadian authors, such as Charles G.D. Roberts's *The Forge in the Forest* (Boston: Lamson, Wolffe, 1896), Ernest Thompson Seton's *Two Little Savages* (New York: Doubleday, Page, 1903), and Arthur Stringer's *The Silver Poppy* (New York: Appleton, 1903).[7] Briggs handled these works no differently than he did those of the best-selling Scottish author Samuel Rutherford Crockett, for example, whom Wallace excludes. This inconsistency misleads the reader into assuming that Briggs published the Canadian works when in fact he merely distributed an American edition of them.

Wallace uses the term *publisher* in the loose sense when he writes that 'William Briggs embarked not only on a policy of printing the work of Canadian authors, but also on a policy of publishing in Canada books that would appeal to the clientèle of the Methodist Book Room. He brought out Canadian editions of books by such writers as J. Jackson Wray, Annie S. Swan, Mrs. G.R. Alden ("Pansy"), E.P. Roe, S.R. Crockett, and Ethel M. Dell.'[8] Precisely, the role Briggs played was that of a distributor. As will become clear below, he issued and sold these works to the Canadian market but had no dealings with the authors and no hand in making their manuscripts into first editions. This popular usage of *publisher* is not uncommon, but it is misleading because it implies a relation with the author. The gravitation of such authors as Roberts, Seton, and Stringer to New York is a clear indication of where they felt the real publishers were.

Lorne Pierce's *The House of Ryerson* also distorts the extent to which William Briggs was a Canadian publisher. As the book editor of the Ryerson Press from 1920 to 1960, Pierce was the heir to Briggs's reputation, and some self-interest colours his history of 'the Mother Publishing House of Canada.'[9] His style swells to the oratorical at times, clearly pulsing with nationalism, Christianity, and literary resolve. One passage surely strays into exaggeration when it concludes that the Methodist Book and Publishing House 'above all ... would not be afraid to go, when necessary, beyond the call of duty – even to forget the cost and all other considerations of costs.'[10] On the contrary, William Briggs appears to have been an astute calculator of costs at all times.

Despite such noble colouring, Pierce's portrait remains valuable for the many details it draws from the company's primary records. One such detail reveals the financial arrangement that was key to the Canadian original editions that the company did publish. About 1846, the editor, George F. Playter, submitted his own manuscript on fine arts for the consideration of the book committee. Pierce relates that the 'Committee approved Playter's book on the fine arts and recommended its publication on a subscription basis' and then adds that this arrangement was 'a formula that became something of a ritual in the publishing house for a half a century.'[11] What Pierce here illuminates is that, from at least the mid-1840s on, the Methodist Book and Publishing House regularly arranged to print original editions, not by investing capital directly but by having payment collected in advance from prospective readers. The printing was contingent upon the securing of subscriptions. Subscription publishing, or the production of an edition conditionally on sufficient advance sales, has long been one of the financial tactics of publishers, normally reserved for large undertakings, but in the dealings of the Methodist Book and Publishing House with local authors it was the long-term standard practice. Moreover, the organizational work of finding the subscribers often fell to the authors themselves. Briggs generally printed the work of a new author on condition that the requisite capital be squeezed from elsewhere.

The Methodist Book and Publishing House did remain a publisher, in the true sense of the term, of religious periodicals. These were generally safe from the uncertainties of copyright that prevailed over trade literature because they were attached to the national churches. The Methodist congregations of Canada constituted a predictable market, and local ministers were obliged to act as agents.[12] Not surprisingly, the records Pierce cites repeatedly place the denominational papers at the centre of the publishing enterprise throughout William Briggs's time. In 1879 the book committee launched a new Sunday school paper, *Sunbeam,* and rebranded the old one as *Pleasant Hours* (formerly *Sabbath School Guardian*). The expansion paid off. Over the next decade the revenue from these two periodicals, together with the flagship *Christian Guardian,* increased greatly. In a pamphlet printed in 1891 the General Conference of the Methodist Church of Canada stressed the indispensability of the *Guardian,* and the book committee responded in 1894 by raising its circulation goal to twenty thousand. Expansion continued with the launching of *The Epworth Era* in 1898, and in 1902 the book committee was once more instructed to concentrate on the periodicals.[13]

Books, however, were another matter. Janet B. Friskney has shed light on the process by which Briggs printed a number of Canadian original editions, and the pattern she has uncovered is that he normally required someone else, usually the author, to pay for the production. In 1880 Briggs offered to publish a book of poems (*Canadian Idylls*) by William Kirby if the author fronted a hundred dollars to do so. Kirby refused. In 1886 Briggs printed *Toronto 'Called Back,' from 1886 to 1850* at the expense of the author, Conygham Crawford Taylor. Taylor remained in debt to the Methodist Book and Publishing House until his death twelve years later. To finance William Canniff's *The Medical Profession in Upper Canada, 1783–1850* (1894), Briggs obliged the author to come up with a minimum number of subscribers before publication and then to apply his share of later sales to any production costs that were outstanding. Friskney points out that the Methodist Book and Publishing House did not merely print this work but also circulated copies for review; still, Canniff was otherwise expected to do his own advertising. Before agreeing to bring out *Pearls and Pebbles; or, The Notes of an Old Naturalist* (1894), the head of Briggs's book-publishing department, Edward S. Caswell, requested that the ninety-two-year-old Catharine Parr Traill find two hundred individuals who would agree to buy the book in advance. She succeeded. The success of *Pearls and Pebbles* emboldened Briggs to publish Traill's next work, *Cot and Cradle Stories* (1895), on a royalty basis, offering the author 10 per cent; unfortunately, it did not sell as its predecessor had, and the experiment failed. The reprinting of Charles Mair's *Tecumseh* in 1901 also proceeded by subscription. Acting on Caswell's suggestion, the author and his friends found three hundred buyers in advance. Caswell's advocacy for Nellie McClung's *Sowing Seeds in Danny* (1908) was unusually warm; still, he could not promise anything until an American firm, Doubleday, Page, and Company, had been found to publish it. Although Briggs eventually offered Robert Service a royalty on the best-seller *Songs of a Sourdough* (1907), he initially printed it only because Service had included with his manuscript a cheque for a hundred dollars.[14] Over and over again, the pattern repeats itself: William Briggs was willing to 'publish' Canadian authors in book form on the condition that someone else foot the bill.

There were exceptions. Briggs offered to publish Service's later books on a royalty basis, for example, once his immense popularity was clear. In general, however, Friskney concludes that 'the expense of publishing books by Canadian authors was always a concern, and the cost of doing so was more often than not absorbed in one way or another by the writers themselves.'[15] Moreover, the number of Canadian-authored works printed by Briggs fell sharply after 1914. Ultimately the bulk of these examples inclines towards the conclusion that William Briggs admirably survived in the treacherous world of the Canadian book trade by avoiding the risk inherent in specialist publishing. Although he may have appropriated the name of publisher, he did not in fact nurture and develop Canadian writing with attractive offers to authors to invest in the production and dissemination of their work in book form.

The imperial and foreign original editions handled by William Briggs have been the subject of far less scholarly interest; nevertheless, it is clear that these constituted most of the books that the Methodist Book and Publishing House supplied to Canadian readers between 1879 and 1919. To make a complete list of them would be, to repeat Wallace's word, 'impossible.' The pages of the trade journals teem with advertisements and blurbs of the American and British books available through Briggs. Pierce writes that Briggs eventually turned away from printing new Canadian works and embraced the role of distributing books from abroad, while consolidating his role as a Canadian publisher of religious periodicals:

> The closing years of Dr. Briggs' régime were marked by smooth-running efficiency, enlarged sales of agency books, expansion of Church papers, and plans for the erection of the present imposing Headquarters of the Church and the publishing House ... In 1912 it was rumoured that the Book Room, through its trade department, had been circulating objectionable literature. It is remarkable that this sort of complaint did not occur more frequently, considering the number of British and American publishers we represented, and the long lists of books they issued, over which we had no control. Book publication by the House itself grew less and less impressive, as the emphasis upon foreign agencies increased.[16]

Although the printing of new Canadian works occurred, distributing imperial and foreign original editions seems to have been at the core of the profitability of the Methodist Book and Publishing House throughout William Briggs's tenure, ultimately winning out as the most viable way to supply the general market for books in Canada.

How exactly did this distribution take place? It varied to some extent since each contract between a British or an American publisher on the one hand and a Canadian distributor on the other would have been the result of unique negotiation. However, copyright law imposed basic limits on this variation, particularly because of the unabated power of imperial copyright. It prevented the Canadian firm from independently reprinting the work. It also left the Canadian market at all times exposed to books from Britain. The following case study of Samuel Rutherford Crockett's *Cleg Kelly* (1896) presents Briggs cooperating with an American publisher to supply an imperial copyright work in Canada. He played the role of printer, binder, and wholesale Canadian distributor of the American edition, carving out a part for himself in relation to imperial copyright and learning to cope with the disadvantages that such copyright entailed for Canadian bookselling. He thus fulfilled the form of Canadian book supply solidified by the decision in *Smiles v. Belford*.

Before turning to the case itself, it is necessary to summarize four developments in the law of copyright after 1877, which affected Canadian bookselling in the 1890s without essentially changing it. In 1886 the United Kingdom joined the Berne Convention, bringing the empire, including Canada, under the rule of international copyright. This action necessitated a levelling of imperial copyright across all British territory. Under the 1842 act, only publication in the United Kingdom had created an imperial copyright, one that extended through the United Kingdom and all of the British colonies; publication in a colony had not. This was the injustice that the 1870 bill had tried, and failed, to redress. Joining the Berne Convention at last required Britain to effect the reform. The International Copyright Act of 1886 therefore included the provision that publication in a colony alone was sufficient to create an imperial copyright.[17] As a result, a Canadian original edition after 1886 was theoretically protected by copyright not only through the whole empire but also through all Berne countries, but because the United States did not join the Berne Convention this development was long of little interest to members of the English-Canadian trade.[18]

In 1889 the issue of Canadian sovereignty in copyright erupted again. In that year the Canadian parliament passed an act aimed once more at reducing the power of imperial copyright in the Dominion. John Ross Robertson, Alexander Belford's former employer, spearheaded the pro-reprint lobby that was responsible for pushing through this legislation.[19] The Canadian Copyright Act of 1889 contained bold measures that would have substantially freed Canadian publishing from outside control, had they taken effect. First, it would have granted Canadian copyright to foreign authors only if they were citizens of countries that had signed an international copyright treaty with the United Kingdom in which Canada was included.[20] This measure would have increased pressure on the United States to sign such a treaty, which in turn would have given Canadian publications what they most needed – copyright in the American market. Second, it would have made simultaneous publication in Canada a condition of obtaining Canadian copyright,[21] such that imperial and foreign publishers would have had to come to terms with their Canadian counterparts in advance if they expected to sell a new book in the Dominion. Third, like the 1872 bill, it would have legitimated the licensed reprinting of British copyright works. If a Canadian, British, or treaty-country author did not secure Canadian copyright by simultaneously publishing in Canada, any Canadian would be allowed to reprint the work, after applying for a license to do so from the Minister of Agriculture and committing to pay the author a 10 per cent royalty on all copies produced.[22] The 1889 act was a straightforward document that demanded yet again independence for the Canadian book trade. Unlike the Copyright Bill of 1872, this act received royal assent, but this time the Governor General never proclaimed a date for its entry into force. Sixteen years later, when the statutes were revised, its clauses were still hanging in suspension before an unspecified start date. The 1889 act never came into effect and therefore did not change the business of selling books in Canada.[23]

In 1891 the United States amended its copyright law to recognize foreign authors. This amendment, known as the Chace Act, removed the condition that the author of a work be a citizen or resident of the United States; instead, it stated that the work of any author could receive American copyright so long as he or she belonged to a country that granted copyright to American authors in return.[24] On 1 July of that year President Benjamin Harrison proclaimed Great Britain and its empire, along with Belgium, France, and Switzerland, to be such countries.[25] What the Chace Act gave with one hand, however, it removed with the other, for it also included strict formalities regarding legal deposit and domestic manufacture. It stipulated that no work would be entitled to American copyright unless two copies were delivered to the Librarian of Congress on or before the date of first publication anywhere; it further specified that those copies had to be printed from type set in the United States or from plates cast from such type.[26] These formalities, which prevented the United States from joining the Berne Convention, effectively made American publication a condition to accessing the American market. If a foreign author wished to control his or her work in the United States, he or she had to ensure that it was printed and deposited there; naturally, an American publisher was best positioned to make these arrangements. The formalities thus deepened the divide between the Berne copyright jurisdiction, including Canada, and the American one. Original publication in Canada alone still guaranteed no protection in the latter. However, through simultaneous publication in London, American editions continued to secure copyright in Canada. In clarifying the rules by which foreign authors could secure American copyright, the Chace Act also solidified the threat of unauthorized reprinting for all foreign-authored works that did not follow those rules. Canadian original editions remained as vulnerable to American reprinting after 1891 as before, as the case of Ralph Connor shows.

Finally, the Foreign Reprints Act lapsed in 1895. The previous year, the Canadian parliament had prepared to drop the 12.5 per cent import duty on American editions of British copyright works. The Duties of Customs Act of 1894 announced that it would be collected only 'until the end of the next session of Parliament,' after which it would fall to six cents per pound, the rate paid on all imported books.[27] The 12.5 per cent import duty was of course integral to the Foreign Reprints Act, and when the duty ceased in 1895, the Foreign Reprints Act lapsed. Of all of the developments in copyright law, this stood to affect Canadian bookselling the most. Theoretically, it made it illegal to import all American editions of British or Berne-country works. It took time for this development to make an impact, however, because the American supply of books to Canada was a pattern that more than a century of practice had ingrained. Moreover, Canadians were not interested in further defending the claims of imperial copyright. Nevertheless, some booksellers became aware that the lapse of the Foreign Reprints Act left them in a vulnerable position: 'An alert bookseller informed us the other day that many of the books on his shelves were American reprints of English authors and might be, as far as he knew, infringements of copyrights. He could, he thought, be put to some inconvenience if copyright were enforced.'[28] This comment was made in 1900, however; it is not clear that William Briggs realized the implications of the lapse of the Foreign Reprints Act when he chose to distribute Samuel Rutherford Crockett's latest novel in 1896. The more pressing concern then was competing against the imperial publisher in the Canadian market.

As Edward Caswell contritely explained to Catharine Parr Traill in 1895, Samuel Rutherford Crockett was an author whose books would be handled by Canadian firms without hesitation.[29] Crockett had begun writing for periodicals while he was a bursary student at Edinburgh

University in the late 1870s. He persisted in journalism while travelling through Europe as a tutor and continued to write while studying divinity. In 1886 he became the minister of a Free Church congregation in the Scottish town of Penicuik, and in the same year he published a volume of poems. He married Ruth Mary Milner in 1887, and the couple had four children. In 1893 *The Stickit Minister,* a compilation of short, ironic pieces on religious life that had previously appeared in a newspaper, became a best-seller and catapulted Crockett into international fame. Following his initial success with *The Raiders* and *The Lilac Sunbonnet* in 1894, he left his job as minister to devote his energies to writing full-time.[30]

William Briggs quickly attempted to become the Canadian distributor of Crockett's works. In February 1894 he signed a contract with Crockett's publisher, Thomas Fisher Unwin of London, for 'the exclusive right to publish the said work [*The Stickit Minister*] in the Dominion of Canada.' The details of the contract indicate the precise meaning of 'publish': Briggs bought a set of stereotype plates from Unwin, the imperial copyright owner, for £20 ($88.80),[31] in order to print a Canadian issue of the 280-page British edition; he took responsibility for other expenses, including binding, advertising, and shipping; and he agreed to pay Unwin 'a Royalty of 10 percent on the published price on all copies sold,' rendering account semi-annually in March and September. The arrangement was to last 'so long as he [Briggs] carries out the conditions of this Agreement.' Last but not least, the final clause restricted Briggs from selling any copies outside of Canada.[32] Thus Briggs printed, bound, advertised, and shipped copies of *The Stickit Minister* in the Dominion but had no relations with the author, did not produce a separate edition of the work, and could not sell his copies elsewhere in the empire, the Berne block, or North America.

Two months later, Briggs and Unwin came to a similar agreement for Crockett's *The Raiders*. This contract, which described Unwin only as the *agent* of the imperial copyright owner, again granted Briggs the 'exclusive right to publish' the work in Canada but this time limited that right to a period of five years beginning on 1 March 1894, after which it could be renewed for the same term again or terminated as the parties saw fit. At about four hundred pages, this work was longer, so the stereotype plates cost £25 ($111.00). Briggs once more took on the associated expenses. As for the royalty, it was higher and appears to have been the object of some strife. At the last minute Unwin agreed to strike out the words *fourteen cents per copy* and substitute instead *fifteen per cent on the published price,* initialling the change *TFU.* In a further departure from the last contract, this one stipulated that the retail price was not ever to be less than 2s 6d (55¢).[33]

If Briggs was content with the 'exclusive' role that he had negotiated for himself in the publication of *The Raiders,* his contentment did not last long. Within months he discovered that cheap copies of Unwin's edition of *The Raiders* were entering Canada and undercutting him.[34] Worse, he had no way to stop them. The same section of the Canadian Copyright Act of 1875 that had caused the Belfords so much grief contained the proviso that 'nothing in this Act shall be held to prohibit the importation from the United Kingdom of copies of any such work lawfully printed there.'[35] Canadian copyright, while it offered protection against an American edition, had no power over the shipment of books from Britain to the Dominion. Nor could Briggs sue Unwin for a breach of contract, because he had no way of proving that Unwin himself was directly responsible for exporting the books to Canada. Briggs's only recourse was to complain to the British publisher. He appears to have done so, for on 7 July Unwin telegraphed a response, granting him permission to 'publish raiders at twenty-one pence' (1s 9d or 39¢).[36] Still, the damage had been done. The initial demand for the work had passed, and Briggs was left scrambling against the competition. His role as 'publisher' had unravelled. He survived the scrum, advertising *The Stickit Minister* and *The Raiders* (paper) at 50¢ and 60¢, respectively, or (cloth) at $1.25 in 1896.[37] However, although he continued to print and bind his own copies, the incident effectively reduced him once more to being only one of a number of local booksellers trying to sell an imperial edition. The cheaper paper editions indicate an inability to maintain a high price.

Crockett's next best-seller was *Cleg Kelly, Arab of the City: His Progress and Adventures,* the story of an Edinburgh street urchin ('arab') that weaves together threads of the social gospel and the gothic romance. Smith, Elder, and Company of London published *Cleg Kelly* in 1896. Spottiswoode and Company of London typeset the text, cast stereotype plates, and printed an edition that ran well over four hundred pages:

Cleg Kelly: Smith, Elder Edition[38]

[red:] CLEG KELLY | [black:] ARAB OF THE CITY | BY | [red:] S. R. CROCKETT | [black:] *SECOND EDITION* | LONDON | SMITH, ELDER, AND CO. | 15 WATERLOO PLACE | MDCCCXCVI

COLLATION [3] a² B–I⁸ K–U⁸ X–2E⁸ 2F⁵ [$ 2 (–a2) signed]. 226 leaves.
Pages *i–vii* viii–ix *x 1* 2–442 [= 452].
CONTENTS *i* half-title. *ii* blank. *iii* title. *iv* blank. *v* dedication: '*To* |
J. M. BARRIE | *with the hand of a comrade* | *and the heart of a friend*'.
vi blank. *vii*–ix contents. *x* blank. *1* head title. *1*–442 text. 442
imprint: 'PRINTED BY | SPOTTISWOODE AND CO., NEW-
STREET SQUARE | LONDON'.
TYPOGRAPHY 34 lines (33 on 275), 143 (152 [154 on 17, 153 on 49]) ×
80 mm; 10 lines = 42 mm; capital 2.5 (x 1.5) mm.
PAPER Leaves 18.8 × 11.6 cm. Machine laid, no watermark. Chain
lines vertical, 2.7 cm apart; wire lines 8/cm. Heavy.

The paper used for this 'Crown 8vo' edition was thick and heavy, and
according to advertisements within the book, the retail price was 6s
($1.32). The work sold steadily in the United Kingdom for a few years.
Smith, Elder had run off four impressions by 1903.

D. Appleton and Company of New York simultaneously published
the American edition. Like the British edition, it is simple and tidy, re-
flecting a well-planned and smoothly executed manufacture. The two
years included in the copyright statement indicate that Appleton was
adroit in registering the copyright. In accordance with the 1891 act,
they began the registration process late in 1895 by printing off a copy
of the title page and depositing it with the Librarian of Congress, and
they completed the registration in 1896 by depositing two copies of the
finished book. The manufacture was straightforward, as the neat collational formula shows, and Appleton was able to save money by reducing the total number of pages and using cheaper paper:

Cleg Kelly: Appleton Edition[39]

[red:] CLEG KELLY | ARAB OF THE CITY | [black:] [ornament,
0.1 × 0.8 cm: two handles] | HIS PROGRESS AND ADVENTURES
| [ornament, 0.1 × 0.8 cm: two handles] | BY | [red:] S. R.
CROCKETT | [black:] AUTHOR OF | THE LILAC SUNBONNET,
BOG-MYRTLE AND PEAT, ETC. | ILLUSTRATED | [ornament,
0.2 × 0.4 cm: leaf] [ornament, 0.2 × 0.4 cm: leaf] | [publisher's or-
nament, 1.6 × 1.4 cm: tree, shield, banner: 'D·A & Co· ·INTER· ·
FOLIA· ·FRUCTUS·'] | [ornament, 0.2 × 0.4 cm: leaf] [ornament,
0.2 × 0.4 cm: leaf] | NEW YORK | [red:] D. APPLETON AND
COMPANY | [black:] 1896

COLLATION 1^8 2–25^8 [\$ 1 signed]. 200 leaves. Pages *i–iv* v–vii *viii 1*
2–388 *389–392* [= 400]. Plates [8] (facing 1_2^a, 2_2^a, 5_5^a, 9_2^a, 12_7^b, 14_4^b,
21_5^a, 23_7^b).
CONTENTS *i* half-title. *ii* advertisement. *iii* title. *iv* copyright
statement: 'COPYRIGHT, 1895, 1896, | BY D. APPLETON AND
COMPANY.' v–vi contents. vii list of illustrations. *viii* blank.
1 head title. *1–388* text. *389–392* advertisements.
TYPOGRAPHY 34 lines, 138 (139 on 41) (148) × 86 mm; 10 lines =
41 mm; capital 2.5 (x 1.6) mm.
PAPER Leaves 18.4 × 12.5 cm. Machine wove, no watermark. Wire
lines 16/cm. Light.

The pagination is free of errors, and no cancellations were necessary. The printers did not have to tamper with the plates to create new pages once collation had begun. Prying a little in the gutter shows that the leaves form the usual conjugate pairs and that the stitching is uniform throughout the book. None of the leaves is blank on both sides. The publisher filled what little white space remained with advertisements. The binding intelligently matches the story. Sixteen green-and-lilac thistles, symbolizing the rough beauty of life in the slums of Edinburgh, adorn the front cover. Appleton engaged T.J. Fogarty to illustrate the narrative. The edition incorporates eight photographic greyscale half-tone blocks of Fogarty's original paintings. All of these details point to uninterrupted control of the production process from start to finish. The book retailed at the high price of \$1.50.[40]

Having recently been stung by a Crockett novel, Briggs took a different approach this time, turning to the American publisher. His priority was certainly to risk as little as possible in his handling of it. Dealing in the American edition presented uncertainties of its own, however, because the lapse of the Foreign Reprints Act had technically rendered American editions of British copyright works such as Appleton's *Cleg Kelly* illegal in Canada. Nevertheless, the Canadian demand for Crockett's latest work would be high, and it was impossible to foretell whether there would be any serious interruption in the age-old flow of American books into Canada. In order not to lose the opportunity to a local competitor, Briggs invented a way to supply the Canadian demand, navigating the perils of the market as best he could. He persuaded the American publisher to contract him to produce a separate, Canadian issue. This got around the lapse of the Foreign Reprints Act in that a locally printed issue of the American edition would not have to be imported. Moreover, the role he carved out for himself was small and safe. He printed, bound, advertised, and shipped the Appleton edition vicariously for the American publisher, collecting immediate payment for each task performed. Briggs did not take a share of each sale and did not pay a royalty; he staked nothing on being the exclusive Canadian dealer and assumed no responsibility for the success or failure of Appleton's edition in Canada.

Briggs registered *Cleg Kelly* for Canadian copyright in Appleton's name.[41] This registration would have warned rival Canadian booksellers not to import the American edition directly themselves (but could not have stopped them from importing the British edition). It also implies that Crockett, the imperial copyright owner, sanctioned the American publisher's taking control of the Canadian market. What the Belfords had railed against had thus come to pass.

On 30 March 1896, using stereotype plates supplied by Appleton, Briggs printed and bound one thousand copies, charging his American client $283.60 in total for the work, including about $70 in make-ready, 13¢ per copy in printing, and 8¢ per copy in binding.[42] Beside the tidy Appleton edition, the first Briggs issue is a sloppy thing. The disorder of its physical form reflects disorder in production, the inevitable result of having to improvise a business strategy in reaction to underlying uncertainties. Briggs's books embody the adverse economic conditions under which they were made. The copyright statement on the back of the title page is cautious and lengthy, taking pains to identify both the proprietor and the local agent of registration. The construction of the book shows signs of last-minute changes:

Cleg Kelly: First Briggs Issue (Appleton Edition)[43]

CLEG KELLY | ARAB OF THE CITY | *HIS PROGRESS AND ADVENTURES* | BY | S. R. CROCKETT | AUTHOR OF | THE LILAC SUNBONNET, BOG-MYRTLE AND PEAT, ETC. | TORONTO: | WILLIAM BRIGGS, | WESLEY BUILDINGS. | MONTREAL: C. W. COATES. [vertical rule, 0.3 cm] HALIFAX: S. F. HUESTIS.
COLLATION [1]^8 ($-1_{1,4}$, $\pm1_2$) [2–24]^8 [25]^8 ($-25_{7,8}$). 196 leaves. Pages *iii–iv* v–vi *1* 2–388 [= 392].
CONTENTS *iii* title. *iv* copyright statement: 'COPYRIGHT, 1896, BY D. APPLETON & COMPANY | [rule, 0.8 cm] | ALL RIGHTS

RESERVED. | [rule, 0.8 cm] | Entered according to Act of the Parliament of Canada, in the year one | thousand eight hundred and ninety-six, by William Briggs, at the Department | of Agriculture.' v–vi contents. *1* head title. *1*–388 text.
typography 34 lines, 138 (139 on 41) (145) × 86 mm; 10 lines = 41 mm; capital 2.4 (x 1.6) mm.
paper Leaves 18.5 × 12.7 cm. Machine wove, no watermark. Wire lines 16/cm. Light.

Four leaves were removed after printing – two in the first gathering and two in the last – and the title page is a substitute. Sixteen stitch punctures and fifteen short threads, set in slightly from the fold, run down the length of the title page, whereas all other gatherings in the book have four stitch punctures and three longer threads set right in the fold. As for the discarded leaves, they included the list of Fogarty's illustrations and some advertisements of the American publisher; as a result, the pagination oddly begins at iii. The unusual stitching and the cancellations emphasize the substantial changes that had to be made to the sheets after they left the press. Such changes must have involved undesirable delays, not to mention additional labour and expense, and they show the trouble that was taken to disguise this American book as a Canadian one. Perhaps there was no time to have the plates altered before publication. Whatever the reason, the post-printing changes to the sheets imply inefficiency in production.

Eliminating the list of illustrations was necessary for the obvious reason that the book had none. Perhaps Appleton could not spare the photographic plates and decided that they were too expensive to duplicate. In any event, in the rush to simultaneously publish, Briggs had to proceed without the illustrations, cutting two leaves from the first letterpress gathering in consequence. Finally, the binding is different. Apart from some simple lines in blind, the covers are blank; the title and the author's surname adorn the spine alone. The design is simple and tasteful but symbolically vapid in comparison to Appleton's thistles.

The retail price of the Canadian impression was $1.25.[44] It seems to have sold well, at least initially. The following blurb in *Bookseller and Stationer* may contain some exaggeration since Briggs himself probably wrote it, but the evidence of subsequent print runs corroborates its positive report: 'GOOD CANADIAN SALES. Crockett's "Cleg Kelly, Arab of the City," is likely to prove by far the most popular of his books. Of the Canadian edition 500 copies were sold within three days. The

American publishers, placing their edition on the market on the 13th inst., had advance orders for 5,000 copies, of which 1,300 were taken up in Boston alone. Bearing in mind the difference in population of the two countries, the Canadian sales were relatively greater than the American.'[45] Emboldened by this initial success, Appleton paid Briggs $203.85 to print off another thousand copies in April. In May, a third impression occurred, doubled to two thousand copies, for $335.40, but thereafter production slowed. Briggs printed a final run of five hundred in December and charged Appleton $137.00. Again, the cost of make-ready was about $70, and the price per copy was 13¢. In summary, between March and December 1896, Appleton invested $959.85 in the production of the Canadian issues of *Cleg Kelly*, and Briggs printed 4,500 copies for Canadian readers.[46]

The second Briggs issue shows a refinement of the production process. Having met the deadline of simultaneous publication, the partners stepped back and made some changes to improve the books while reducing expenses. The stereotype plates were altered to eliminate the cancellations, yielding a product that was much simpler in construction:

Cleg Kelly: Second Briggs Issue (Appleton Edition)[47]

CLEG KELLY | ARAB OF THE CITY | *HIS PROGRESS AND ADVENTURES* | BY | S. R. CROCKETT | AUTHOR OF | THE LILAC SUNBONNET, BOG-MYRTLE AND PEAT, ETC. | *ILLUSTRATED* | TORONTO: | WILLIAM BRIGGS, | WESLEY BUILDINGS. | MONTREAL: C. W. COATES. HALIFAX: S. F. HUESTIS.

COLLATION $[1-25]^8$. 200 leaves. Pages *[2] i–iv* v–vi *1* 2–388 *389–392* [= 400]. Plates [8] (facing 1_2^a, 2_2^a, 5_5^a, 9_2^a, 12_7^b, 14_4^a, 21_5^a, 23_6^b; plates [6] and [8] differ in placement from Appleton edition).

CONTENTS *[1–2]* blank. *i* half-title. *ii* blank. *iii* title. *iv* copyright statement: 'COPYRIGHT, 1896, BY D. APPLETON & COMPANY. | [rule, 0.8 cm] | ALL RIGHTS RESERVED. | [rule, 0.8 cm] | Entered, according to the Act of the Parliament of Canada, in the year one | thousand eight hundred and ninety-six, by WILLIAM BRIGGS, Toronto, in the | Office of the Minister of Agriculture, at Ottawa.' *v–vi* contents. *1* head title. *1–388* text. *389–392* advertisements.

TYPOGRAPHY 34 lines, 138 (139 on 41) (145) × 86 mm; 10 lines = 41 mm; capital 2.4 (x 1.6) mm.

PAPER Leaves 18.8 × 13.0 cm. Machine wove, no watermark. Wire lines 16/cm. Light.

As the collational formula makes clear, all twenty-five gatherings consist of eight leaves, with no eliminations or substitutions. The pagination and stitching are regular throughout. More important, Fogarty's eight illustrations are included as in the Appleton edition, with minor differences in their placement. Either Appleton was now at liberty to send the photographic plates to Toronto so that Briggs could print the illustrations or they had the illustrations printed in the United States and then sent to Briggs to be tipped in, unconcerned if eight of four hundred pages were not printed in Canada; at any rate, the differences in placement suggest that Briggs's books were not bound at the same time or in the same place as Appleton's regular lot. The use of paper is not quite as economical as that of the Appleton edition, in that the book commences with a blank leaf, but Briggs made good use of the final leaves of the last gathering ($25_{7,8}$), filling them with his own, distinctly Canadian, advertisements. Finally, the cover design, featuring the green-and-lilac thistles, is the same as the Appleton edition. Appleton probably shipped pre-stamped covers to Toronto in order to trim expenses from their Canadian bill.

There was one other firm involved in the publication of *Cleg Kelly*. This final complication in the publishing history confirms Briggs's wisdom in limiting himself to the printing, binding, and distribution of the novel. Sometime in 1896, Macmillan and Company of London acquired the right to distribute *Cleg Kelly* to the empire – to the imperial market outside of the United Kingdom. As an internationally expanding firm, Macmillan was better situated to supply the overseas demand. The collational formula indicates that they obtained a set of plates from the Smith, Elder edition to produce their own issue:

Cleg Kelly: Macmillan Issue (Smith, Elder Edition)[48]

[GOTHIC AND UNDERLINED:] MACMILLAN'S COLONIAL LIBRARY |
CLEG KELLY | ARAB OF THE CITY | BY | S. R. CROCKETT |
[*gothic:*] *London* | MACMILLAN AND CO., LTD | NEW YORK:
MACMILLAN & CO. | No. 270 1896
COLLATION [3] a² B–I⁸ K–U⁸ X–2E⁸ 2F⁵ [$ 2 (–a2) signed]. 226 leaves.
Pages *i–vii* viii–ix *x* 1 2–442.
CONTENTS *i* half-title. *ii* disclaimer: '*This Edition is intended for circulation only in India | and the British Colonies*'. *iii* title. *iv* blank.
v dedication: '*To | J. M. BARRIE | with the hand of a comrade | and the heart of a friend*'. *vi* blank. *vii–*ix contents. *x* blank. *1* head title.

1–442 text. 442 imprint: 'PRINTED BY | SPOTTISWOODE AND
CO., NEW-STREET SQUARE | LONDON'.
TYPOGRAPHY 34 lines (33 on 275), 143 (152 [154 on 17, 153 on 49]) ×
80 mm; 10 lines = 42 mm; capital 2.5 (x 1.5) mm.
PAPER Leaves 17.7 × 11.5 cm. Machine wove, no watermark. Wire
lines 16/cm. Light.

Macmillan had this colonial edition printed on much lighter, poorer
paper than that of the original, and it probably sold for much less than
6s. The noteworthy disclaimer facing the title page clarifies the relation between the British publishers: one had the home market while the
other took the imperial one. Nothing could have prevented this issue
from being imported into the Dominion of Canada and undercutting
the high-priced Appleton edition there. In any case, this disastrous
possibility would have mattered little to the Canadian firm that only
printed, bound, and distributed Appleton's books. Briggs had insured
himself against the possibility of again being undercut by the subtleties
of imperial copyright; he had abandoned the role of exclusive Canadian
publisher. Whether or not Canadians bought his books over the competitor's, he would turn a profit.

The roles of the American and the Canadian firms in the publication of *Cleg Kelly* differed sharply. Both participated in bringing Samuel
Rutherford Crockett's rough-mannered, practical Christianity to North
American readers, but Appleton was the one that made the crucial initial investment and shouldered more of the risk. In the United States,
where the law of copyright was transparent and where, after 1891, the
congealing of texts into property was more solid, book publishing bore
heavier investments and yielded larger returns. American publishers,
more sure both of the exclusivity and the longevity of their textual
property, were able to throw more money into production and then
await its trickling back in ultimately greater quantities. Their mode of
operation therefore comprehended everything from the setting of type
for the manufacture of stereotype plates to the advance payment of authors. As the publisher and the proprietor of the copyright, Appleton
strove to recoup a large initial investment by 'booming' an expensive
edition, maximizing its sales by expanding its territory. Canada may
have been a relatively small market, but it was still a significant one; to
the American as well as the British publishers of the late nineteenth century, it offered *additional* thousands of sales – additional returns on an
investment that had already paid for itself at home. William Briggs, by

contrast, made little investment in *Cleg Kelly* and secured a potentially smaller but more reliable return in the form of immediate payment. He stood to profit less from the work, but the payment he did earn as printer and distributor was certain. By unloading the costs of production onto another firm, Briggs escaped responsibility for the success or failure of the edition. He thus practised a clever way of doing business that was more or less immune to the copyright-induced unpredictability of the Canadian trade.

This way of doing business had consequences. The most important was that Briggs evolved a conservative financial policy with respect to book publishing. He developed strategies that avoided investing in the independent production of writing by new authors. These strategies included vanity publishing, in which the author paid for the printing; subscription publishing, in which readers paid for production through advance purchases; and international deals, in which collaboration with foreign capital allowed for a minimization of production costs. In the next decade, as the subsequent chapter will show, he also developed a brilliant form of import piracy, in which he secured exclusive distribution contracts from a British publisher and then undercut them himself by importing illegal American editions. All in all, William Briggs would print and bind if authors paid him to do so, he would refer them to an American publisher, and he would distribute their books, but he would not publish them.

Briggs's long-lived success encouraged others to follow his example. John McClelland was one. McClelland's partnership with Frederick Goodchild began in 1906 with the supplying of books to libraries. Both he and Goodchild had entered the book trade as employees of the Methodist Book and Publishing House, and like Briggs they did not shy away from styling themselves 'publishers' at times, but the term that accurately describes them is *publisher-agent*. Through the First World War their business consisted chiefly of distribution. They incorporated in 1911, and George Stewart joined the firm in 1914. 'They were wholesale agents,' judges George Parker: 'even during the war years their McClelland, Goodchild and Stewart letterhead still carried the phrase "Wholesale and Import Booksellers."'[49] They learned the tricks of import-distribution from William Briggs, and when competition grew stiff, they put their lessons to good use. Again, the next chapter will show that they used Briggs's hard-won knowledge of the way in which to undercut a rival Canadian firm by importing a British colonial edition at just the right moment. Under

McClelland's son, the firm would ultimately become, thoroughly and primarily, an original Canadian publisher, but this would not occur until the 1960s.

The publishing history of *Cleg Kelly* sheds light on the origins of the agency system. It is a good example of the complementary but profoundly different roles of an American and a Canadian firm in producing an edition and selling it in Canada. It also pinpoints the problem of multiple editions of the same work competing in the Canadian market. Thanks to the fifteenth clause of the 1875 act, Canada remained exposed to British book exports irrespective of the contractual arrangements that a wholesaler like Briggs might make in order to be the exclusive national supplier. By solving this problem, the Canadian Copyright Amendment of 1900 would usher in the era of the publisher-agent.

5 The 1900 Amendment, the Agency System, and the Macmillan Company of Canada

A precious window onto the twentieth-century Canadian book trade exists in the extensive papers of the Macmillan Company of Canada. Macmillan branched into Canada shortly after the Canadian Copyright Amendment of 1900 had come into force, and the operations of the company thus reflect, first in unconscious and then in conscious ways, the effect of it. The intention of the amendment was to stabilize book prices by allowing a Canadian firm to become the exclusive distributor of a British copyright work to the national market. It thus aimed to eliminate what William Briggs had suffered with *The Raiders* – rival booksellers' importing of cheap copies directly from abroad, despite his possessing a contract to be the sole Canadian supplier. British publishers, politicians, and authors mainly welcomed it as a sign that Canada, abandoning the confrontational stance of the 1889 act, was willing to continue to work within the framework of imperial copyright and the Berne Convention.[1] The amendment, sometimes called 'the Fisher Act' for Sydney Arthur Fisher, the agriculture minister in Wilfrid Laurier's government, passed in July 1900. It took effect as Canadian booksellers one by one implemented or paid heed to it. What took shape on the basis of it was the agency system, the practice of trade whereby the books of foreign publishers were available in Canada through a local firm (the publisher-agent) who acquired a monopolistic and enforceable licence to distribute them.[2] The publisher-agent was not a mere branch of a foreign publisher; it was in general a Canadian-owned company, and it offered a mixed plate as opposed to a single brand, supplying a number of the books of various foreign publishers to the Canadian market, rather than all of the books of one alone. Branches like the Macmillan Company of Canada were set up to monitor only their principal's interests, but as time passed they too learned to use the 1900 amendment to sell any attractive book published abroad, thus adapting to the role of the publisher-agent. Indeed, like the faith of a convert, Macmillan's knowledge of the 1900 amendment became exemplary precisely because of the company's initial friction with it. The story of this friction, compelling in itself, offers an illuminating view of the copyright-governed pattern that would govern the Canadian book trade for much of the twentieth century. The agency system did not suddenly appear fully formed; it accreted around the statute as people in the book trade figured out how it worked.

The Macmillan Company of Canada was incorporated under Ontario law on 15 December 1905. Its capital stock was $20,000.[3] Its original shareholders were Frederick Macmillan, chairman of the London-based parent firm, Macmillan and Company, and son and nephew, respectively, of the company's founders, Daniel and Alexander Macmillan; George Platt Brett, president of the Macmillan Company of New York; George Augustin Macmillan; Charles Coleman Nadal; and Frank Wise, president of the new Canadian branch.[4] On 1 January 1906 Wise commenced business in Toronto with a small staff, renting an office at 27 Richmond Street West.[5] His initial salary, $2,500 per annum, increased to $6,000 in 1913. The shareholders expected him to do two things: distribute the trade books of the London and New York houses to the Canadian market and publish textbooks for Canadian schools. At the end of his first year in Toronto, Wise reported that the sale of Macmillan books in Canada had yielded a profit of $2,185.57, which the principals duly divided among themselves. In March 1908 the annual profit had quadrupled to $8,114.98, and in 1910 it peaked at $17,814.33. The buying out of the Morang Educational Company in 1912 necessitated the deferral of dividends for a few years, but from 1915 through 1918 the company was again delivering annual profits in the range of $10,000, despite the war.[6] Judged by these results, the expansion was an undeniable success.

Founded in 1843, the parent, Macmillan and Company, had grown into a major literary publisher by the end of the nineteenth century. Alfred Tennyson, Thomas Hardy, Henry James, Lewis Carroll, and Charles Kingsley are a handful of the many authors of poetry and fiction upon whom the company affixed its imprint. After 1891 the Macmillan Company of New York also distinguished itself in publishing literature, with American novelists such as Winston Churchill, Owen Wister, and Jack London. Original literary publishing was not, however, among the founding reasons for the Macmillan enterprise in Canada. Frederick Macmillan made this explicit in a letter to Frank Wise in 1910: 'You say something about the necessity of having money in hand in case some profitable publishing venture came in sight, but as to this I may say at once we should be more than a little surprised and displeased if you embarked on any "publishing venture" of importance without first consulting us. The primary business of the Macmillan Company of Canada is to sell the publications of the New York and London houses, and the only kind of publishing which ought to originate in Canada is the production of school books authorized by one or other of the Provincial governments.'[7] The financial structure of the company ensured the carrying out of Frederick Macmillan's dictates, for a time at least. Since imperial or foreign shareholders skimmed most of the profit made by the Toronto branch, it could hardly accumulate the capital necessary for an independent publishing program. Apparently, Frank Wise did manage to publish some thirty original trade books for the Canadian market before his resignation in 1921, including one novel, W.H.P. Jarvis's *As Others See Us: Being the Diary of a Canadian Debutante* (1915), and one book of jingoistic verse, T.A. Browne's *The Belgian Mother and Ballads of Battle Time* (1917).[8] His principal tasks, however, remained those laid out by Frederick Macmillan. Foremost among the foreign books that he was to sell in Canada were those of Rudyard Kipling, a highly prized Macmillan author.

Elizabeth James has chronicled the growth of the Macmillan Company of New York across the United States, from a single distribution office in 1869 to a corporate network controlled by multidivisional headquarters with a subsidiary in Chicago and agencies in Boston, Atlanta, and San Francisco by 1907.[9] The move into Canada should be understood as part of this continental growth. For the first two years the Toronto branch sold mostly books on consignment from New York. This stock remained the property of the New York company; Wise could return volumes that did not sell, at no loss to his branch. In February 1908 the relation changed from consignment to outright purchase, but this change did not alter the fact that for the most part Toronto still distributed books from New York. In that month Wise accepted an offer of George Platt Brett, agreeing to buy the currently consigned stock at a discount of 5 per cent off the regular wholesale price. He also arranged to pay for all books to be sent from New York in future at the same discount. Brett allowed Wise to make the initial purchase in four quarterly payments and also to exclude any books 'that you consider slow of sale or unsaleable'; he further promised to continue sending 'presentations' (advertising copies) free of charge so long as Wise kept their number under personal control.[10] These arrangements show the way in which the New York company launched the Toronto one. In supplying stock on consignment, Brett carried the bulk of the risk for the first two years; thereafter, Wise received favourable terms, chief among them the universal discount, on which to continue distributing Brett's books.

The growth of the American company at the beginning of the twentieth century was undoubtedly one factor behind establishing the Toronto branch. Another was the opening up of the English-Canadian schoolbook market. In the year 1906 an important contract for the printing of educational texts expired. For two decades three Toronto printers had enjoyed the exclusive right to produce the Ontario Readers, the only reading series authorized for schools in that province. When this much-envied contract finally reached its term, others had the chance to compete for the next one.[11] It is likely that Macmillan planned its expansion to coincide with this opportunity, although landing a government school-book contract was not as easy as it might have seemed from afar.

Competing in the distribution of trade books was also more complicated than expected. The Canadian Copyright Amendment of 1900 was in place, and in some cases it prevented Macmillan from shipping popular books to its new Toronto office. The heart of the amendment lay in the first clause, which allowed a Canadian firm to obtain a prohibition order against the importation of all editions of a work, including the British, if it had a 'licence' (contract) from the imperial copyright owner to reproduce the work in Canada. Making the prohibition order, which was enforceable, contingent upon the contract, which was not, was the key innovation. It conferred a monopoly on the local firm, thereby decreasing competition and stabilizing the industry, while recognizing the imperial copyright owner, who retained proprietorship of the work and could determine through the terms of the contract how it would be produced for the Canadian market:

> If a book as to which there is subsisting copyright under *The Copyright Act* has been first lawfully published in any part of Her Majesty's dominions other than Canada, and if it is proved to the satisfaction of the Minister of Agriculture that the owner of the copyright so subsisting and of the copyright acquired by such publication has lawfully granted a license to reproduce in Canada, from movable or other types, or from stereotype

plates, or from electroplates, or from lithograph stones, or by any process for facsimile reproduction, an edition or editions of such book designed for sale only in Canada, the Minister may, notwithstanding anything in *The Copyright Act,* by order under his hand, prohibit the importation, except with the written consent of the licensee, into Canada of any copies of such book printed elsewhere.[12]

In other words, if a Canadian firm acquired a contract from the British copyright owner to reproduce an imperial copyright work for the Canadian market, all other copies of the work printed elsewhere could be stopped from entering Canada; any importation would have to have the written permission of the Canadian firm. The one exception was public libraries. The section quoted above ends with the proviso that 'any public free library or any university or college library, or . . . the library of any duly incorporated institution' could freely import two copies from abroad for its 'bona fide use' without the permission of the Canadian distributor. Libraries would make extensive use of this proviso, leading publisher-agents to complain frequently about the practice of 'buying-around.'

In 1901 George N. Morang arranged for a Canadian issue of *Kim,* Rudyard Kipling's introspective narrative of religious cross-pollination and racial rapprochement in British India. Morang had originally come to Toronto as the representative of an American publisher but soon launched out on his own. *Kim* was one of the first books to implement the 1900 amendment. Morang had lobbied the government of Wilfrid Laurier to enact the legislation and had helped ease it past the British publishing industry with a persuasive address on the subject.[13] Understandably, he was one of the first to put its provisions to use after it received royal assent. Since 1898 Morang had issued a dozen of Kipling's works with his own title page in a strategic effort to dominate the Canadian market, but *Kim* was one of the first to benefit from the new law.

Cassell's Magazine (London) and *McClure's Magazine* (New York) began publishing *Kim* simultaneously in instalments in December 1900. The serializations ran until October 1901, illustrated with drawings by H.R. Millar, a wash drawing by E.L. Weeks, and photographs of bas-reliefs by John Lockwood Kipling, Rudyard's father. Macmillan and Company of London, Kipling's usual publisher, contracted R. and R. Clark of Edinburgh to print the novel in book form. By mid-August 1901 Kipling had corrected and returned the printer's proofs.[14] A copy of this set of proofs was then sent to Doubleday, Page and Company of

New York for the American edition, which was published on 1 October. It is a book of thirty unsigned gatherings, the first with four leaves and the rest with eight, bound in green cloth and stamped in black with the image of a ship:

Kim: Doubleday, Page Edition[15]

COLLATION $[1]^4$ $[2–30]^8$. 236 leaves. Pages [8] 1–460 *461–464* [= 472]. Plates [10] (facing 1_3^a, 5_3^b, 6_8^b, 9_3^b, 11_7^b, 12_8^b, 20_4^b, 24_3^b, 26_8^b, 29_8^b). CONTENTS *[1–2]* blank. [3] half-title. [4] ornament, 2.6 × 2.6 cm: circle enclosing swastika and author's name. [5] title. [6] copyright statement: 'COPYRIGHT, 1900, 1901, | BY | RUDYARD KIPLING.' [7] list of illustrations. [8] blank. 1–460 text. *461–464* blank. TYPOGRAPHY 28 lines, 144 (157) × 84 mm; 10 lines = 52 mm; capital 2.6 (x 1.6) mm.

Of the periodicals' illustrations it contains only the ten bas-reliefs. Kipling then made more alterations, especially in chapters 5 through 10; consequently, the chapter headings and text of the British edition differ substantially from the American. The British edition appeared on 17 October, illustrated by the ten bas-reliefs. It consists of twenty-seven signed gatherings:

Kim: Macmillan Edition[16]

COLLATION A^4 $B–I^8$ $K–U^8$ $X–2D^8$ [$ 1 signed; B1 signed 'E']. 212 leaves. Pages *[8]* 1 2–413 *414–416* [= 424]. Plates [10] (facing $A3^a$, $C3^a$, $D1^a$, $G1^a$, $H2^b$, $K8^a$, $R4^b$, $S6^b$, $2B5^b$, $2D2^b$). CONTENTS *[1–2]* blank. [3] half-title. [4] ornament, 2.6 × 2.6 cm: circle enclosing swastika and author's name. [5] title. [6] blank. [7] list of illustrations. [8] blank. *1–413* text. 413 imprint: '*Printed by* R. & R. CLARK, LIMITED, *Edinburgh.*' *414* blank. *415–416* publisher's advertisements. TYPOGRAPHY 33 lines, 140 (150) × 84 mm; 10 lines = 42 mm; capital 2.7 (x 1.7) mm.

It is bound in red cloth stamped in gold with Kipling's insignia of Anglo-Indian unity – an elephant's head accompanied by a swastika. The second impression of the American edition, which followed on 23 October, added the British chapter headings.[17]

In June 1901 Morang announced that he had secured the author's permission to 'publish' *Kim* for the Canadian market.[18] In licensing Morang to be his Canadian distributor, Kipling retained ownership of the imperial copyright in his novel. It is the author's name, not the British publisher's, that appears in the copyright statement on the back of the title page of Morang's *Kim*. Having obtained permission to print the novel, Morang then acquired the means to do so. It is clear that, like William Briggs in the case of *Cleg Kelly*, he turned to the American publisher, for his books are clearly an issue of the Doubleday, Page edition:

Kim: Morang Issue (Doubleday, Page Edition)[19]

COLLATION $[1]^4(-1_4)$ $[2–29]^8$ $[30]^6$. 233 leaves. Pages [6] 1–460 [= 466].
Plates [10] (facing 1_3^a, 5_3^b, 6_8^b, 9_3^b, 11_7^b, 12_8^b, 20_4^b, 24_3^b, 26_8^b, 29_8^b).
CONTENTS [1–3] blank. [4] publisher's advertisement. [5] title. [6] copyright statement: 'Entered according to Act of the Parliament of Canada, | in the year Nineteen Hundred and One, by RUDYARD | KIPLING, at the Department of Agriculture.' 1–460 text.
TYPOGRAPHY 28 lines, 144 (157) × 84 mm; 10 lines = 52 mm; capital 2.6 (x 1.6) mm.

When Doubleday's letterpress plates were manufactured at the end of the summer, Morang purchased a duplicate set and had them altered slightly to include his own advertisements and his imprint on the title page. He did not bother to remove the Doubleday ornament from the space above his name on the title page. He did, however, remove the list of illustrations (leaf 1_4), perhaps because (somewhat like Briggs in the case of *Cleg Kelly*) he had not received enough copies of the illustrations from the American publisher to include all ten in every copy of the book. The letterpress plates weighed 474 pounds – about eight pounds per octavo forme for a book made from sixty formes.[20] Despite their weight, these plates were shipped to Toronto; Morang did not merely import sheets from Doubleday's printer. Like the Canadian Copyright Act of 1875, the 1900 amendment required that a copyright work be printed in Canada. Once printed, the books were bound in green cloth stamped in black with the image of a ship, identical to Doubleday's books, or in paper. Morang began advertising his issue in September at the price of $1.50 (cloth) or 75¢ (paper).[21]

The books were ready by October, and orders for them began to pour into Morang's office at 90 Wellington Street West in Toronto from booksellers across the country. The best-seller lists published in *Bookseller and Stationer* from November 1901 through May 1902 give an indication of the success of Morang's *Kim*. It sold well in Ontario: readers demanded it at bookstores in Toronto, Guelph, Belleville, Kingston, London, and St Catharines. It was the second best-selling English-language book in Montreal in October. Its popularity extended across the Prairies: readers in Regina called for it, and in Winnipeg it outsold every other trade book. By November, when *Kim* ascended to the top of the list in the United Kingdom, Morang boasted that it would be 'the largest seller in Canada of any of Kipling's works.'[22] It was now among the top four books in Ottawa and Hamilton and had arrived at the third position on the national list of Canadian best-sellers, following Hall Caine's *The Eternal City*, also distributed by Morang, and Gilbert Parker's *The Right of Way*. Sales continued strong over the Christmas season, and in January readers in Vancouver and Victoria bought it in great quantities. By April the wave was subsiding in England, and readers in Canada were turning to Ralph Connor's *The Man from Glengarry*, but *Kim* continued strong in the bookstores of the Maritimes, particularly in Charlottetown and Moncton.

By distributing *Kim* in this way, Morang fulfilled the terms of the 1900 amendment. He selected a book under imperial copyright, he negotiated a contract with the imperial copyright owner, and he had his books printed in Canada. He thereby acquired the right to prohibit any other edition from entering Canada – an unprecedented accomplishment with regard to an imperial copyright work. Morang's issue of *Kim* achieved the legal status to debar both the American and the British editions from the Canadian market; all copies of Kipling's novel bought and sold in Canada (except library copies) had to be ordered from George N. Morang. He negotiated a similar arrangement for Kipling's *Stalky and Co.* (London: Macmillan; New York: Doubleday, Page, 1899), which was published, however, before the 1900 amendment took effect, and *Just So Stories* (London: Macmillan; New York: Doubleday, Page, 1902).

Since 1891 Macmillan had striven to become the sole publisher of Kipling in the British Empire. After 1893 most of Kipling's new works had appeared under the Macmillan imprint, and in 1895 the company acquired the right to republish earlier ones such as *Soldiers Three, Under the Deodars,* and *The Phantom 'Rickshaw*. Under previous copyright acts Macmillan's books had had access to the Canadian market, and recapturing that market was one of the first tasks of Frank Wise. Morang's contract appears to have expired after a few years, and when it did, Wise took possession of three sets of plates belonging to Morang – those used to produce the Canadian impressions of *Kim, Stalky and Co.*, and *Just So Stories*. In a letter to Kipling's London-based literary agent, A.P. Watt and Son, Wise complained that he had no room to store them in his cramped office on Richmond Street and recommended that they be sold as scrap metal.[23] Caroline Kipling consented on behalf of her husband, and in his reply Alexander Strahan Watt (the 'Son') reminded Wise to forward to her any payment he received for them.[24] The plates for *Stalky and Co.* weighed 325 pounds and those for *Just So Stories* 326 pounds. All told, Wise sold 1,125 pounds of metal at 2.5¢ per pound. He sent $25.31 to Caroline after subtracting 10 per cent of the proceeds for his own role in the transaction.[25]

The Canadian publication of *Puck of Pook's Hill* differed sharply from that of *Kim*. The stories ran in periodicals from January to October 1906. In the United Kingdom they appeared in *The Strand* (London) alongside illustrations by Claude A. Shepperson; in the United States they began in *The Ladies' Home Journal* (Philadelphia) with illustrations by Charlotte Harding but then switched to *McClure's Magazine* with illustrations by André Castaigne in May. Publication in book form occurred simultaneously on 2 October, though, again, substantial discrepancies exist between the American and British texts.[26] The Doubleday, Page edition consists of eighteen unsigned eight-leaf gatherings accompanied by four colour half-tone photographic plates of ink drawings by Arthur Rackham:

Puck of Pook's Hill: Doubleday, Page Edition[27]

COLLATION [1–18]^8. 144 leaves. Pages [10] 1–277 *278* [= 288]. Plates [4] (facing 1_2^a, 1_8^b, 11_1^b, 14_7^b).
CONTENTS [1] half-title. [2] list of author's works. [3] title. [4] copyright statement: 'Copyright, 1905, 1906, by | RUDYARD KIPLING | Published, October, 1906 | *All rights reserved,* | *including that of translation into foreign languages,* | *including the Scandinavian* | [frame, 2.9 × 5.8 cm: enclosing all of the following] 'ROBIN GOODFELLOW – HIS FRIENDS | By RUDYARD KIPLING | I. A Centurion of the Thirtieth. | II. On the Great Wall. | III. The Winged Hats. | IV. Hal o' the Draft. | V. Dymchurch Flit. | VI. The Treasure and the Law. | Copyright, 1906, by RUDYARD KIPLING.'

[5] contents. [6] blank. [7] list of illustrations. [8] blank. [9] half-title. [10] blank. 1–277 text. 278 blank.
TYPOGRAPHY 35 lines, 147 (155) × 84 mm; 10 lines = 42 mm; capital 2.9 (x 1.8) mm.

Like previous works, it was bound in green cloth stamped in black with the image of a ship. The Macmillan and Company edition, again printed by R. and R. Clark of Edinburgh, has twenty-one gatherings, the first with six leaves, the last with two, and the rest with eight:

Puck of Pook's Hill: Macmillan Edition[28]

COLLATION *A*⁶ B–I⁸ K–U⁸ X² [$ 1 signed; B1 signed 'E']. 160 leaves.
Pages [2] *i–vi* vii *viii* ix–x *1–2* 3–306 *307–308* [= 320]. [All half-title pages of chapters are numbered except the first (*1*).]
CONTENTS [*1–2*] blank. *i* half-title: 'PUCK OF POOK'S HILL'.
ii ornament, 2.6 × 2.6 cm: circle enclosing swastika and author's name. *iii* blank. *iv* frontispiece. *v* title. *vi* copyright statement: 'COPYRIGHT, 1906 | BY RUDYARD KIPLING'. vii contents.
viii blank. ix–x list of illustrations. 1–306 text. 306 imprint: '*Printed by* R. & R. CLARK, LIMITED, *Edinburgh*'. *307–308* publisher's advertisements.
TYPOGRAPHY 33 lines, 140 (150) × 84 mm; 10 lines = 42 mm; capital 2.8 (x 1.7) mm.

The twenty engravings of drawings by H.R. Millar were incorporated into the letterpress plates.

In June 1906 Frank Wise announced that the Macmillan Company of Canada would 'publish' *Puck of Pook's Hill*.[29] He advertised steadily through the summer, exploiting the opinion among some critics that this narrative of the rise of English civilization was Kipling's best work since *Kim*. In August he billed it as his 'leading Fall book.'[30] Unlike Morang's impression of *Kim,* the printing of the Canadian issue of *Puck of Pook's Hill* occurred in the United Kingdom as part of the British edition. The twenty-one gatherings signed *A* through *X* are almost identical to the British edition, including its imprint and advertisements:

Puck of Pook's Hill: Macmillan Company of Canada Issue (Macmillan Edition)[31]

COLLATION *A*⁶ B–I⁸ K–U⁸ X² [$ 1 signed; B1 signed 'E']. 160 leaves.
Pages [2] *i–vi* vii *viii* ix–x *1–2* 3–306 *307–308* [= 320]. [All half-title
pages of chapters are numbered except the first (*1*).]
CONTENTS [*1–2*] blank. *i* half-title: '[*gothic:*] *Canadian Edition* | PUCK
OF POOK'S HILL'. *ii* ornament, 2.6 × 2.6 cm: circle enclosing swastika and author's name. *iii* blank. *iv* frontispiece. *v* title. *vi* blank.
vii contents. *viii* blank. ix–x list of illustrations. *1*–306 text. 306
imprint: '*Printed by* R. & R. CLARK, LIMITED, *Edinburgh*'. *307–308*
publisher's advertisements.
TYPOGRAPHY 33 lines, 140 (150) × 84 mm; 10 lines = 42 mm; capital
2.8 (x 1.7) mm.

The only differences are the half-title (which declares the issue to be
the Canadian edition), the title page (which bears the name and city
of the Canadian branch instead of the London firm), and the verso of
the title page (which is blank in place of the British copyright statement). A separate plate was cast to produce these changes in the first
gathering, which has no cancellations. The plates were not, however,
wholly duplicated for shipment to Toronto. Writing two years later to
refuse Caroline Kipling's request for author copies, Wise illuminated
the entirely British production of his book:

> In regard to your postscript we may state that we are sending to-day
> to Mrs. Kipling a copy of 'Puck of Pook's Hill', which is the only book of
> Mr. Kipling's which bears our imprint. We supposed you were aware of
> the fact that we only import the various titles in lots of 25 from our London
> house from their regular stock, so that our so-called 'editions' – cloth and
> leather – are identical with the London ones, and for that reason we pre-
> sume Mrs. Kipling will not wish to have us submit complete sets. As far
> as 'Puck' is concerned, it is identical with our London edition, merely
> having the title-page imprinted for us by them and bound with their
> regular lot.[32]

The Canadian issue was bound in red cloth stamped in gold with
an elephant's head and a swastika, uniform with the British edition.
Macmillan attempted to increase its profit by not offering an inexpensive alternative in paper. Published on 2 October, *Puck of Pook's Hill* was
available in cloth only at the price of $1.50.[33]

It did not take off. According to the best-seller lists, sales were good
in Toronto and appreciable in Winnipeg in November, but in the rest of

the cities of the country demand was unremarkable.[34] Canadian readers preferred Robert W. Chambers's *The Fighting Chance,* Marie Corelli's *The Treasure of Heaven,* and Robert E. Knowles's *The Undertow.* In the new year Ralph Connor's latest, *The Doctor: A Tale of the Rockies,* shot to the top of the best-seller lists, leaving all competitors behind.

Wise took the precaution of registering *Puck of Pook's Hill* for Canadian copyright in the author's name in October 1906,[35] but as the production process of his issue shows, he did not yet understand how to wield Canadian copyright. Unlike Morang, he did not fulfil the conditions of the 1900 amendment; he did not acquire a special Canadian contract from the imperial copyright owner, and he had not printed *Puck of Pook's Hill* in Canada. Had he needed to rely on this Canadian copyright, he probably would have discovered that it was of little value. He was an effective distributor but had not yet learned how to become a publisher-agent.

Although *Puck of Pook's Hill* was not an immediate Canadian bestseller, the accumulating works of Kipling remained highly valuable. The advertisements in the British edition boast that *The Jungle Book* had sold over 72,000 copies in the British Empire since its first publication, *Kim* over 67,000, *The Day's Work* over 63,000, *Plain Tales from the Hills* over 55,000, *The Light That Failed* over 52,000, *Just So Stories* over 48,000, *Stalky and Co.* over 39,000, and so on through the author's two dozen works to date. Regardless of the individual success or failure of the author's latest work, Kipling's opus as a whole was proving to be steadily and immensely lucrative. Macmillan and Company had carefully positioned itself to enjoy the returns on its investment in him over the long term, and it was Wise's purpose to ensure that Canada kept up its contributions to the imperial account.

A six-month period in 1908 is representative of the financial function of the Canadian branch as a distributor within Macmillan's Kipling empire. Between 1 January and 30 June the Macmillan Company of Canada sold 1,482 copies of Kipling's books. They were available in two bindings: the 'uniform edition,' advertised as 'extra crown 8vo,' was bound in red cloth; the 'edition de luxe' was bound in leather. Of the former, 525 copies sold, and of the latter, 957. The retail price per book was $1.50 (cloth) or $2.50 (leather). This compared to the retail price in the United Kingdom, which was 6s. (cloth) or 10s. 6d. (leather), a Canadian quarter being roughly equivalent to an English shilling. The wholesale price, at which the publisher distributed the books to retail shops, would have been something less. For every book that Wise sold, whether cloth or leather, he owed Kipling 37.5¢ – an amount that equates to a royalty of 25 per cent on the cloth but only 15 per cent on the leather. The account that Wise rendered to A.P. Watt and Son in July 1908 included twenty titles. The six most popular books were the following: *The Jungle Book,* of which 159 copies sold (74 cloth and 85 leather); *The Second Jungle Book,* 129 sold (48 and 81); *Just So Stories,* 122 sold (52 and 70); *Kim,* 113 sold (36 and 77); *Stalky and Co.,* 108 sold (26 and 82); and *From Sea to Sea,* a two-volume work, of which a total of 173 volumes sold (30 and 143). *Puck of Pook's Hill* continued to lag behind, coming in midway down the list of sales, at 62 copies sold (0 and 62). The total amount of royalties payable to the author for this six-month period was $555.74 (£114 3s. 11d.). The Canadian office did not pay this amount directly. Wise attached to his account a remittance, drawn on the London firm, from whom Watt could collect the author's money in pounds sterling.[36]

These figures exemplify the steady though not overwhelming demand for Kipling's works in Canada as well as Macmillan's meeting of it. The remittance emphasizes the subordinate role of the Canadian office; Wise was one line in the ledger of an imperial publishing operation financially controlled by London. It seems that Wise went to greater lengths to sell the more expensive leather-bound books, for almost twice as many of those sold as the cheaper cloth-bound, and in some cases, such as that of *Puck of Pook's Hill,* none of the cloth-bound sold at all. In addition, these figures indicate that in offering expensive books, Wise ignored important factors in the Canadian book trade and may therefore have failed to tap a broader demand. The figures above summarize only the legal purchases of Kipling in Canada in the first half of 1908 and should not be mistaken for a complete account of all Canadian sales. In laying claim to the Canadian market, Wise had not only to take over Morang's authorized Canadian production but also to expose and stop the importation of American copies. Such importation, though illegal since 1895, had been deeply ingrained in the Canadian book trade for over a century. Seasoned Canadian booksellers had a great deal of experience in evading monopolies imposed from London and in dealing in cheaper American books. The less Wise knew about Canadian copyright and the higher he drove his prices, the more tempting a cheaper alternative became. An added twist was that Kipling remained the proprietor of his copyrights rather than assigning them to his publisher. Macmillan and Company therefore could not sue for infringement on their own; rather, they were obliged to bring infringement to the copyright owner's attention and then stand by while he decided whether or not to act.

Around April 1908, Frank Wise became aware that one of his chief competitors, William Briggs, was illegally importing American editions of Kipling into Canada. Some, but not all of these, the Century Company of New York was supplying. The Century Company had managed to reprint some nine of Kipling's books during the 1890s, one of which was *The Jungle Book,* which missed qualifying for copyright in the United States under the U.S. Copyright Act of 1891. When Wise travelled to London in the late spring, one of his goals was to obtain Kipling's authorization to litigate in defence of the Macmillan monopoly in Canada. The matter was not a priority for the author, however, and during his short stay Wise failed to obtain the interview he desired with Alexander Pollock Watt. Upon his return to Toronto, he wrote to Watt in frustration, 'There were a number of matters which should have been talked over and settled, not the least of which was your attitude on the question of the prevention of the invasion of Mr. Kipling's copyrights in Canada.'[37] Before an answer could arrive, Wise importuned Watt for legal support again: 'I have just had an offer from a subscription house here for payment of about $50.00 a week for the time being at the rate of $1.00 per set, on a set of Kipling in ten volumes, published by some unauthorized house in the States. I hope you will agree with me that I have best served Mr. Kipling's interests by refusing absolutely to even consider the matter. I should be glad to hear from you on this point. I am apprising the Collectors of the Ports in Canada to keep a specially close watch for the attempted importation of any of these sets.'[38] A Toronto firm was importing a set of Kipling's collective works from an American reprinter and selling them through the mail to Canadians who wanted to read Kipling but were unable to afford Macmillan prices. The sets were selling tremendously, at the rate of about fifty per week, and the firm was now seeking Wise's sanction of the enterprise, offering him a share of the profits. Macmillan's Kipling empire was under attack, and it was vulnerable because Wise had neither the imperial nor the Canadian copyright under control.

To the former letter Alexander Strahan Watt answered on behalf of his father that Wise must be patient since consulting an author always entailed delay.[39] Upon receipt of the latter letter Watt replied that Wise's first paragraph was confusing, but that he had done right in refusing to collude with pirates.[40] In a third letter Watt reported the result of his own enquiry into the illegal editions in Canada, enclosing a reply he had received from William Briggs. Briggs's words are deferential but circumspect; they were surely weighed carefully.

According to Watt's report, Briggs admitted that a '"representative of a New York House"' had come to Toronto in the summer of 1907 and sold him '"a number of lines of books,"' including *The Story of the Gadsbys, Under the Deodars, The Phantom 'Rickshaw, In Black and White,* and *Departmental Ditties.* Briggs claimed that he purchased the books innocently: '"At the time of purchasing these titles the fact that they were copyright books here was overlooked by our buyer, not intentionally I assure you, but quite inadvertently."' True, his travelling representative had tried to sell them in British Columbia as recently as January 1908, but when Briggs subsequently learned that they could not legally be sold in Canada, he stopped advertising them and had them '"packed away in a case ready to re-ship to the United States."' Then he received an unexpected visit from someone from the Macmillan Company of Canada:

'Sometime ago our attention was drawn to the fact that the books were copyrighted and we immediately withdrew the samples from our travellers. That our statement is correct is quite borne out by the fact that when a representative of Messrs. MacMillan Co., of Toronto, called on us about April 27th last and asked us for any books we had in stock by Mr. Kipling, we informed him that we had none for sale (this because we had withdrawn the samples.[)] At the time he called there were two old samples which you had evidently in your hands at the time of writing. The representative of Messrs. MacMillan Co. stated that these two would answer his purpose as he wished them only for his personal use, as he was a great admirer of Mr. Kipling. Under these circumstances we let him have them at 6¢ each. This is speaking from memory, in other words we gave them to him at less than cost, merely as an act of courtesy. We would have given the two copies free of charge but he insisted on paying for them. The two books purchased were "Departmental Ditties", and "Barrack Room Ballads". The latter book we have not had in stock excepting for the one single copy which we delivered. We have therefore sold no copies of this book.'

To the accusation that he had been selling pirated editions of Kipling for the past five years, Briggs answered, '"This information is not correct as we have not had the books in stock a year yet, and in fact have distributed only about 53 books in all."' He closed his letter by promising to return the books to the New York supplier, adding, '"and I wish to assure you that there was no intention on our part to infringe the British copyright. We are always most zealous in upholding the same."' After quoting Briggs, Watt concluded his third letter by informing Wise that Briggs's promises had satisfied Kipling. The copyright owner did not wish to pursue the matter any further.[41]

The length of Briggs's explanation is in itself an admission. Wise's accusations, relayed through Watt, had caught him at something, and he took pains to acquit himself prudently. His claim to have been ignorant of the imperial copyright in Kipling's works in the summer of 1907 is not plausible. Kipling's fame was enormous by then, and Macmillan's exclusive association with him was the envy of the trade. That Briggs sold copies of five early works only is unlikely. For the most part, the works he names were originally published before 1891; therefore, they were in the public domain in the United States, and the unauthorized reprinting of them there, though lamentable from the author's point of view, was inevitable. The filtering of some such copies into Canada would not have been of grave concern. It is far more probable that Briggs was dealing in Kipling's more recent and more popular works, such as the Century edition of *The Jungle Book,* and that he had sold hundreds of copies to a broad demand. His struggle to answer the allegation of illegal sales in British Columbia hints that his travelling salesmen were selling his illicit American editions all across the country during their regular trips. Wise attempted to obtain proof by sending someone to the Methodist Book and Publishing House to buy some copies, but Briggs anticipated him and disposed of two negligible volumes at the absurd price of 6¢ apiece. Wise dutifully sent these two books to Kipling's agent, but they hardly amounted to the hoped-for proof. Having these details of his failed trap repeated back to him by Watt in a letter that also denied his request for legal backing must have been humiliating for Frank Wise.

Venting all his frustration at being refused, Wise interpreted Briggs's careful statements for Watt, sketching out the real proportions of the infraction that he was convinced lay beneath them. 'I am glad,' he stated sarcastically, 'that our neighbour has promised to return to America his supply of pirated Kipling books.' He then clarified that the total of '"53 books"' that Briggs had confessed to selling could only refer to the latest of innumerable cross-border shipments. Briggs had confessed only to what might be proven against him, according to Wise:

I have proved to my own satisfaction that he has been selling this edition for years, in fact the draper shop, whose Book Manager I brought to account in the spring for selling this pirated edition, claims that they did not know they were violating any copyright since for years they had purchased this same edition through the Methodist Book house, and furthermore if this concern, its buyer, and its travellers only learned this spring that the lines were being drawn tight at the customs around any improper importation it must have taken the information a long time to sift through since we have been notifying them for over two years that we intended to uphold Mr. Kipling's copyright interest against all invasion.

Wise fumed that the Methodist Book and Publishing House was 'a byword here for untruthfulness, and invasion of rights,' passionately wishing that Watt and Kipling would inflict some 'good stiff' punishment on them. Before reluctantly agreeing not to raise the matter again, he lobbed one final accusation, asking, 'What do you think of a concern that obtains the Canadian right on a well-known line of English juvenil[e] copyrights, and for every one authorized book purchased purchases at the same time at least three pirated books from the States [?]'[42]

One must pause to admire the cleverness that Wise wrathfully attributed to his competitor by way of this last question. Almost thirty years of experience in the treacherous Canadian book trade had made William Briggs an expert in navigating the complex commercial terrain between imperial copyright and American supply. The suggestion that he had learned to bargain for Canadian distribution contracts from British publishers in order to turn around and import the American edition instead – thereby fusing into a practical amalgam the opposite roles of partner and pirate – is a fascinating testament to the quandaries in which copyright law left the Canadian industry at the beginning of the twentieth century. A decade or so after having been tripped up by the cheap British edition of Crockett, Briggs had perfected the role of Canadian distributor, deceptively placating the British publisher on the one hand while dealing undercover for American books on the other.

Wise's letter articulates what was one of his most pressing concerns in the early years of the Macmillan Company of Canada – the intention 'to uphold Mr Kipling's copyright interest against all invasion.' Kipling's agent ultimately asked the Century Company of New York not to export its editions to Canada, and it expressed willingness to comply.[43] Wise himself, however, could not prosecute either the American exporters or the Canadian importers of the editions that were undercutting the Macmillan copyright. He did work some damage on Briggs, for his interference caused Watt to call the latter to account, and he was successful in threatening a lowly retailer into no longer selling the books that he had sold for years. Nevertheless, against the standard of the new publisher-agent set by Morang through knowledgeable implementation of the 1900 amendment, Wise failed to measure up.

Frank Wise did not learn how to use the 1900 amendment until he had been in Canada for a decade. In May 1913 the London and New York Macmillan houses simultaneously published *The Inside of the Cup* by the American novelist Winston Churchill, a tale of the transformation of a parish from atrophy caused by capitalism and orthodoxy to rebirth in historical criticism and Christian socialism. The Toronto branch of Macmillan distributed the American edition in Canada. A year later Wise discovered himself in an all-too familiar situation, though strangely inverted. McClelland, Goodchild, and Stewart of Toronto, who had trained under Briggs, were undercutting Wise's Canadian sales by importing from London the cheap colonial edition designed for sale in India.[44] The 'Empire Edition' was printed on the poorest of paper, and the author had accepted a lower royalty on it so that the publisher could market it as an ephemeral. The irony is that the publisher of it was none other than Macmillan and Company of London. Although it intended this edition for India, it could not ensure that the various exporters to whom it transferred its shipments did not divert copies to other destinations. When this cheap book filtered into Canadian bookstores in the summer of 1914, it undercut the American edition. Frank Wise reacted by ordering his lawyer, John Moss, to sue.[45] To his astonishment, Moss replied that the action was impossible: as the American edition was not registered at Stationers' Hall in London, no legal action could be taken to defend its copyright.[46] This was exactly the kind of situation that the 1900 amendment had been devised to prevent.

In 1915 Macmillan published Churchill's next novel, *A Far Country*. This time, Wise troubled himself to find out how to stop a competitor under Canadian law. A letter to his lawyer crystallizes his new knowledge. It summarized the 'very valuable copyright inside information' that he had recently received from the office of the registrar of copyrights and trademarks in Ottawa, stating his registration of *A Far Country* for Canadian copyright and then explaining the acquisition of a prohibition order against other editions:

> We also asked for protection against a cheap edition published by our London house for sale in the Colonies other than Canada. The Department

refused to prohibit any such attempted importation saying that they were not justified in doing so. After a good deal of correspondence I got a Licence from our London house granting us the sole right to sell their edition in Canada; that, however, I found was not accepted by the Customs Department at Ottawa unless we first assigned our copyright to our London house. This, we did, duly registering it at Ottawa, and the Department has now sent us a copy of the circular which has been sent to their Ports of Entry telling them to prohibit the importation of any English edition.[47]

Fourteen years after Morang's impression of *Kim* and nine years after Macmillan's expansion into Canada, Frank Wise learned to conform to the 1900 amendment. He selected a book for Canadian publication and, upon advice, made sure that it was under imperial copyright. He obtained a contract from the imperial copyright owner to publish that book in the Canadian market and then a prohibition order to enforce it.[48] He distributed a Canadian issue, which, though probably printed in the United States, bore no legal evidence of having been produced outside of Canada. He thereby discovered an effective Canadian copyright, at last finding the stone upon which others were already building the agency system.

6 The North American Copyright Divide: *Black Rock* and the Magnification of 'Ralph Connor'

As the preceding chapters have argued, British imperial copyright hindered the development of a book-publishing industry in the Dominion of Canada. It precluded unauthorized reprinting and thus closed off the possibility of the Dominion becoming a competitive centre of book production within the North American context. The post-Confederation campaign to make Canada sovereign in copyright hit stiff resistance from the elite at the centre of the imperial book trade – the London publishers – and when reform finally came in the Canadian Copyright Act of 1875, it reinforced rather than supplanted the rights of the imperial copyright owner, much to the dismay of the flourishing Toronto reprinters. The 1875 act also left Canada exposed to British book exports irrespective of a Canadian bookseller's possessing an exclusive distribution contract, causing turmoil and uncertainty among wholesalers who strove to supply the national market. This lasted until the early 1900s when the Canadian Copyright Amendment, which was also designed to function in concert with imperial copyright, gradually put a stop to the problem of importing competing editions. Owing to the domination of Canada by imperial copyright and then by the Berne Convention, Canadian printers and booksellers tended to evolve internationally cooperative, rather than radically independent, strategies for producing literature in Canada, and accordingly they distributed issues rather than publishing editions, looking more to the foreign publisher than to the local author to supply them with texts. Instead of specialist publishers they became publisher-agents.

Imperial copyright, however, was only half of the problem. Just as formidable a barrier to original Canadian publishing, if not a greater one, was the protectionism of the United States with regard to its own printing and publishing industries. Until 1962 books originally printed and published in Canada alone automatically forfeited copyright in the United States because of the strict formalities of the latter country as to domestic manufacture and registration. Indeed, the main reason Canada ratified the Universal Copyright Convention in that year was so that books first published in Canada alone might finally enjoy American copyright. The royal commissioners appointed in 1954 to examine this very issue noted that most Canadian writers turned to American publishers, and hoped that ratification might reverse this trend: 'Although, as we understand, many Canadian authors now have their works printed in the United States, the time may come when a great many more of them will print first in Canada and in that event it would be a substantial advantage to them to be free of the United States' requirements as to registration, notice and printing. The Canadian printing trade can only benefit from Canada ratifying the Universal Copyright Convention.'[1] However, until this watershed moment in the history of the book in Canada arrived, Canadian publisher-agents shied away from original publishing except in conjunction with an American publisher, who could secure copyright in the United States. The *North American copyright divide* designates the tectonic incompatibility of the United States with Britain and then the Berne Union, an incompatibility, felt keenly by Canada, that endured from the American Revolution until the later-twentieth century. It impelled experienced Canadian authors to take steps to have their work published in the great republic.

It is often said that the United States embraced international copyright with the Copyright Act of 1891 (the Chace Act). True, the 1891 act removed all reference to the nationality of the author and thereby extended the possibility of American copyright to foreigners, but the copyright divide persisted because this extension of privileges was made conditional upon first publication in the United States. The 1891 act was a far cry from the aim of the Berne Convention: national treatment for works first published elsewhere. For the generation of Canadian writers and booksellers who came of age in the early twentieth century, what taught them to be mindful of the copyright divide was the sensational case of Ralph Connor.

It has been claimed that Charles William Gordon (1860–1937) set an early precedent for career authorship in Canada. As 'Ralph Connor' he earned enormous amounts of money writing novels with Canadian characters and settings, and he not only lived in Canada all his life but also published in Toronto. At first glance, he seems to have been something of a Canadian literary pioneer, apparently disproving the generalization that literary authorship in Canada was not viable. A closer look, however, shows him rather to be the exception that proves the rule.

There is no doubt that Gordon could spin a good yarn, but his success as an author was inordinate. The *Literary History of Canada* labels him 'the most widely read Canadian writer' in the first two decades of the twentieth century,[2] and sales estimates substantiate this claim. From 1898 to 1906 his first five novels sold over two million copies worldwide;[3] by the time he wrote his autobiography in the mid-1930s, his books had sold 'over five million.'[4] By contrast, L.M. Montgomery, the next most popular author who remained in Canada, sold approximately two million books between the publication of *Anne of Green Gables* in 1908 and her death in 1942.[5] Over the course of her life her entire opus eventually crept up to the mark that Gordon's first books surpassed within eight years. Then there were the encounters with public figures. President Theodore Roosevelt welcomed Gordon to the White House in 1905 and told him that he could ' "pass an examination in *Black Rock* and *The Sky Pilot*," ' he had enjoyed them so much. In 1917 Prime Minister Robert Borden selected Gordon to go on a speaking tour of the United States to persuade Americans to join the Allies in the First World War, because ' "from your popularity as a writer you have the entree to the hearts of the common people of America." ' In 1932 Gordon attended a meeting of the League of Nations in Geneva and delivered a sermon as part of the opening session.[6]

What caused Gordon's spectacular fame? A critical tradition based in the method of reading his novels has ascribed it to their frontier settings, the authenticity of the portrayed experience, their action-packed plots, and their social-gospel ideology. Susan Wood states that Gordon's success stemmed from 'the synthesis of social and religious values with adventurous plots and colourful descriptions of western life.' She adds that his writing from experience, combined with the 'simplicity of [his] morality,' also helped ensure his popularity.[7] F.W. Watt takes note of the humour that flowed from Gordon's 'essential good-will,' but then chalks up his success to the 'timeliness' of his writing about the West during a period of expansionism.[8] Clarence Karr states that Gordon was an attractive guide through the cultural upheaval of the modern world – one who offered a much-needed evangelical message in a broadly appealing form: 'Connor's immense popularity resulted from his ability to link popular fiction in the form of gripping adventure novels with

[a] progressive reform spirit and the religious needs of the age.'[9] These explanations more or less accord with the reasons that Gordon himself came up with in his autobiography. Although confessing some surprise even years later at the 'amazingly enthusiastic' reception of *Black Rock: A Tale of the Selkirks* (1898) and *The Sky Pilot: A Tale of the Foothills* (1899), Gordon judged it to be a result of their authenticity, setting, and ideology; written 'from personal experience,' they presented a view of 'the great and wonderful new country in Western Canada,' while setting forth religion 'in its true light as a synonym of all that is virile, straight, honorable and withal tender and gentle in true men and women.'[10] The characters, places, and events of Gordon's novels leap out as causes of his great popularity when one reads the texts with this question in mind.

There was, however, another cause. Reading a text is only one step in historically accounting for its social existence; a full explanation of its proliferation must also take into account the processes and circumstances of its production and dissemination. The publishing and reception history of *Black Rock*, Gordon's first novel, shows that his success stemmed from more than the qualities of his writing. *Black Rock* was by far the most popular novel Gordon ever wrote;[11] none of the others that came afterwards matched its popularity, although he returned to western settings repeatedly with an unswerving commitment to the social gospel. 'Ralph Connor' became a household name in the early twentieth century because the physical form of his ideas intersected with the continental fault line between North American copyright regimes in just the right way. As his publishers well knew, an anomaly lay at the foundation of his career. Gordon's first novel forfeited copyright in the United States. Apart from Frank Luther Mott, who mentions Gordon only briefly,[12] critics have generally viewed this anomaly as a regrettable intrusion onto a successful author's property. On the contrary, the lack of copyright was a crucial element in making Gordon a successful author in the first place. *Black Rock* entered the American public domain the moment it was first printed in Toronto, because no simultaneous American edition had been arranged. Owing to this error, American firms were free to reprint the novel without authorization, and they soon realized this opportunity, as the number of surviving editions indicates. From the unusually rapid profusion of editions it is clear that North American readers had greater access to *Black Rock* than to other new popular novels. A far greater number of people in both the United States and Canada bought and read it than otherwise would have done so, because Gordon's first novel fell beyond the pale of American copyright. Charles William Gordon became a famous Canadian author because his first novel was pirated in the United States.

A contemporaneous case, one that doubtless fed the *Black Rock* fire, encapsulates the correlation of copyright with reception. In 1896 Charles M. Sheldon, a minister in Topeka, Kansas, wrote a series of sermons in the form of a narrative. The *Chicago Advance* serialized the narrative and then published it as a book entitled *In His Steps; 'What Would Jesus Do?'* (1897). Demand for it proved strong, and by 1899 the *Advance* was offering it at a variety of prices ranging from 10¢ to $1.25. About that year, a number of American reprint houses noticed that, although the book had been properly registered in the United States, the serialization had not; the text, therefore, was in the public domain. The unauthorized reprinting of *In His Steps* soon began, with over a dozen American firms entering the fray. It was reprinted in England and translated into twenty foreign languages. Eight million copies of the book sold worldwide in the first half of the twentieth century, including at least two million in the United States.[13]

Once the appeal of the novel was obvious, its lack of copyright became a major factor in the colossal augmentation of its production and reception. In fact, *In His Steps* shot into worldwide prominence because it missed copyright twice. American reprinting began after the discovery that it did not have a perfect American copyright. Then, when its popularity among readers in the United States had grown too large for British and foreign publishers to ignore, it avalanched into the public domain of the Berne Convention, for it had not been simultaneously published in any Berne country. The obvious popularity of this social-gospel novel primed publishers both in the United States and in the rest of the English-speaking world to be ready for the next such opportunity.

Lack of copyright increases the reading of a work by eliminating the need for publishers to deal with one another for permissions. The number of producers increases freely, and the rate of replication rises accordingly. Competitive publishing increases the access of readers to a text by removing any one publisher's ability to fix price, thus allowing it to fall to the most attractive level. Generally, the price of a book drops when it passes out of copyright. William St Clair's study of English book production, prices, and reading from the sixteenth to the twentieth centuries assembles a vast amount of data to show that there is 'a clear consequential link between the governing intellectual property structures on the one hand and the provision of texts, the supply of books, prices, access, and reading on the other.'[14] The link, briefly, is that when the copyright is comprehensive and explicit in scope and long in term, the price rises, the supply slows to a trickle, and reading is restricted to an elite class; when the copyright is poorly defined and short or non-existent, the price falls, the supply flows, and reading spreads through the population. In this case, it seems that the *Advance* was already offering *In His Steps* cheaply before the competition had begun, but, whether or not this was so, the important development was the initial publisher's loss of control: the *Advance*'s price hierarchy was swept away in the torrent of editions in 1899. In its relation to copyright, price varies not only in the simple amount but also in organization and location. A text's being in the public domain removes one publisher's control over the timing of the release of different editions as well as over the markets to which they are distributed. The key difference in copyright and non-copyright publishing is the number of producers, which affects the ability of any one of them to control price in all its aspects.

The publishing and reception of *Black Rock* followed the pattern set by *In His Steps*. It too involved an unassuming writer, a popular Christian message, a forfeiture of copyright, and free competition in production. Like Sheldon, Gordon was first and foremost a minister. He donned the mantle of authorship reluctantly, and then only to further a religious cause. He had been a Presbyterian missionary in Banff and the surrounding area from 1890 to 1894, and although he left the mountain missions for a church in Winnipeg, he remained deeply committed to their success. After a bleak report from the missions committee in 1896, James Alexander Macdonald convinced him to drum up support with a fictional account of his years there. Macdonald, a friend of Gordon's from university, was the editor of a new Presbyterian magazine, *The Westminster: A Paper for the Home,* which was produced in Toronto. He promised to publish the story in the Christmas issue. Gordon procrastinated but finally managed to write a piece entitled 'Christmas Eve in a Lumber Camp.' When Macdonald received it, he telegraphed that it was too long and recommended that Gordon break it into three parts. Although too late now for December publication, Gordon complied, and the first instalment of 'Tales from the Selkirks' appeared in *The Westminster* in January 1897.[15]

It hit the mark. Macdonald wrote to Gordon promptly to say that the story was generating a favourable response: 'The "tale" in the January number is taking splendidly.' His letter also makes clear how hard he was working to transform his friend into an author. He not only had to hold Gordon to the equally important tasks of composition and timely submission but also had to edit Gordon's writing substantially:

> We have a good thing here if we work it vigorously and prudently, but you must unfold the next tale without delay; it will not do for us to miss a month, and it will not do if the manuscript reaches me at the last hour. It must be carefully revised before it is printed. I should have the February manuscript by this time, all things go to making it a success; I cannot get the illustrations made unless I have the manuscript in good time. You have a good subject and it will bear working up. I have staked my Editorial reputation on these 'Tales From the Selkirks', if they do not come up to the mark, as the preacher said to old man Nelson, 'it will be hell for all of us;' But they will come up to the mark.[16]

Mixing praise and exhortation, Macdonald braced the novice for the pressure of writing regularly for a magazine. He insisted on a schedule that would allow him to edit Gordon's submissions substantially.

The text shows signs of this editorial intervention. An anecdote surrounds the origin of Gordon's nom de plume, and in looking at the January instalment in light of it, one discovers a passage that Macdonald 'carefully revised.' The anecdote goes that just before publication Macdonald had to send a telegraph to Winnipeg to inform Gordon that he had neglected to sign the piece. What name should it appear under? Toying with some letterhead, Gordon made up the pseudonym *Cannor* from 'British Canadian Northwest Mission.' The telegraph operator silently corrected this to *Connor*. Perplexed by the Irish choice, Macdonald added the name *Ralph* and proceeded with publication.[17] Turning to the text of the first instalment, one finds the name *Ralph Connor* only in the headline; the body of the text never mentions the first name, and this absence accords with the anecdote. However, the last name, *Connor*, does occur in the text, in an exchange between Leslie Graeme and Mr Craig: '"Let me introduce my friend, Mr. Connor, sometime medical student, now artist, hunter, and tramp at large, but not a bad sort." "A man to be envied," said the minister, smiling. "I am glad to know any friend of Mr. Graeme's." '[18] If the anecdote is true, and there is no reason to doubt it, then Gordon did not write this passage. It centres on the narrator's name, Connor, but this name was an accident, a last-minute addition, the result of a miscommunication that occurred after the author had finished composing his story. Besides adding the pseudonym to the headline, Macdonald must have inserted these sentences into the text.

Nor was this the only substantial editorial change. After receiving the manuscript of the second instalment, Macdonald delicately explained that he had altered it, too:

> The sketches so far are good – capital – but they will bear touching up at little points when you have them all finished. E.G. in the first you are so affected by Campbell's playing in the camp that you 'wish he would stop'; you use the same words regarding the effect of Mrs Mavor's singing. I edited that sentence – not improved, but changed the wording. There may be other little points that would be better of a touch. These things do not shew in articles a month apart but brought together in a book they will be prominent. I hope you understand me, and appreciate my kindness thoughtfulness and cheek in giving you a chance to revise or correct before making your book.
>
> Now this does not mean that subsequent sketches are to be less carefully done. That would be ruinous for the real writing must be done at first, while the fire burns, only revision can be done afterwards.[19]

A glance at the February issue confirms that he made the change described above. Nowhere does it include the wish that Mrs Mavor 'stop'; the closest it comes is the narrator's saying that her song was so beautiful that 'my heart ached for some relief.'[20] Macdonald downplayed his activity as editor by rejecting the term *improved,* by jesting about his own 'cheek,' and by distinguishing the trifles of revision ('touching up at little points') from the 'fire' of 'real writing,' but these protestations ultimately emphasize his contributions all the more. Strong editing guided Gordon's first novel into print. Karr does not exaggerate when he judges that, 'without [Macdonald], there would have been no Ralph Connor.'[21]

The Westminster printed the 'Tales from the Selkirks' in ten instalments from January to November 1897. In his autobiography Gordon wrote that neither he nor his editor thought to publish them in book form until the serialization was almost complete, but this claim must stem from either a faulty memory or false humility.[22] Already in January Macdonald was thinking of a book:

> Now about subsequent publication. I decided after receiving the proof of last month's back from you not to make plates of the type set up for The

Westminster; and so the type of the first was distributed as will be that of the second. I have done this because of two things: 1. I believe these sketches are deserving of being put out in better form than would be possible from The Westminster type. This type is too small and the columns rather wide for good effect. I am copyrighting each sketch to prevent reprinting, and when the series is complete will make arrangements for printing them in book form both in Canada and the old country. I may also negotiate with Revell, or Dodd Mead also in New York. I am shewing you plainly what I purpose. I am sure I am right. The cost of the book will be more but it will be also more satisfactory.[23]

The germ of Gordon's accidental and tremendous fame lies in these lines. As his preoccupation with the type shows, Macdonald's concept of publishing the book centred on printing it in Canada; he even toyed with casting plates from the very type used in Toronto to print the magazine. He expected to arrange a British edition too, but he clearly did not imagine that having the work printed in the United States might be an indispensable part of the venture. Macdonald was anxious to preserve Gordon's copyright, but in putting American publication on the back burner he ignored the North American copyright divide and so exposed the text to unrestricted reprinting in the United States. After 1886, mere publication anywhere in the British Empire had automatically created an imperial copyright, and registration in a British possession was deemed equivalent to registration at Stationers' Hall in London.[24] By publishing the 'Tales' in a Canadian magazine, then, Macdonald was in a sense 'copyrighting' them, but the copyright extended only as far as the rule of British law. However, it is not clear whether or not he also registered them.[25] Moreover, original Canadian publications were disqualified from American copyright because they did not fulfil the U.S. formalities that two copies of a work, printed from type set in the United States, be deposited at the Library of Congress upon or prior to publication of the work anywhere.[26] When he wrote that he was 'copyrighting each sketch to prevent reprinting,' Macdonald was aware of the need for copyright but not of the means to achieve it in different jurisdictions.

Apparently, he did make one attempt to find an American publisher: he took the text to New York but was told that it 'would never go in America. It was "too religious," "too temperance." '[27] He did succeed, however, in persuading Hodder and Stoughton of London to publish an edition, and in so doing he achieved the goal envisioned in his letter to see the text published in Canada and Britain. *The Westminster* proudly announced the agreement he had struck: 'The sketches by Ralph Connor, "Tales from the Selkirks," which charmed readers of The Westminster when they first appeared in serial form, are to be published this year in book form in Canada, the United States, and Britain. Messrs. Hodder & Stoughton, London, England, have secured the British and American markets... The Westminster Co., Toronto, will introduce it to the Canadian public.'[28] How exactly did the British company assure Macdonald that they had 'secured' the American market? Whatever the proposed means were, they would prove inadequate.

At a meeting of the Westminster Company's board of directors on 18 October 1898, Macdonald laid out his plan for the first edition of *Black Rock*. The run would be one thousand copies, the retail price $1.00, and the estimated unit cost of production 25¢.[29] Since Westminster had no printing establishment of its own, the printing must have been contracted out to another firm.[30] Neither the minutes of this meeting nor the books themselves name the printer.

Gordon later boasted that 'leading Canadian booksellers' advised Macdonald to publish an edition of eight hundred copies but he dared a thousand, and that the 'first edition' ultimately rose to 'the hitherto unapproached figure of 5,000 copies.'[31] What neither the autobiography nor any other source admits is that the Westminster edition was beset with so many problems that Macdonald had to replace it promptly. Westminster published its edition on 4 November 1898.[32] Gordon had revised the text, expanding the ten serial instalments into sixteen chapters. The eleven unsigned gatherings and the dimensions of the type clearly set this edition apart from those that would follow:

Black Rock: Westminster Edition[33]

COLLATION [1–10]¹⁶ [11]⁴. 164 leaves. Pages [2] *1–10* 11–29 *30–32* 33–57 *58* 59–77 *78 79 80* 81–97 *98* 99 *100* 101–119 *120–121* 122–136 *137–138* 139–154 *155–156* 157–176 *177–178* 179–195 *196–198* 199–223 *224–226* 227–243 *244–246* 247–259 *260–262* 263–275 *276* 277–295 *296–298* 299–305 *306* 307–311 *312* 313–317 *318* 319–322 *323–326* [= 328].
TYPOGRAPHY *Chapters 1–14, 16.* 26 lines, 124 (131) × 80 mm; 10 lines = 48 mm; capital 2.6 (x 1.8) mm. *Chapter 15.* 27 lines, 122 (130) × 80 mm; 10 lines = 45 (46 on 301) mm.

The Westminster edition is a poorly executed product. The pagination is irregular, appearing sporadically on the chapter title pages and disappearing from pages of text; the first chapter lacks its own title page; the typography of the fifteenth chapter, 'With the Shield, or On It,' is denser, thereby revealing it to be a late addition; in place of endpapers, the first and last leaves of the letterpress sheets are pasted directly to the boards and naturally have torn away over time; and, in the copies I have seen, the faded and fragile paper is almost as light as newsprint. There are no illustrations, contrary to Macdonald's initial wish: 'We will have illustrations made for the book. I have a very good one in my mind: Old Man Nelson on his knees in the snow. Picturesque!'[34] In the end, this would be the only image to adorn the shabby Westminster edition: a kneeling lumberjack, raising his face and arms to the sky, is stamped on the front cover. All in all, the first edition of *Black Rock* was an embarrassment.

Meanwhile Hodder and Stoughton appear to have produced their edition simultaneously in November as planned, and apart from minor oversights it reflects the veteran stature of the publisher and the expertise of the printer, T. and A. Constable of the Edinburgh University Press:

Black Rock: Hodder and Stoughton Edition[35]

COLLATION a⁶ A–I⁸ K–U⁸ X⁴ [$ 1 signed; a3 signed 'a2']. 170 leaves. Pages *i–v* vi *vii* viii–ix *x–xii 1* 2–21 *22–24* 25–50 *51–52* 53–73 *74–76* 77–94 *95–97* 98–115 *116–118* 119–135 *136–138* 139–155 *156–158* 159–180 *181–182* 183–201 *202–204* 205–232 *233–234* 235–252 *253–254* 255–268 *269–270* 271–284 *285–286* 287–307 *308–310* 311–327 *328* [= 340] [i.e., the first page of each chapter is numbered, except in chapter one (*1*) and five (*97*)].
TYPOGRAPHY 25 lines, 129 (140) × 78 mm; 10 lines = 52 mm; capital 2.5 (x 1.5) mm.

The pagination is regular, with two or three exceptions; all chapters have a title page; and the typography is uniform throughout. The most important difference, however, is that it consists of only fifteen chapters, omitting 'With the Shield, or On It.' The reason for this major omission is unknown.

Macdonald bought a duplicate set of plates of the Hodder and Stoughton edition and produced a Canadian issue on 15 December

1898, six weeks after the ill-fated Westminster edition had appeared. A note on the back of the title page attempts to hide the gravity of the substitution by declaring that a 'First Impression' had preceded this 'Second Impression,' but in fact the books constitute entirely different editions, stemming as they do from separate settings of type. Compared to the Westminster edition, the Westminster *issue* is a better book, with paper of a higher grade. For some reason, however, there are gaps in the signatures. Nevertheless, it is possible to identify this book with its parent, the Hodder and Stoughton edition:

Black Rock: Westminster Issue (Hodder and Stoughton Edition)[36]

COLLATION ⁴ [A–H]⁸ I⁸ K–M⁸ [N–O]⁸ P–Q⁸ [R–U]⁸ X⁴ [$ 1 signed]. 168 leaves. Pages *i–v* vi *vii–viii* 1 2–21 *22–24* 25–50 *51–52* 53–73 *74–76* 77–94 *95–97* 98–115 *116–118* 119–135 *136–138* 139–155 *156–158* 159–180 *181–182* 183–201 *202–204* 205–232 *233–234* 235–252 *253–254* 255–268 *269–270* 271–284 *285–286* 287–307 *308–310* 311–327 *328* [= 336].
TYPOGRAPHY 25 lines, 129 (140) × 78 mm; 10 lines = 52 mm; capital 2.6 (x 1.6) mm.

The variations in the typography are small enough to be negligible – attributable to slight differences in the duplicate plates or the paper used, if not to measurement error. Like its parent, the Westminster issue omitted 'With the Shield, or On It.' As a result, almost from the beginning two substantially different texts of *Black Rock* circulated simultaneously in the Canadian market.

Westminster duly registered *Black Rock* for Canadian copyright in early November 1898.[37] Again, this registration put the company in a good position to defend the Canadian and imperial copyright but did nothing to secure the American. Mott states that Fleming H. Revell published *Black Rock* simultaneously in New York, Chicago, and Toronto in 1898, but this was not the case.[38] At the end of that year it existed only in the form of the Westminster and the Hodder and Stoughton editions. Thus, on the north shore of Lake Ontario *Black Rock* was theoretically a property to be enjoyed exclusively by the author and the publisher at controlled prices for forty-two years from the date of publication or the life of the author plus seven years, whichever was more.[39] On the southeast shore it was ripe for the picking by any number of reprinters at once.

Black Rock came to the attention of a few readers in the United States in the first half of 1899.[40] In the summer George Doran persuaded Fleming H. Revell of Chicago to test the American market with an issue of five hundred copies bought from Westminster. Revell was a seasoned evangelical publisher in touch with the Midwest's demand for religious books; nevertheless, it seems that he was not interested in *Black Rock* until his vice-president, the Canadian-born Doran, urged him to take it on, and then he did so only 'as a courtesy gesture.'[41]

The original Revell issue of August 1899 is almost identical to the impression from which it derived – the third impression, printed in June, of the Westminster issue.[42] The Revell issue differs only in its preliminary pages, its paper, and its casing:

Black Rock: First 1899 Revell Issue (Hodder and Stoughton Edition)[43]

COLLATION [6] [A–H]^8 I^8 K–M^8 [N–O]^8 P–Q^8 [R–U]^8 X^4 [$ 1 signed]. 170 leaves. Pages [*1–5*] iv [i.e., *6*] [*7–9*] vi [i.e., *10*] [*11–12*] 1 2–21 *22–24* 25–50 *51–53* 54–73 *74–76* 77–94 *95–97* 98–115 *116–118* 119–135 *136–138* 139–155 *156–158* 159–180 *181–182* 183–201 *202–204* 205–232 *233–234* 235–252 *253–254* 255–268 *269–270* 271–284 *285–286* 287–307 *308–310* 311–327 *328* [= 340]. TYPOGRAPHY 25 lines, 129 (140) × 78 mm; 10 lines = 52 mm; capital 2.6 (x 1.6) mm.

There are three errors in the pagination of the third impression of the Westminster issue: the first page of each chapter is numbered, except of chapters 1, 3, and 5 (pages [1], [53], and [97]). The first Revell issue has exactly these errors. Evidently Revell bought five hundred copies of the twenty-one sheets of text ([A] through X) but substituted a new preliminary sheet for Westminster's so that the books would have a Revell title page without the Canadian copyright statement. Obvious differences in the cover indicate that Revell then had the books bound locally with its name on the spine rather than Westminster's. Once the issue was ready, the distribution was national. The copy I examined had the ticket of a retail bookseller of Springfield (Massachusetts), Henry R. Johnson, on the back pastedown. From his shop it found its way into the hands of a married couple, Ysabelita H. and Martin E. Kranz, who glued their bookplate to the front pastedown.

Besides shipping copies of *Black Rock* for sale in the United States, Revell sent out some for publicity, and the *St. Louis Globe-Democrat* was the first, in Doran's words, 'to recognize its quality.'[44] The review that appeared in the *Globe-Democrat* on 6 August 1899 was pivotal. It looked past both the Christian didacticism and the Canadian nationalism of the story to hail it as a romance of the frontier. The review does not so much as mention religion, let alone the finer points of social-gospel conversion; rather, it marvels at the resilience and expansionism of the 'Anglo-Saxon' settler, seeing both the American migration beyond the Appalachian Mountains in the early nineteenth century and the influx of British settlers into the Canadian North-West at that century's end as part of one racial tide flowing across the world. It lauds the courage of the Anglo-Saxon, who 'severs, almost without a pang, the ties which bind him to the old and goes forth to a new and often little-known region to find a fortune or die of a fever.' Passing over the minor French-Canadian and Celtic characters and Gordon's vilification of the gun-toting American, 'Idaho Jack,' this reading of *Black Rock* saw the novel as a frontier romance with a racial message consonant with the American ideology of manifest destiny.[45]

More important, the review signalled the novel's lack of American copyright: ' "Black Rock" (Revell), by "Ralph Connor," known to his friends as Rev. Chas. W. Gordon, was already familiar to a limited circle in this country through the English edition ere the American publishers took it in hand.' To any publisher with even a rudimentary understanding of copyright law, this remark amounted to a proclamation that the text was in the public domain. As *Black Rock* had not been published first in the United States, it could be reprinted there with impunity. Whether this remark directly touched off the rush of unauthorized American editions is hard to say; other public indications of the lack of copyright followed. *Publishers' Weekly* announced the first Revell issue as a 'new publication' in August and again in September. The retail price was $1.25. Both listings disclosed that *Black Rock* was not private property, for neither included the all-important *c.* that designated copyright.[46] Of course, *Black Rock*'s being in the public domain was obvious after the first unauthorized reprint met no legal resistance from Revell. Once that had occurred, the way was clear for other reprinters to follow, and the unauthorized books themselves became announcements of the open season on the text.

American readers quickly exhausted the first issue, and Revell soon moved to a more permanent method of supply. In the late summer or early fall of 1899, it acquired a duplicate set of plates from Westminster in order to re-impress the work as the need arose. The second 1899 Revell issue is very similar to the first: the title page is the same; the pagination is identical apart from the preliminary pages; the sporadic signatures are the same; the chapter title pages are unchanged; the typography varies slightly in three of seven dimensions; and except for the colour of cloth, the binding is the same. The main differences are the reduction of the preliminaries (the preface was eliminated) and the gathering of the book in fours rather than eights:

Black Rock: Second 1899 Revell Issue (Hodder and Stoughton Edition)[47]

COLLATION [1]⁶ [2–42]⁴ (129 signed 'I', 145 'K', 161 'L', 177 'M', 225 'P', 241 'Q', 321 'X'). 170 leaves. Pages [2] *i–v* v [i.e., vi] *vii–viii 1* 2–21 *22–24* 25–50 *51–53* 54–73 *74–76* 77–94 *95–97* 98–115 *116–118* 119–135 *136–138* 139–155 *156–158* 159–180 *181–182* 183–201 *202–204* 205–232 *233–234* 235–252 *253–254* 255–268 *269–270* 271–284 *285–286* 287–307 *308–310* 311–327 *328–330* [= 340]. TYPOGRAPHY 25 lines, 129 (141) × 79 mm; 10 lines = 52 mm; capital 2.5 (x 1.6) mm.

These differences are sufficient to indicate that Revell did not continue to issue Westminster sheets but instead began to produce new impressions of its own.

Marginalia in the copy of the second 1899 Revell issue that I inspected testify that young people were among the readers of *Black Rock*. The morality of the novel doubtless made it a prime gift to the young from those who wished to shape their character. A teacher presented a copy to an exemplary pupil at the end of the school term. Inscribed to 'Fred Goetz from his teacher, Mrs. McEwan, for perfect lessons in the year 1900,' it indicates that adolescents and perhaps even older children had Ralph Connor thrust upon them. Likewise, a certain 'John Haines' received a copy of the novel 'From his Teacher, Zaida Hurlburt. Christmas 1901.'[48] In fact, *Black Rock* made such a good gift to the young that one publisher, David C. Cook of Illinois, eventually produced an illustrated, lavishly bound, large-format edition for this very purpose. One copy bears proof that a buyer used it as intended: 'To dear Gussie, on her sixteenth birthday, with best wishes for the day, from Charlotte.'[49] Young people constituted an important category of Gordon's readership, and the appropriateness of the novel as a gift was another factor in its success.

The unauthorized reprinting of *Black Rock* began in the fall of 1899. Mott states that the bulk of it occurred in 1901.[50] The surviving books do not contradict this proposition, but many of them cannot be dated with certainty. Moreover, there are reasons for believing that the reprinting was well underway shortly after the *Globe-Democrat* review appeared. Doran recalls that the success of *Black Rock* 'was immediately so great that many pirated editions appeared.' According to his recollection, Revell issued *Black Rock* in the summer of 1899, pirated editions soon appeared, Ralph Connor became a well-known author, and consequently *The Sky Pilot* met with instant success when it came out in November 1899.[51] A private statement by Gordon suggests the same chronology. In a letter dated 27 May 1912 he wrote that 'the pirates helped me; gave me unlimited introduction, so that when the Sky Pilot came along there was no further trouble about publishers.'[52]

Another reason for dating the earliest reprints thus is the transformation that Revell's books underwent early in 1900. Revell abandoned its 1899 issues, purchased a new set of plates from Westminster, and thereafter produced new issues. D.T. McAinsh at Westminster wrote to Gordon in December 1899, informing him of the change: 'I am just in receipt of a letter from Mr. Revell in which he indicates that there is a likelihood of a cheap edition of "Black Rock" in the United States to head off a "pirate". Unfortunately, the book does not enjoy copyright there.'[53] McAinsh did not specify how cheap this issue would be, but by mid-June 1900 Revell was offering a paper-covered impression of it for 25¢ – a fifth of the company's original price.[54] The 1900 issue also carried a false copyright statement in its first two impressions, designed to scare off the reprinters: 'Copyright 1900 by Fleming H. Revell.' It failed to do the trick.

The plates that Westminster sold to Revell this time derived from the inferior Westminster edition, not the superior Hodder and Stoughton edition:

Black Rock: 1900 Revell Issue, First Impression (Westminster Edition)[55]

COLLATION [1–20]⁸. 160 leaves. Pages *1–10* 11–29 *30–32* 33–57 *58* 59–77 *78 79 80* 81–97 *98* 99 *100* 101–119 *120–121* 122–137 *138* 139–154 *155–156* 157–177 *178* 179–195 *196* 197 *198* 199–223 *224* 225

226 227–243 *244* 245 *246* 247–259 *260–262* 263–275 *276* 277–295 *296*
299–305 *306* 307–311 *312* 313–317 *318* 319–322 [= 320].
TYPOGRAPHY *Chapters 1–14, 16.* 26 lines, 124 (131) × 80 mm; 10 lines =
48 mm; capital 2.6 (x 1.8) mm. *Chapter 15.* 27 lines, 122 (130) × 80 mm;
10 lines = 45 (46 on 301) mm.

The differences between the 1900 Revell issue and the Westminster edition are numerous enough – clearly, Revell was manipulating a new set
of plates – but not so great as to hide the genealogical relation. The collation is different but related, consisting of twenty gatherings of eights
instead of ten gatherings of sixteens. The pagination repeats most of
the previous errors besides introducing new ones, such as skipping
numbers 297 and 298 altogether. Some chapter title pages have been
awkwardly squeezed onto the verso of leaves. The next impression of
this issue would clean up these errors and return to the ten gatherings
of sixteens:

Black Rock: 1900 Revell Issue, Second Impression (Westminster
Edition)[56]

COLLATION [1–10]¹⁶. 160 leaves. Pages *3–10* 11–322 [= 320].
TYPOGRAPHY *Chapters 1–14, 16.* 26 lines, 124 (131) × 80 mm; 10 lines =
48 mm; capital 2.6 (x 1.8) mm. *Chapter 15.* 27 lines, 122 (130) × 80 mm;
10 lines = 45 (46 on 301) mm.

In both of these impressions, as well as in subsequent ones, the typography is identical to that of the Westminster edition – again becoming
suddenly denser at chapter 15 – so their descent from it is indisputable.
Most important of all, unlike their previous issues, the 1900 Revell issue
comprises sixteen chapters, including 'With the Shield, or On It.'
   Why this change? The plates of the Westminster issue had worn
out by the end of 1899, and Westminster was obliged to resurrect
the plates of the Westminster edition to meet the ongoing demand.
'We shall make a new edition of "Black Rock" here early next year,' wrote
McAinsh in December, 'but the plates are almost worn out. I do not
well see how we can afford to make a new set because another small
edition is about all we can reasonably expect to sell.'[57] A few weeks
later he added, 'We have been obliged here to patch up the old plates
at considerable expense, as we require another small edition.'[58] A copy
of the novel dated 1902 confirms that Westminster did indeed return

to re-impressing their original edition, patching up and re-using 'the old plates':

Black Rock: Westminster Edition, 1902 Impression[59]

COLLATION [1]² [2–21]⁸ [22]². 164 leaves. Pages [4] *1–10* 11–322 *323–324* [= 328] [pagination 11–322 identical to first impression].
TYPOGRAPHY *Chapters 1–14, 16.* 26 lines, 124 (131) × 80 mm; 10 lines = 48 mm; capital 2.6 (x 1.8) mm. *Chapter 15.* 27 lines, 122 (130) × 80 mm; 10 lines = 45 (46 on 301) mm.

The irregular pagination of the text (from 11 to 322) is identical to that of the first impression, as is the typography. This change of plates in Canada may be one reason for the same in the United States. It should be added, too, that in the letter quoted above McAinsh vastly underesti-mated the continuing demand. Four and a half years later, in June 1904, Westminster agreed to a proposal from Revell to produce yet another issue of the Westminster edition,[60] this time an illustrated one with a joint Canadian-American imprint:

Black Rock: Westminster-Revell Illustrated Issue (Westminster Edition)[61]

COLLATION [1–20]⁸. 160 leaves. Pages [8] 11–29 *30–32* 33–57 *58* 59–77 *78* 79 80 81–97 *98* 99[faint] *100* 101–119 *120–121* 122–137 *138* 139–155 *156* 157–177 *178* 179–195 *196* 197 *198* 199–223 *224* 225 *226* 227–243 *244* 245 *246* 247–259 *260–262* 263–274 *275–276* 277–295 *296–298* 299–304 *305–306* 307–317 *318* 319–322 [= 320]. Plates [8] (facing [1]₁ʳ, [2]₆ʳ, [4]₂ᵛ, [9]₆ᵛ, [12]₄ʳ, [13]₁ʳ, [14]₄ʳ, [15]₅ᵛ).
TYPOGRAPHY *Chapters 1–14, 16.* 26 lines, 124 (131) × 80 mm; 10 lines = 48 mm; capital 2.6 (x 1.8) mm. *Chapter 15.* 27 lines, 122 (130) × 80 mm; 10 lines = 45 (46 on 301) mm.

The retail price of this illustrated subedition was 50¢.

Another reason for the fundamental change in the 1900 Revell issue was that it was a counter-attack. Despite its typographical faults, the Westminster edition had a sixteenth chapter; therefore, Revell could tout it as authorized, complete, and unabridged in contrast to the reprints, which followed the fifteen-chapter text of Hodder and Stoughton. In the end, the effect of the change was to perpetuate the same textual split in the American editions of *Black Rock* as in the Canadian. Ironically, the books of the authorized American publisher were the ones saddled with the worse flaws. Revell did try dropping 'With the Shield, or On It' in its third impression but later reinstated it.[62] Meanwhile, the reprinters – all of them – sprang away with the shorter, cleaner text of the English edition.

While the freedom of reprinting allows for a choice of existing texts, it also allows the evolution of new ones; each new edition introduces a possibility of variation. Some variants are unintentional errors, but others are deliberate attempts at improvement – to modify the text to suit it better to a perceived audience or purpose. One of the most interesting changes that *Black Rock* underwent during the initial scrum was the addition of three short stories in the edition of A.L. Burt of New York.[63] Oddly, neither the title page nor the table of contents mentions them, and the head title before each story declares no author. The three stories – 'Ethan Brand,' 'John Inglefield's Thanksgiving,' and '[My Kinsman,] Major Molineux' – are the work of Nathaniel Hawthorne. The suppression of the rightful author's name might mislead one into assuming that they are by Ralph Connor. The stories, originally published a half-century before *Black Rock*, contrast with it marvellously. Whereas Gordon justifies Christianity in a new age of science, emphasizing its social value, Hawthorne's stories explore the dark realm of pre-Darwinian Christian superstition, mingling suggestions of diabolical forces with the narration of objective events. Moreover, the New England stories counterbalance the Canadian novel and imbue the whole book with a more American flavour, thereby suiting it better to Burt's perceived audience. It would be a mistake to dismiss this variation as mere 'corruption'; it is important evidence of adaptation to a new niche. Unauthorized reprinting accelerates the evolution of texts to reader-defined environments.

The reprinting hit full stride early in 1900. American editions and issues of *Black Rock* increased sharply in that year and proliferated rampantly in 1901 and the years following. The copying of *Black Rock* declined after the First World War, but editions continued to appear at intervals, in forms showing a free fluctuation in the reading and marketing of the novel. Avon Books packaged it as a paperback romance in 1973, and it now exists in a number of electronic forms.

As had happened with *In His Steps*, the unauthorized reprints wrenched the novel out of the publisher's control and undercut the original price, at first moderately but then drastically. In the lead-up to Christmas 1899 Revell was still advertising *Black Rock* at the single price of $1.25 (cloth), a sum commonly asked for a new copyright novel.[64] Burt sold its illustrated edition for $1. New York's J.S. Ogilvie went a step further, probably offering *Black Rock* for 75¢ (cloth) or 50¢ (paper).[65] The Donohue issue of the Street and Smith edition probably ranged from $1 (presentation cloth) or 75¢ (cloth) down to 25¢ (paper).[66] By 1901 the price competition had grown fierce. Grosset and Dunlap of New York managed to bring out a cloth-bound edition for only 50¢,[67] but Henry Altemus of Philadelphia soon surpassed them, buying a set of Grosset and Dunlap's plates and producing an issue for 40¢ (cloth).[68] Then W.B. Conkey of Chicago advertised an edition 'printed on a good quality of book paper, durably bound in cloth, and stamped with neat design in attractive colors' that cost only 20¢.[69] Hurst of New York advertised *Black Rock* in a catalogue of titles that ranged from $5 (leather) down to 10¢ (paper).[70] According to an indignant editorial in *The Westminster,* by mid-1902 the book had hit the low of 5¢.[71] It would be an understatement to observe that this extreme, equivalent to 4 per cent of the original American price, was something of a bargain.

These prices indicate that all classes of the American reading public had unusually great access to *Black Rock* shortly after its publication. The production records of the reprinters have not come to light, but their books speak for themselves: an American reader with a dime to spare could buy a copy of *Black Rock.* Table 1 summarizes the sales of only the authorized editions of *Black Rock.* The low figure for the United States in contrast to that of Gordon's next books suggests the extent to which the reprinters cut into Revell's market. Nor were American readers the only ones to benefit from low prices. Hodder and Stoughton quickly moved to protect the British market against the American reprints by producing its own cheap edition of *Black Rock,* priced at 6 d.[72] Over 75 per cent (68,599) of the 90,816 copies it sold were of this cheap edition. The company did not produce cheap editions for *The Sky Pilot* or *The Man from Glengarry,* Gordon's next most popular novels, in the period covered by the table. Thus it appears that the American reprints pressured the British publisher to lower prices too. Furthermore, marks of ownership in individual books attest that Canadian readers benefited directly from the American reprints. One man residing in a town in southwestern Ontario purchased a copy of the Burt edition, which was illegal in the British Empire. His name and address on the front endpaper locate his reading of the American book in Canada: 'C H Roberts 159 Brant ave Brantford.'[73]

Predictably, the ordering of American reprints by Canadian readers, or the importation of them by Canadian booksellers, had become a

Table 1
Authorized Sales of First Ralph Connor Novels, 1898–1905

	Edition	Quantity of Books Sold		
		By Edition	By Country	Total
Black Rock				
Canadian	$1.00	11,419		
	$0.50	2,891	14,310	
American	$1.25	31,605	31,605	
English	6s.	10,808		
	Collector	11,409		
	6d.	68,599	90,816	136,731
Sky Pilot				
Canadian	$1.00	15,388		
	Paper	1,000	16,388	
American	$1.25	123,896		
	Cheap	50,000	173,896	
English	6s.	21,485		
	Collector	17,357	38,842	229,126
Man from Glengarry				
Canadian	$1.25	28,311	28,311	
American	$1.50	131,176	131,176	
English	6s.	11,047		
	Collector	13,484	24,531	184,018

Transcribed from W.E. Robertson to C.W. Gordon, 1 January 1906, folder 12, box 32, Gordon Papers, MSS 56, PC 76. Note: Robertson makes no attempt to calculate the unauthorized sales of *Black Rock.*

real problem for Westminster by mid-1902. The editor of the magazine reported that 'attempts have been made to introduce these American pirated editions into Canada, contrary to the copyright laws, and thousands of copies have been confiscated.'[74] In December 1902, for example, Westminster paid Gordon the royalties owing on 377 additional copies of *Black Rock* that had come into its possession in that month but were part of neither its 'ninth impression,' printed in 1902, nor its 'tenth impression,' printed in 1903.[75] Thousands may have been confiscated, but thousands more doubtless slipped through unnoticed. Whether authorized editions or public-domain reprints, books published in the United States had a sphere of dissemination that normally, not exceptionally, included Canada. The cheap American editions significantly contributed to the popularization and hence the canonization of Ralph Connor throughout the English-speaking world.

A positive feedback loop occurs as the price falls through each class of readers. The more a text is read and discussed, the greater the demand for and production of it grows. The fact that Revell produced a cheap impression or that Altemus bit the hand that fed him is very significant. Both are evidence that price competition stimulated production. In the former case, it impelled the authorized publisher to supply a demand that had initially been negligible. In the latter, it encouraged yet another reprinter to enter the fray, with thousands more copies of the novel finding their way into the hands of thousands more readers. For this reason the lack of copyright cannot be viewed as a regrettable accident in what would in any event have been a successful publication, let alone a successful career; rather, it was the fundamental and determining factor not only in the production and dissemination of this author's books but also in his ultimate lionization *as* an author. Ralph Connor was so widely read because *Black Rock* was so freely reprinted. By the same token, the Canadian publisher had little control over the wild literary phenomenon that it had unleashed; Westminster could neither recapture the massive revenue that had escaped it nor very well repeat the botched process by which it had published this text. Westminster did not mature into a stable Canadian publisher; it vanished long before the career of its first and only famous author was over.[76] The unauthorized reprinting of *Black Rock* was a Pandora's box that could not be closed, and it worked powerful and opposite effects on Canadian author and Canadian publisher.

Advertisements of 'publisher's libraries' (reprint series) amount to another category of evidence for the argument that reprinting caused more reading. Every reprint series is an act of canonization, in so far as it claims that the works included have value despite the passage of time since original publication. The canonization may be strong or weak depending on the success of the series, and one cannot assume that all the works in a series were produced and read in the same numbers. Nevertheless, reprint series do confer a certain status, claiming that their titles are 'classics.' Within a year or two of his fortuitous invention Ralph Connor had joined the greatest authors of English and American literature from the Renaissance to the nineteenth century on the reprinters' canons. Conkey's Amaranth Series and Burt's Home Library, for example, listed *Black Rock* among the works of Shakespeare, Milton, Bunyan, Scott, Browning, Tennyson, Dickens, Longfellow, Poe, and Stowe. By including *Black Rock* in their series, the reprinters canonized it. This process was not essentially different from what a modern literary anthology does when it encloses *Beowulf* and a poem by Margaret Atwood in one set of volumes, presenting them in the same font with the same sort of introduction. The aura of each work rubs off on the next, and greatness arises from the combination. The reprint series were another contributing factor to the magnification of Ralph Connor.

Not long after being written, *Black Rock* was a classic. For a time, as this first novel plummeted in price and flowed to an ever-wider readership, each successive Ralph Connor book was assured of success because nothing could destroy the popular recognition of the author's name. Charles William Gordon cruised to a public career because *Black Rock* missed American copyright. For the same reasons, however, he cannot be recuperated as an early type of stay-at-home Canadian literary success without severe qualifications. He was guided, if not pushed, into the role of author by a strong editor, and his triumph was as much due to the North American copyright divide as to literary talent. These complexities cancel the simple value that Gordon could have had as a model author. Subsequent Canadian writers may have envied the money that Gordon later made from writing without abandoning his native country, but he had not paved a way that they could follow. Publication in the United States remained as indispensable as ever to aspiring writers from north of the border. Moreover, the Canadian publisher, Westminster, which had invested in and was largely responsible for creating the author Ralph Connor, was left in the unenviable position of fighting a losing battle against the flood of cheap, unauthorized reprints from the United States. Thanks to the copyright divide, a Canadian Presbyterian minister had achieved international renown, and a distinctly Canadian text had quickly become an icon of American western expansionism, but in general the publishing of original literature in Canada remained as precarious and unrewarding a calling as ever. The publisher-agents of the twentieth century took note of Westminster's blunder and avoided the pitfalls of printing and publishing literature in Canada alone.

Conclusion

The foregoing study explains the manner in which Canada, at the moment of its inception as a modern state, absorbed a fundamentally unnational model for the production of literature. In the wake of Confederation, Canadian politicians, under pressure from their constituents, urged the imperial government to reform the law of copyright so that Canada could become the site of an inexpensive, rapid reprint industry. Canadian printers hoped to begin producing their own editions of popular books in order to compete with the ubiquitous American reprints in what was essentially one continental market. They argued that once literary book production had been established on a secure commercial basis, it would lead to the publication of original literature, which the new country needed in order to assert an identity. Canada encapsulated this logic in its ill-fated 1872 bill. In London the Board of Trade admitted the justice of the Canadian position but drafted an alternative measure, the 1873 bill, which would have liberalized book production throughout the empire by means of state-licensed reprinting. The major publishing houses of London, however, mobilized against this threat to the principle of authorial property and proceeded to steer the reform instead towards layered definitions of imperial and colonial copyright. This layering allowed them to get what they wished in a Canadian statute (the exclusion of American reprints) without relinquishing what they held through the imperial statute (the right to suppress colonial editions). Changes of government in Canada and Britain in 1873 and 1874, respectively, gave them the advantage, and when reform arrived in 1875, it corresponded to their imperial, mercantilist vision.

The new act was subtle. Its crucial clause, which did not purport to allow the Canadian reprinting of British books, echoed the defunct

1872 bill, which had. Its true import did not become clear until an eager Toronto reprinter became ensnared in its complexity. Alexander Belford had grasped the key to Canadian trade publishing in producing popular editions for the North American market, but in 1876 he was sued for infringing an imperial copyright, and the final ruling in the case of *Smiles v. Belford* confirmed Canada's constitutional lack of sovereignty in copyright. A disequilibrium resulted: while Americans could obtain copyright in Canada by virtue of simultaneously selling copies in Britain, Canadians could not obtain copyright in the United States, even after 1891, unless they printed there. The intense but abortive struggle for self-governance in copyright eventuated in the adoption on the part of the Canadian book trade of risk-averse practices of importation, printing, and distribution – practices that acknowledged, albeit reluctantly, the rights of authors and publishers abroad to control Canadian editions of their works. These practices, initially tentative and scattered, coalesced after 1900 around a functional model – the agency system – whereby a Canadian (invariably Toronto-based) firm obtained permission to be the sole channel of supplying a foreign book (usually the American edition) to the Canadian market. By the time Britain gave its self-governing colonies full jurisdiction over copyright in 1911, international copyright (imperfect though it was, given the fault line of American protectionism) had superseded imperial copyright as an overarching framework, and the agency system was well established. The 1875 act and the 1900 amendment, the only Canadian copyright legislation to receive royal assent and be proclaimed in this period, should therefore be construed as instrumental in cementing international authors' rights in Canada during the early years of the Berne Convention. Through their recognition of the rights of distant authors, these acts shaped the basic character of the Canadian book trade for the next century, orienting it firmly towards American and British centres of production.

The agency system, though stable, failed to patriate the process of book publishing, and those who undertook to create a national literature inevitably ran into dispiriting practical problems. Inferior technology and techniques in book manufacture, the forfeiting of American copyright, and the expatriation of Canadian writers proved to be potent obstacles. Charles William Gordon and James Alexander Macdonald discovered to their surprise that independently publishing new writing in Canada was a sure path to being reprinted without authorization in the United States. The North American copyright divide generated the fame of Ralph Connor but undermined the profit of his publisher, and the Canadian book trade, taking due note of the example, sought out more predictable and less spectacular ways of handling manuscripts with commercial potential. Henceforth, publishing Canadian literature would paradoxically depend on finding an American publisher.

Certain Canadian writers learned to cross the rugged international legal divide. Sara Jeannette Duncan, Charles G.D. Roberts, Nellie McClung, L.M. Montgomery, Marshall Saunders, Morley Callaghan, Irene Baird, and A.J.M. Smith all found their way to American publication, with or without the assistance of a Canadian publisher-agent. Such success came with varying degrees of exile. To understand much Canadian writing of the post-Confederation period, therefore, we must strive to follow each of these figures across the international turf that he or she traversed. Duncan, for example, wrote more than *The Imperialist,* and a number of her 'non-Canadian' novels have recently been recovered in new editions.[1] Nevertheless, the above imperative bears repeating because it is counter-intuitive. The study of Canadian literature often begins with the desire to know what Canada is; the answer, surprisingly, lies in discovering the narrowness and mutability of the term. There have been many and vastly different *Canadas;* this study has illuminated the relative inefficacy of one, which consisted of little more than a newly minted federal government perched artificially upon a powerful international reality. This is not to say that the study of Canada is pointless; on the contrary. But illuminating the changing and limited substance of this particular nation, as well as its drifting place in the world, is crucial to understanding the life and work of past figures and the cultured spaces that they inhabited and crossed.

Other Canadian writers of the post-Confederation period did not navigate well the complex terrain of international publishing, and their literary achievements are regrettably less than what they might have been. The defeat of Archibald Lampman is emblematic. While Lampman was a student at Trinity College, Toronto, in the early 1880s (where he worked on the college paper, *Rouge et Noir*), he encountered Joseph Edmund Collins and Charles G.D. Roberts. Their articulation of the Romantic nationalist idea that a country must be built in letters galvanized his poetic talent. Thanks to Roberts's position as the inaugural editor of *The Week* (Toronto), Lampman gained entry to that magazine; he then went on to place poems in several others south of the border, including *Scribner's, Independent, Century, Harper's, Youth's Companion,* and *Atlantic Monthly.*[2] He moved to Ottawa to take a job in the civil service, married, and in 1888 published his first book privately. *Among the Millet, and Other Poems* was critically acclaimed but not remunerative; although it bore the imprint of the Ottawa bookseller John Durie, it was financed by the author. In 1892 Lampman began submitting the manuscript of his second book, *Lyrics of Earth,* for commercial publication. It was rejected by several American houses before a friend in Boston, Edward William Thomson, persuaded Copeland and Day to take it; they agreed, provided it was cut down to include nature lyrics only. Frustrating errors and delays then dogged the printing, and when the book finally appeared in March 1896, the author was disappointed. Worse, its poor sales hardened the publisher against accepting any more of Lampman's work.[3] 'If someone had some money a magazine of our own might now be run without going beyond our borders for any of the material,' Lampman had mused hopefully to Thomson in 1890, but by 1897 this outlook had changed to a grim, self-dismissing cheer: 'Intellectually I am a moss covered wreck – have written nothing since Xmas, and don't expect to write anything more. I wish I were not a married man. In that case I think I should take to running dangerous rapids in a small birch bark.'[4] His death at the age of thirty-seven in 1899 cut short the promise evinced by his early achievements, and his legacy, restricted to a handful of nature poems, has been tainted by the shadow of unfulfilled potential ever since. The proximate, sympathetic publishing that he briefly tasted in Toronto never truly materialized, and without a publisher his dreams ended up going as 'an ant slow-burrowing in the earthy gloom.'[5]

Writers of the post-Confederation period needed local publishers in order to realize the regionally reflective works of which they dreamed; instead, what they had were national publisher-agents at some remove and international publishers still farther away. The aspiring Fredericton poet Dorothy (Gostwick) Roberts felt the curse of inhabiting a zone devoid of autonomous book publishers when she wrote to Toronto in 1925. Lorne Pierce at the Ryerson Press had looked at her manuscript and offered to have it printed if she would underwrite the costs. She declined: 'I fully understand that the poet's market is the slowest in the world, and that volumes by unknown writers are put in it at considerable risk. I am sorry to refuse your offer to publish a book subsidized by me for I am more unable than unwilling to further the scheme.'[6] The disadvantages of distance and anonymity that characterized the internationally centralized empire of publishing were great; many could not overcome them.

It was with some regret that the Canadian publisher-agent turned down the hopeful Canadian writer, and this sentiment signals an important ramification of the agency system. It both pre-empted and exacerbated nationalism. As the independent production of Canadian literature grew more precarious and attenuated, the desire for it waxed all the stronger. The economic pattern of and the cultural desire for Canadian literature were thus locked together in inverse proportion. A cultural dilemma asserted itself with relentless regularity, in which national merit fluctuated between total existence and total non-existence. On the one hand, there was the bullish celebration of Canadian writing regardless of its quality; on the other hand, there was the espousing of international standards of excellence with snobbish disregard for local tradition. In the caustic rhetoric of A.J.M. Smith and the McGill Group, these polarities went by the labels *native* and *cosmopolitan*. In later struggles over canonicity, anxiety expressed itself over whether a work was merely 'Canadian' or truly 'classic.'[7] Whatever the labels, these categories are but opposite manifestations of a single condition – worry at the overshadowing of local cultural production. The perennial calls for a national literature that characterized Canadian writing and criticism through much of the twentieth century should be construed, in this light, as a corollary of the agency system, which thrived on supplying other books to Canadian readers. The ardent literary nationalism of figures like Pierce and the bristling contempt for early Canadian writing articulated by Smith began to fade after the 1960s, when original Canadian publishing increased in volume and diversified. Eventually there was more Canadian literature than could be accounted for by either extreme of the nationalist polarity.

Nevertheless, the agency system remains with us to this day.[8] Despite its indubitable logistical success in smoothing commercial relations, there is a cultural unease with it that persists. A teenage girl drifting in a small town on the Prairies bumps up against it: 'I dream of escaping into the *real* world. If I'm forced to read one more Narnia series book I'll kill myself. I would love to read the diary of a girl my age – a girl from the city. Or a textbook on urban planning. Or a New York City phone book. I would kill to own a New York City phone book.'[9] Briefly but unmistakably, Miriam Toews here allows an edge of the contemporary Canadian book trade to break the surface of her character's unconscious. The adolescent protagonist floats through a cultural texture that is at once rich and unreal. Inundated by censored cultural products from abroad, she thirsts. And she is not alone. In large part, what most

Canadians read, listen to, and view is less like the diary of a peer than it is like a C.S. Lewis book: the former contains an immediate truth directly relevant to one's position, while the latter consists of ideas first constituted in a different time and place, approved by a distant authority, mass-produced, and showered over global markets. The effect is a longing to be somewhere else, somewhere closer to the heart of things.

Local literature is conducive to a thoughtful and responsible public. However, if good literature is the product of authorial perseverance, and authorship vitally relies on the strength, frequency, and intimacy of its connection to an audience, then the emergence of such a public depends on the development of local publishing. The aim of the present study has been to demonstrate the seminal importance of copyright policy to the development of what we now call the cultural industries and, beyond that, to the formation of culture itself. The lesson illuminated by the case of Canada in the post-Confederation period is not one of absolute authorial property. Rather, it is that such property is only one of a number of conflicting principles that are intrinsic to copyright – the sociality of language and the interests of regional development are two others – and that every reformulation of the law should freely adjust the balance among them in order to achieve a regionally appropriate result. The fact that copyright exists finally not to shore up private wealth but to enrich the public sphere must never be lost from view. Indeed, the statutory demarcation of the public domain is foundational to our concept of the public sphere. In the nineteenth century a sparseness of literary creativity and a poverty of local publishing slowed the development of cultural self-awareness in Canada, because the Dominion enshrined or was made to enshrine the rights of imperial and foreign owners to the detriment of its own interests in printing and publishing. In a sense, it protected authors before it had established a culture of authorship worth protecting. As we approach the challenge of reforming copyright for each new generation of media technology, let us avoid repeating the mistake, in the words of one commentator, of protecting ourselves to death.[10]

Notes

Introduction

1 Cambron and Gerson, 'Literary Authorship,' 129.
2 Mount, *When Canadian Literature Moved to New York*, 21.
3 Bentley, *The Confederation Group of Canadian Poets*, 242.
4 Davey, 'Economics and the Writer,' 108.
5 Frye, conclusion to *Literary History of Canada*, 333 and 334–5.
6 Gaskell, *A New Introduction to Bibliography*, 179–83, 297–300.
7 Michon, 'Book Publishing in Quebec,' 199.
8 Bourinot, *Our Intellectual Strengths and Weakness*, 46.
9 Moodie, *Roughing It in the Bush*, 141.
10 An Act to Amend the Law of Copyright (UK), 5 & 6 Vict., c. 45.
11 An Act to Amend and Consolidate the Law Relating to Copyright, S.C. 1921, c. 24. This act entered into force in January 1924.
12 An Act to Amend the Law Respecting International and Colonial Copyright (UK), 49 & 50 Vict., c. 33.
13 Warren McDougall, 'Copyright Litigation in the Court of Session, 1738–1749,' 2–31.
14 Pollard, *Dublin's Trade in Books*, 1–31; Johns, *Piracy*, 145–77.
15 Act of 31 May 1790, c. 15 §5, 1 Stat. 124 at 125.
16 St Clair, *The Reading Nation in the Romantic Period*, 374–93.
17 Altbach and Rathgeber, *Publishing in the Third World*, 54.
18 Johns, *Piracy*, 1–15. The following account of the origin of copyright is based on Johns, 109–43.
19 An Act for the Encouragement of Learning, by Vesting the Copies of Printed Books in the Authors or Purchasers of Such Copies, During the Times Therein Mentioned (GB), 8 Anne, c. 19.

20 Johns, *Piracy*, 7.
21 An Act to Amend the Law Relating to the Protection in the Colonies of Works Entitled to Copyright in the United Kingdom (UK), 10 & 11 Vict., c. 95.
22 Wiseman, 'Silent Companions,' 17–50.
23 L.M. Montgomery, *The Green Gables Letters*, ed. Wilfrid Eggleston (Toronto: Ryerson, 1960), 80. Quoted in Carole Gerson, ' "Dragged at Anne's Chariot Wheels," ' 143–59.
24 An Act to Amend the Copyright Act, S.C. 1900, c. 25.
25 Robert Darnton, 'What Is the History of Books?' *Daedalus* 111, no. 3 (1982): 65–83, reprinted in *The Book History Reader*, ed. David Finkelstein and Alistair McCleery (New York: Routledge, 2002), 9–26 (12).

1. The Principles of Copyright

1 Parker, *The Beginnings of the Book Trade in Canada*, 102.
2 An Act to Amend the Law of Copyright (UK), 5 & 6 Vict., c. 45, s. 15.
3 Fraser, 'John Murray's Colonial and Home Library,' 339–408.
4 United Kingdom, House of Commons, 'Colonial Copyright: Copies or Extracts of Correspondence Between the Colonial Office, the Board of Trade, and the Government of Canada' (339), in *Sessional Papers*, vol. 43 (1872) 277 at 3 (no. 1), *House of Commons Parliamentary Papers* (Cambridge: Chadwyck-Healey, 2005–).
5 An Act to Amend the Law Relating to the Protection in the Colonies of Works Entitled to Copyright in the United Kingdom (UK), 10 & 11 Vict., c. 95.
6 Seville, *The Internationalisation of Copyright Law*, 86–7; An Act to Impose a Duty on Foreign Re-Prints of British Copyright Works, S. Prov. C. 1850 (13 & 14 Vict.), c. 6.
7 Allan Smith, 'American Publications in Nineteenth-Century English Canada,' 15–29.
8 Seville, *Internationalisation of Copyright Law*, 88.
9 Barnes, *Authors, Publishers and Politicians*, 151–2.
10 Fraser, 'John Murray's Colonial and Home Library,' 382.
11 British North America Act 1867 (UK), 30 & 31 Vict., c. 3, s. 91.
12 An Act to Impose a Duty on Foreign Reprints of British Copyright Works, S.C. 1868, c. 56; An Act Respecting Copyrights, S.C. 1868, c. 54.
13 Parker, *Beginnings of the Book Trade*, 79–88, notes Lovell's success with newspapers, directories, and government contracts and describes his involvement through the 1840s and 1850s in original literary publishing, in which he usually ensured that 'the financial risk was taken by someone else' (83).

14 *Debates of the Senate,* 15 May 1868 at 319 (Cauchon).

15 *Debates of the Senate,* 12 May 1868 at 285.

16 *Debates of the Senate,* 12 May 1868 at 286.

17 Minute, Thomas Henry Farrer, 17 June 1868, C803 in Board of Trade Papers, 22/17 Canadian Copyright Part 2, National Archives of the United Kingdom (hereafter cited as BT 22/17); Board of Trade to Colonial Office, 18 June 1868, C803, BT 22/17, printed in UK, House of Commons, 'Colonial Copyright' (1872), 17 (no. 19).

18 John Lovell to John Rose, 11 June 1868, C857, BT 22/17, printed in UK, House of Commons, 'Colonial Copyright' (1872), 18 (no. 20, enclosure 2).

19 Memorandum, 'Canadian Copyright,' by John Rose, 30 June 1868, C857, BT 22/17, printed in UK, House of Commons, 'Colonial Copyright' (1872), 17–18 (no. 20, enclosure 1).

20 Minute, Louis Mallet, 8 July 1868, C857, BT 22/17.

21 Johns, *Piracy,* 264, 282–3. Johns argues that the concept of *intellectual property* itself was first articulated in response to the Victorian anti-patent campaign: by comparing patents to copyright, proponents of patenting asserted a deep proprietary essence in all creative work (248).

22 Minute, Thomas Henry Farrer, 9 July 1868, C857, BT 22/17; Board of Trade to Colonial Office, 22 July 1868, BT 22/17, C857, printed in UK, House of Commons, 'Colonial Copyright' (1872), 21–2 (no. 27).

23 Memorandum, 'Copyright Law in Canada,' by John Rose, 30 March 1869, printed in UK, House of Commons, 'Colonial Copyright' (1872), 34–7 (no. 38, enclosure).

24 *Routledge v. Low* (1868), L.R. 3 H.L. (English and Irish Appeal Cases) 100.

25 For a detailed publishing history of *The Clockmaker,* see Parker, introduction to *The Clockmaker*; Panofsky, 'A Bibliographical Study of Thomas Chandler Haliburton's *The Clockmaker.*'

26 Minute, Louis Mallet, 26 May 1869, C687, BT 22/17.

27 Minute, Thomas Henry Farrer, 15 June 1869, C687, BT 22/17.

28 Board of Trade to Colonial Office, 27 July 1869 (final draft), printed in UK, House of Commons, 'Colonial Copyright' (1872), 26–30 (no. 33). Canada received this answer in the fall: Earl Granville (Colonial Secretary) to John Young, Baron Lisgar (Governor General), 20 October 1869, C1266, BT 22/17, printed in UK, House of Commons, 'Colonial Copyright' (1872), 30 (no. 35).

29 Minute, Louis Mallet, 23 June 1869, C687, BT 22/17.

30 Board of Trade to Colonial Office, 27 July 1869 (first draft and annotations), C687, BT 22/17.

31 Circular, F.R. Daldy to John Rose, 23 June 1869, C78, BT 22/17.

32 Edward Thornton to Earl of Clarendon (Foreign Secretary), 5 March 1870, printed in UK, House of Commons, 'Colonial Copyright' (1872), 48–9 (no. 48, enclosure).

33 Board of Trade to Colonial Office, 7 March 1870, C304, BT 22/17; Colonial Office to Board of Trade, 31 March 1870, C418, BT 22/17; both letters, along with the first two drafts of the 1870 bill, are printed in UK, House of Commons, 'Colonial Copyright' (1872), 41–4 (nos. 45–6).

34 Thomas Longman and John Murray to W.E. Gladstone, March 1870, C399, BT 22/17, printed in UK, House of Commons, 'Colonial Copyright' (1872), 46–7 (no. 47, enclosure).

35 Minute, Thomas Henry Farrer, 9 April 1870, C399, BT 22/17.

36 Board of Trade to Colonial Office, 25 April 1870, C399, BT 22/17, printed in UK, House of Commons, 'Colonial Copyright' (1872), 44–5 (no. 47).

37 Minute, Louis Mallet, 23 June 1869, C687, BT 22/17.

38 Circulars, Earl Granville (Colonial Secretary) to governors of colonies, 1 and 2 June 1870. These two circulars and all the responses to them are printed in UK, House of Commons, 'Colonial Copyright' (1872), 49–65 (nos. 50–69).

39 Brownlow Gray (Attorney General) to W.F. Brett (Acting Governor of Bermuda), 29 July 1870, printed in UK, House of Commons, 'Colonial Copyright' (1872), 55 (no. 57, enclosure).

40 Minute, Louis Mallet, 24 May 1871, C421, BT 22/17.

41 Memorandum, Francis Hincks and Christopher Dunkin, 30 November 1870, C21, BT 22/17, printed in UK, House of Commons, 'Colonial Copyright' (1872), 58 (no. 60, enclosure).

42 Minute, Louis Mallet, 9 January 1871, C21, BT 22/17.

43 John Murray to Louis Mallet, 8 March 1871, C198, BT 22/17.

44 Roberton Blaine to Louis Mallet, 9 March 1871, C199, BT 22/17.

45 Thomas Longman to Louis Mallet, 28 March 1871, C261, BT 22/17.

46 Minute, Louis Mallet, 29 March 1871, C261, BT 22/17.

47 *Debates of the Senate,* 5 May 1869 at 90, and 11 May 1869 at 103; Canada, Parliament, 'Correspondence Respecting the Copy-Right Law in Canada,' in *Sessional Papers,* no. 11 (1869).

48 *Debates of the Senate,* 16 March 1870 at 56, and 10 May 1870 at 222; Canada, Parliament, 'Return to an Address to the Senate, dated 16th March, 1870,' in *Sessional Papers,* no. 50 (1870).

49 *Debates of the Senate,* 28 February 1871 at 53 and 54; Canada, Parliament, 'Return to an Address of the Senate, dated 28th February, 1871,' in *Sessional Papers,* no. 43 (1871), and 'Return to an Address of the Senate, dated 23rd April, 1872,' in *Sessional Papers,* no. 54 (1872) (not printed).

50 Seville, *Internationalisation of Copyright Law,* 98.

51 Copyright Association, 'Memoranda on International and Colonial Copyright,' March 1872, 2404, BT 22/17, reprinted in UK, House of Commons, 'Colonial Copyright' (1872), 68–75 (no. 70, enclosure).

52 'The Copyright Law,' *The Gazette* (Montreal), 5 January 1872.

53 John Lovell, letter, 'To the People of British North America,' *The Daily News* (Montreal), 12 January 1872, clipping preserved in C30, BT 22/17.

54 John Lovell, letter to the editor, 'John Lovell's Printing Office,' *Publishers' Weekly* 3, no. 5 (30 Jan. 1873): 107–8.

55 Stern, *Imprints on History*, 261–2; Parker, *Beginnings of the Book Trade*, 172–5.

56 Thomas Farrer to John Rose, 1 February 1872, C30, BT 22/17. The first five letters in this correspondence (up to Farrer's of 31 May) were printed for confidential use under the title 'Private Correspondence Between the Hon. Sir J. Rose and T.H. Farrer Esq.'; one copy is preserved in BT 22/17 (annotated by F.R. Daldy) and another in the John A. Macdonald Papers, Library and Archives Canada (according to Parker, *Beginnings of the Book Trade*, 173n15).

57 John Rose to Thomas Farrer, 11 March 1872, 2477, BT 22/17.

58 Thomas Farrer to John Rose, 26 March 1872, 2477, BT 22/17.

59 John Rose to Thomas Farrer, 9 April 1872, 2477, BT 22/17.

60 Murray and Trosow, *Canadian Copyright*, 74.

61 C.E. Trevelyan to Thomas Longman, 8 February 1872, printed in Trevelyan, *Compromise Offered by Canada*, 3; all three of Trevelyan's letters are reprinted in UK, House of Commons, 'Copyright Commission: The Royal Commissions and the Report of the Commissioners,' C. 2036, in *Sessional Papers*, vol. 24 (1878) at 327–8, *House of Commons Parliamentary Papers* (Cambridge: Chadwyck-Healey, 2005–).

62 C.E. Trevelyan to Thomas Longman, 12 February 1872, *Compromise Offered by Canada*, 8.

63 Thomas Farrer to John Rose, 31 May 1872, printed in 'Private Correspondence Between the Hon. Sir J. Rose and T.H. Farrer Esq.,' BT 22/17.

2. The London Publishers Prevail

1 Copyright Association, 'Copyright Association [Announcements of Formation],' printed in UK, House of Commons, 'Colonial Copyright: Copies or Extracts of Correspondence Between the Colonial Office, the Board of Trade, and the Government of Canada' (339), in *Sessional Papers*, vol. 43 (1872), 277, at 66–7 (no. 70, enclosure), *House of Commons Parliamentary Papers* (Cambridge: Chadwyck-Healey, 2005–); 'Memoranda on International and Colonial Copyright,' March 1872, 2404, BT 22/17, reprinted in UK, House of Commons, 'Colonial Copyright' (1872), 68–75 (no. 70, enclosure).

2 Thomas Longman, 'Copyright Association,' letter to the editor, *The Times* (London), 21 March 1872.

3 Thomas Farrer to Thomas Longman, 27 March 1872, 2823, BT 22/17.

4 *Debates of the Senate*, 23 April 1872 at 30.

5 'Copyright Question: The Compromise Offered by Canada in Reference to the Reprinting of English Copyright Works,' *Mail* (Toronto), 4 May 1872.

6 *Debates of the Senate*, 8 May 1872, at 65–7.

7 'Bill: An Act to Amend the Act Respecting Copyrights,' in UK, House of Commons, 'Copyright (Colonies): Copies of or Extracts from Any Correspondence Between the Colonial Office and Any of the Colonial Governments on the Subject of Copyright' (144), in *Sessional Papers*, vol. 51 (1875) 635, at 5–7 (no. 2, enclosure), *House of Commons Parliamentary Papers* (Cambridge: Chadwyck-Healey, 2005–).

8 *Journals of the House of Commons*, 11 June 1872, at 314–15.

9 John Rose to Thomas Farrer, 19 June 1872, BT 22/17.

10 Baron Lisgar (Governor General) to Earl of Kimberley (Colonial Secretary), 7 June 1872, 4512, BT 22/17.

11 John Rose to Thomas Farrer, 23 July 1872 (confidentially printed, separately from previous letters), BT 22/17.

12 Undated memorandum, Alexander Campbell, enclosed in Baron Lisgar (Governor General) to Earl of Kimberley (Colonial Secretary), 4 June 1872, 4512, BT 22/17.

13 Minutes, 'Notes of Talk with Messrs. Lovell and Adam' and 'Notes of Talk with Mr. Daldy,' Thomas Farrer, 7 August 1872, BT 22/17.

14 'Private Correspondence Between the Hon. Sir J. Rose and T.H. Farrer Esq.' 13, BT 22/17.

15 'Scheme of Compromise of the English Copyright-Owners,' enclosed in F.R. Daldy to Chichester Fortescue (President of the Board of Trade), 19 July 1872, 4884, BT 22/17.

16 John Lovell and Graeme Mercer Adam, *A Letter to Sir John Rose, Bart., K.C.M.G., on the Canadian Copyright Question by Two Members of the Native Book Trade* (London: 15 August 1872).

17 F.R. Daldy to Thomas Farrer, 29 October 1872, BT 22/17.

18 Undated note, Louis Mallet to Thomas Farrer, in Board of Trade Papers, 22/16, Canadian Copyright Part 1, National Archives of the United Kingdom (hereafter cited as BT 22/16).

19 'Draft of a Bill to Amend the Law of Copyright,' 29 March 1873, BT 22/16. For the final draft of the 1873 bill, see UK, House of Commons, 'Correspondence Respecting Colonial Copyright,' C. 1067, in *Sessional Papers*, vol. 44 (1874), 539, at 2–7 (no. 1, enclosure 2), *House of Commons Parliamentary Papers* (Cambridge: Chadwyck-Healey, 2005–).

20 Memorandum, 'Copyright,' Henry Ludlow, 20 March 1873, BT 22/16.

21 An Act to Amend the Law of Copyright (UK), 5 & 6 Vict., c. 45, ss. 6–10.

22 Ibid., s. 5.

23 John Rose to Thomas Farrer, March 1873, BT 22/16.

24 Henry Reeve to Thomas Farrer, 24 April [1873], BT 22/16; Thomas Farrer to Henry Reeve, 24 April 1873, BT 22/16.

25 Louis Mallet to Thomas Farrer, 5 May 1873, BT 22/16.

26 Thomas Farrer to John Rose, 26 April 1873, BT 22/16.

27 Memorandum, 'Colonial Copyright,' Copyright Association, 28 April 1873, BT 22/16.

28 Thomas Farrer to F.R. Daldy, 14 May 1873, BT 22/16.

29 'Anglo-Canadian Copyright Act,' enclosed in F.R. Daldy to Board of Trade, 19 June 1873, 3850, BT 22/17; undated memorandum, 'Mr. Daldy's Colonial Copyright Bill,' Thomas Farrer, 3850, BT 22/17; 'Memorandum on Bill of Copyright Association,' John Rose, 21 June 1873, 3950, BT 22/17.

30 Memorandum, F.R. Daldy, 28 November 1873, BT 22/16.

31 Circular, Earl of Kimberley (Colonial Secretary) to governors of colonies, 29 July 1873, printed in UK, House of Commons, 'Correspondence Respecting Colonial Copyright' (1874), 1–7 (no. 1 and enclosures).

32 Dawson Brothers to J.C. Taché (Deputy Minister of Agriculture), 2 January 1874, in Copyright Association, *Report of the Copyright Association for the Year 1874–5*, 14–17.

33 Memorandum, Alexander Mackenzie, 7 January 1874, enclosed in Earl of Dufferin (Governor General) to Earl of Kimberley (Colonial Secretary), 9 January 1874, printed in UK, House of Commons, 'Correspondence Respecting Colonial Copyright' (1874), 9–10 (no. 3).

34 *Debates of the Senate*, 24 April 1874 at 96–8.

35 Alfred H. Dymond, 'International Copyright,' *Canadian Monthly and National Review,* April 1872, 289–99.

36 'The Copyright Law,' *The Globe* (Toronto), 14 May 1874.

37 Ibid.

38 Earl of Dufferin (Governor General) to Earl of Carnarvon (Colonial Secretary), 16 May 1874, printed in UK, House of Commons, 'Copyright (Colonies)' (1875), 7 (no. 3); Richard Baggallay and John Holker (law officers of the Crown) to Earl of Carnarvon (Colonial Secretary), 22 May 1874, 4275, BT 22/16.

39 Earl of Carnarvon (Colonial Secretary) to Earl of Dufferin (Governor General), 15 June 1874, printed in UK, House of Commons, 'Copyright (Colonies)' (1875), 12–13 (no. 4); An Act to Remove Doubts as to the Validity of Colonial Laws (UK), 28 & 29 Vict., c. 63, s. 2.

40 F.R. Daldy to Earl of Carnarvon (Colonial Secretary), 1 June 1874, 4275, BT 22/16.

41 *Report of the Copyright Association*, 13.

42 'Bill: An Act Respecting Copyrights,' enclosed in Earl of Dufferin (Governor General) to Earl of Carnarvon (Colonial Secretary), 16 February 1875, 2017, BT 22/16.

43 *Debates of the Senate*, 23 February 1875, at 110–11.

44 'Copyrights Bill,' unidentified newspaper clipping, enclosed in Earl of Dufferin (Governor General) to Earl of Carnarvon, 9 April 1875, 3854, BT 22/16.

45 *Debates of the Senate*, 25 February 1875, at 202.

46 *Journals of the Senate*, 26 February 1875, at 65–7.

47 *Debates of the Senate*, 3 March 1875, at 256–7.

48 *Debates of the House of Commons*, 18 March 1875, at 777–81.

49 Alexander Mackenzie to Earl of Dufferin (Governor General), 20 April 1875, 3854, BT 22/16.

50 F.R. Daldy to Robert G.W. Herbert (Undersecretary, Colonial Office), 17 May 1875, 3854, BT 22/16.

51 W.R. Malcolm (Undersecretary, Colonial Office) to Attorney General and Solicitor General, 21 May 1875, 3854, BT 22/16.

52 An Act to Give Effect to an Act of the Parliament of the Dominion of Canada Respecting Copyrights (UK), 38 & 39 Vict., c. 53.

53 Memorandum, Thomas Farrer, 12 June 1875, 4603, BT 22/16.

54 Robert G.W. Herbert to Thomas Farrer, 21 June 1875, 4603, BT 22/16.

55 UK, House of Lords, *Parliamentary Debates*, vol. 225, col. 85 (17 June 1875), col. 423–8 (24 June), col. 706–7 (29 June), col. 994 (6 July).

56 Thomas Farrer to Robert G.W. Herbert, 22 June 1875, 4603, BT 22/16.

57 UK, House of Commons, *Parliamentary Debates*, vol. 225, col. 1234 (9 July 1875), col. 1554 (15 July), col. 1764 (21 July), col. 1905 (23 July).

58 An Act Respecting Copyrights, S.C. 1875, c. 88.

3. The Stunting of Belford Brothers

1 County of Kerry Retirement Certificate, William Belford, 18 September 1856, file 1, Charles Belford Fonds, MG29-D98, R7834-0-7-E, Library and Archives Canada.

2 Isabella Blackburn to Charles Belford, 25 September 1865, file 2, Charles Belford Fonds.

3 Testimonial, Peter George Fitzgerald, 11 September 1856, file 1, Charles Belford Fonds.

4 Testimonial, Thomas H. Bentley, 16 September 1856, file 1, Charles Belford Fonds.

5 'Mr. Belford,' *Mail* (Toronto), 21 December 1880. Two obituaries appeared after Charles's death: that in the *Mail*, and 'Death of Mr. Charles Belford' in the *Daily Citizen* (Ottawa), 21 December 1880. The latter appears unreliable in the details of Charles's early life: he could not have been born 'in Cork, Ireland, on the 25th April, 1837' if he was 'about the age of fourteen' when his family emigrated.

6 McCalla, 'Beaty, James,' 71–4.

7 *Caverhill's Toronto City Directory, for 1859–60* (Toronto: W.C.F. Caverhill; Lovell & Gibson, Printers, 1859), 23.

8 George William Curtis to Charles Belford, 13 November 1860, file 6; Joshua R. Giddings to Charles Belford, 1 October 1860, file 7; L.K. Lippincott to Charles Belford, 26 November 1860, file 7; Thomas D'Arcy McGee to Charles Belford, 24 December 1860, file 8, Charles Belford Fonds.

9 For a discussion of the dimensions and significance of literary societies in early Canada, see Heather Murray, *Come, bright Improvement!*, 8–16.

10 Isabella Blackburn to Charles Belford, 25 September 1865, file 2, Charles Belford Fonds; *Hutchinson's Toronto Directory, 1862–63* (Compiled by Thomas Hutchinson; Toronto: Lovell & Gibson, Printers and Publishers), 30; *Mitchell's Toronto Directory, for 1864–5* (Toronto: printed by W.C. Chewett & Co., 1864), 11; *Mitchell & Co.'s General Directory for the City of Toronto, and Gazetteer of the Counties of York and Peel for 1866* (Toronto: Mitchell & Co., Publishers; Lovell & Gibson, Printers, 1866), 128; *C.E. Anderson & Co.'s Toronto City Directory for 1868–9* (Henry McEvoy, Compiler; C.E. Anderson & Co., Publishers; Provincial Gazetteer and General Directory; Toronto: Daily Telegraph Printing House, 1868), 190.

11 Newspaper clipping [1928], file 5, Charles Belford Fonds.

12 *Robertson & Cook's Toronto City Directory for 1870* (W.H. Irwin, Compiler; Toronto: Daily Telegraph Printing House, 1870), 9. Much of what has been written about Alexander's early years is based on his obituary, 'Alexander Belford – In Memoriam,' *Publisher's Weekly*, 20 October 1906, 1098–9, which, however, contains errors in dates. It is unlikely that Alexander was 'not yet thirteen' when he founded the Canadian News and Publishing Company; all surviving books with this imprint date from 1871 or 1872. It further states that the Belford imprint began in 'the year 1872,' that James Clarke joined them 'about 1875,' and that the Belfords launched their magazine 'in 1873' – all of which is incorrect.

13 John A. Macdonald to Charles Belford, 16 October 1871, file 3, Charles Belford Fonds.

14 *Toronto Directory for 1875* (Toronto: Fisher & Taylor, Publishers; printed by the Globe Printing Co.), 234; *Toronto Directory, for 1876, Corrected to January*

1st, 1876 (Toronto: Fisher & Taylor, Publishers; printed by the Globe Printing Company), 199.

15 'Alexander Belford – In Memoriam,' *Publisher's Weekly*, 20 October 1906, 1098.

16 Athey, 'Leland, Charles Godfrey,' 462–3; Genzmer, 'Leland, Charles Godfrey,' 158–60.

17 Longtin, *Three Writers of the Far West*, 5–6; Blanck, *Bibliography of American Literature*, vol. 6, 182–217.

18 Roper, 'Mark Twain and His Canadian Publishers,' 33.

19 Advertisement, *The Globe* (Toronto), 20 October 1870; Elizabeth Hulse, *A Dictionary of Toronto Printers*; Roper, 'Mark Twain and His Canadian Publishers,' 36n4.

20 Copy examined: Queen's University (Kingston), W.D. Jordan Special Collections, call no. Lorne Pierce PS8468 E64 G5 1871.

21 Copy examined: Eli MacLaren, personal copy. This paperbound copy advertises two prices on its front cover: 'Cloth 50 Cents: Paper 25 Cents.'

22 'The Copyright Question,' *Mail* (Toronto), 4 May 1872.

23 Hulse, *Dictionary of Toronto Printers*, 18.

24 Copy examined: University of Toronto, Thomas Fisher Rare Book Library (hereafter cited as RBSC), call no. B–10 07220.

25 Certificate of partnership, Robert James Belford and Alexander Beaty Belford, 4 December 1875, file 17, Ontario Publishing Partnership Collection, William Ready Division of Archives and Special Collections, Mills Memorial Library, McMaster University; 'New Publication,' *Mail* (Toronto), 31 July 1875; copy examined – University of Toronto, RBSC, call no. B–10 07073.

26 Copy examined: University of Toronto, RBSC, call no. canlit F55 N66 1875a.

27 Hulse, *Dictionary of Toronto Printers*, 19, 65, 128–9; advertisement, *Mail* (Toronto), 30 October 1875; 'New Publications,' *Mail*, 8 November 1875; advertisement, *Mail*, 12 August 1876.

28 'New Publications,' *Mail* (Toronto), 10 December 1875.

29 'New Publications,' *Mail* (Toronto), 23 December 1875.

30 Roper, 'Mark Twain and His Canadian Publishers,' 45.

31 Advertisement, *Mail* (Toronto), 25 March 1876.

32 Advertisement, *Mail* (Toronto), 15 April 1876 and 6 May 1876.

33 Advertisement, *Mail* (Toronto), 9 June 1876 and 24 June 1876.

34 Roper, 'Mark Twain and His Canadian Publishers,' 47–9.

35 Samuel L. Clemens to Moncure D. Conway, 2 November 1876, in *Mark Twain's Letters to His Publishers*, ed. Hamlin Hill, 105–6.

36 Conway to Clemens, 16 November and 9 December 1876, in *Mark Twain's Letters to His Publishers*, 106n1.

37 Clemens to Conway, 13 December 1876, in *Mark Twain's Letters to His Publishers*, 106–7.

38 *Debates of the House of Commons*, 18 March 1875, at 780.

39 Matthew, 'Smiles, Samuel,' in *Oxford Dictionary of National Biography*.

40 *Smiles v. Belford* (1876), 23 Grant's Chancery Reports 590 at 598.

41 'Legal Intelligence,' *Mail* (Toronto), 13 September 1876.

42 Copy examined: University of Toronto, RBSC, call no. B–12 07062.

43 *Smiles v. Belford* (1876), 23 Grant's Chancery Reports 590 at 590.

44 Copyright Act 1842 (UK), 5 & 6 Vict., c. 45, s. 24.

45 Copies examined: Eli MacLaren, two personal copies; Université de Sherbrooke, call no. BJ1533 E2 S5 T 1875.

46 'The Copyright Question,' *Mail* (Toronto), 10 October 1876.

47 Copies examined: Queen's University (Kingston), W.D. Jordan Special Collections, call no. Lorne Pierce BJ1533 E2 S6 1876t c.2; Library and Archives Canada, call no. BJ1533 E2 S6 1876; University of Toronto, RBSC, call no. B-13 03049.

48 *Smiles v. Belford* (1876), 23 Grant's Chancery Reports 590 at 591, 605.

49 'List of Members,' in *Report of the Copyright Association for the Year 1874–5* (London: Longmans, Green, 1875), 5–6.

50 Beatty, Miller, and Biggar to Belford Brothers, 21 June 1876, printed in 'In the Court of Error and Appeal, Appeal from the Court of Chancery, Between Robert James Belford & Alexander B. Belford, Defendants and Appellants; and Samuel Smiles, Plaintiff and Respondent' (Toronto: Dudley & Burns, 1876) (hereafter cited as Appeal Book), 15, file 185, BT 22/16.

51 Beaty, Hamilton, and Cassels to Beatty, Miller, and Biggar, 24 June 1876, printed in Appeal Book, 15, file 185, BT 22/16.

52 'Legal Intelligence,' *Mail* (Toronto), 2 August, 6 September, and 13 September 1876; 'The Copyright Question,' *Mail* (Toronto), 26 September 1876.

53 The following description of the arguments and judgment is based on *Smiles v. Belford* (1876), 23 Grant's Chancery Reports 590.

54 British North America Act 1867 (UK), 30 & 31 Vict., c. 3, s. 129.

55 *Smiles v. Belford* (1876), 23 Grant's Chancery Reports 590 at 597–8.

56 *Smiles v. Belford* (1876), 23 Grant's Chancery Reports 590 at 605.

57 Certificate of partnership, Charles Belford and Alexander Beaty Belford, 7 October 1876, file 19, Ontario Publishing Partnership Collection.

58 'The Copyright Question,' *Mail* (Toronto), 26 September 1876.
59 Ibid.
60 'Copyright,' *Mail* (Toronto), 27 September 1876 (reprinted from the *Hamilton Spectator*).
61 Ibid.
62 'Canadian Copyright,' *Globe* (Toronto), 26 September 1876.
63 'Canadian Copyright,' *Herald* (Montreal), 4 October 1876.
64 Circular, Belford Brothers, 26 September 1876, file 7607, BT 22/16.
65 Joseph-Charles Taché, letter to the editor, *Mail* (Toronto), 10 October 1876, italics in the original.
66 Ibid.
67 John Rose to Thomas Farrer, 12 October 1876, BT 22/16.
68 'Legal Intelligence,' *Mail* (Toronto), 16 December 1876.
69 'Smiles v. Belford,' *Mail* (Toronto), 19 March 1877; *Smiles v. Belford* (1877), 1 Ontario Appeal Reports 436.
70 'Prospectus, Belford's Monthly Magazine,' *Mail* (Toronto), 10 October 1876.
71 Advertisement, *Mail* (Toronto), 28 April 1877.
72 Copy examined: Dalhousie University, Killam Memorial Library, call no. PS2199 L5 E4.
73 Copies examined: University of Western Ontario, Archives and Research Collections Centre, call no. PN6161 L35 E4 1877 (spine recovered with brown binding tape); Library and Archives Canada, call no. PN6161 L355 (rebound).
74 L. de la Ramé (Ouida) to Belford Brothers, 6 May 1877, file 3, Charles Belford Fonds.
75 Copy examined: University of Toronto, Robarts Library, call no. PR4527 A7 (rebound).
76 Copies examined: Library and Archives Canada, call no. PR4527 A8 copies 1 and 2.
77 Advertisement, *Mail* (Toronto), 20 December 1877.
78 Advertisement, *Mail* (Toronto), 28 February 1878.
79 Letters patent for the Rose-Belford Publishing Company, 8 April 1878, box 1, Hunter Rose Papers, MS Coll 217, Thomas Fisher Rare Book Library, University of Toronto.
80 Jaszi and Woodmansee, 'Copyright in Transition,' 97.
81 'The Belford, Clarke & Co. Failure,' *Publisher's Weekly,* 28 September 1889, 478.
82 'New Publication,' *Mail* (Toronto), 6 January 1877.
83 'The Belford, Clarke & Co. Failure,' *Publisher's Weekly,* 28 September 1889, 478; 'Alexander Belford – In Memoriam,' *Publisher's Weekly,* 20 October 1906, 1098.
84 Doran, *Chronicles of Barabbas,* 97–8.

85 'Ruined Life Near End,' *Record-Herald* (Chicago), 4 September 1906.
86 *Belford v. Scribner,* 144 U.S. 488 (1892).
87 Editorial, *Books and Notions,* October 1889, 3–4.
88 'The Belford, Clarke & Co. Failure,' *Publisher's Weekly,* 28 September 1889, 478.
89 'Belford, Clarke & Co.'s Proposition to their Creditors,' *Publishers' Weekly,* 19 October 1889, 568; 'Belford, Clarke & Co. To Resume,' *Publisher's Weekly,* 26 October 1889, 596; 'The Belford, Clarke & Co. Failure,' *Publisher's Weekly,* 2 November 1889, 637; 'The Belford, Clarke & Co. Failure,' *Publisher's Weekly,* 9 November 1889, 662.
90 'Alexander Belford – In Memoriam,' *Publisher's Weekly,* 20 October 1906, 1098.
91 'Ruined Life Near End,' *Record-Herald* (Chicago), 4 September 1906; 'Belford Taken From Hospital,' *Record-Herald,* 6 September 1906; 'Alexander Belford Dies in Los Angeles,' *Record-Herald,* 8 September 1906. Roper states that Alexander took a job as a 'clerk in a hotel' but identifies no source for this information ('Mark Twain and His Canadian Publishers,' 44n10).

4. William Briggs, Printer, Binder, and Distributor

1 Parker, 'Distributors, Agents, and Publishers, Part I,' 45–7.
2 Wallace, *The Ryerson Imprint,* 22–65. Janet B. Friskney clarifies the year of his retirement, in 'Beyond the Shadow of William Briggs, Part I,' 141–2.
3 Wallace, *The Ryerson Imprint,* 3.
4 Friskney, 'Beyond the Shadow of William Briggs, Part II,' 169.
5 Wallace, *The Ryerson Imprint,* 2.
6 Ibid., 4.
7 Ibid., 40, 49.
8 Ibid., 2.
9 Pierce, *The House of Ryerson,* 2.
10 Ibid., 9.
11 Ibid., 14.
12 This is not to say, however, that Canada had been untouched by American religious publishers. Early Canadian Methodism, for example, nourished itself on books published by the U.S.-based Methodist Book Concern: see McLaren, 'Books for the Instruction of the Nations.'
13 Pierce, *The House of Ryerson,* 22–4.
14 Friskney, 'Beyond the Shadow of William Briggs, Part II,' 165, 167, 173–9, 182–3, 188–92.
15 Ibid., 199.
16 Pierce, *The House of Ryerson,* 27.
17 International Copyright Act, 1886 (UK), 49 & 50 Vict., c. 33, s. 8.

18 Bannerman, 'Canada and the Berne Convention.'

19 Parker, *Beginnings of the Book Trade*, 220–2.

20 Copyright Act, S.C. 1889, c. 29, s. 1.

21 Ibid.

22 Ibid., ss. 3–4.

23 For more on the 1889 act and the constitutional embers it stirred see Seville, *The Internationalisation of Copyright Law*, 116–30; Meera Nair, 'The Copyright Act of 1889,' 1–28.

24 U.S.C. tit. 60 §4952 (1873); Copyright Act 1891, c. 565, §1, 26 Stat. 1106 at 1107, and §13 at 1110. Seville, *Internationalisation of Copyright Law*, 221–52, describes the origin of the Chace Act in detail.

25 Proclamation of 1 July 1891 (no. 3), 27 Stat. 981 at 982.

26 Copyright Act 1891, c. 565, §3, 26 Stat. 1106 at 1107.

27 Duties of Customs Act, S.C. 1894, c. 33, s. 4 and Schedule A, no. 101.

28 'Current Notes and Comments of Interest to the Trade,' *Bookseller and Stationer*, January 1900, 1.

29 Friskney, 'Beyond the Shadow of William Briggs, Part II,' 177–8.

30 Donaldson, *The Life and Work of Samuel Rutherford Crockett*, 16–51.

31 George Oates, *Tables of Sterling Exchange* . . . (Montreal: William V. Dawson, 1898). The value of Canadian currency was $4.44 per British pound sterling.

32 Agreement, T. Fisher Unwin, 22 February 1894, file 245, box 9, accession 83.061C, United Church of Canada Board of Publication Papers, United Church / Victoria University Archives, University of Toronto.

33 Agreement, T. Fisher Unwin, 2 April 1894, file 245, box 9, accession 83.061C, United Church of Canada Board of Publication Papers.

34 Parker, *Beginnings of the Book Trade*, 228.

35 Copyright Act, R.S.C. 1886, c. 62, s. 6. (Section 15 of the 1875 act became section 6 when the statutes were revised in 1886.)

36 Cablegram, C.S.X. Fisher Unwin to Methodist Book House, 7 July 1894, file 245, box 9, accession 83.061C, United Church of Canada Board of Publication Papers.

37 Advertisement in Briggs's later impressions of *Cleg Kelly*. Copies examined: Eli MacLaren, personal copies 1 and 2.

38 Copies examined: University of Guelph Library, call no. PR4518 C3 C53 1896 ('second edition,' i.e., second impression, 1896; rebound); York University (Toronto), Scott Library, call no. PR4518 C3 C57 1903 ('fourth edition,' i.e., fourth impression, 1903).

39 Copies examined: University of North Carolina at Chapel Hill, Davis Library, call no. PR4518 C3 C55 1896; University of Saskatchewan Library, call no. PR4518 C3 C62.

40 Advertisement in *His Honour, and A Lady* by Mrs Everard Cotes (Sara Jeannette Duncan) (New York: Appleton, 1896), 323; copy examined: University of North Carolina at Chapel Hill, Davis Library, call no. PR4507 C678 H57.

41 'Copyrights,' *Bookseller and Stationer,* March 1896, 21.

42 Index book of printing jobs, October 1895 to July 1901, box 4 (see entries for 'Appleton'), accession 83.061C, United Church of Canada Board of Publication Papers. The breakdown of costs is estimated with the equation $y = c_1 + xc_2$, using all of the total costs that Briggs charged Appleton from March through December, where y is the total cost, c_1 the cost of make-ready, c_2 the printing cost per copy, and x the number of copies printed. Only the total cost in March ($283.60) does not fit into this formula; only the total cost in March included binding work as well.

43 Copy examined: York University (Toronto), Scott Library, call no. PR4518 C3 C57 1896.

44 'Book Reviews,' *Bookseller and Stationer,* March 1896, 18.

45 *Bookseller and Stationer,* March 1896, 14.

46 Index book of printing jobs, October 1895 to July 1901, box 4, accession 83.061C, United Church of Canada Board of Publication Papers.

47 Copies examined: Eli MacLaren, personal copies 1 and 2.

48 Copies examined: York University (Toronto), Scott Library, call no. PR4518 C3 C57 HN8248; University of Alberta, Rutherford Library, call no. PR4518 C3 C62 1896 (rebound).

49 Parker, 'Distributors, Agents, and Publishers,' 46–50.

5. The 1900 Amendment, the Agency System, and the Macmillan Company of Canada

1 Seville, *The Internationalisation of Copyright Law,* 130–5.

2 'The 1900 Amendment to the Copyright Act of 1875 permitted the formal development of the agency system, which more or less worked well enough up to the 1950s.' Parker, 'Distributors, Agents, and Publishers,' 16.

3 Whiteman, 'The Early History of the Macmillan Company of Canada,' 68–9.

4 Minutes of Shareholders' Meetings 1905–31, file 13, box 441, Macmillan Company of Canada Fonds, William Ready Division of Archives and Special Collections, Mills Memorial Library, McMaster University. All references to archival materials in this chapter are to this fonds.

5 Whiteman, 'The Early History,' 69.

6 Minutes of Shareholders' Meetings 1905–31, file 13, box 441.

7 Frederick Macmillan to Frank Wise, 11 October 1910, file 16, box 6.

8   Hamelin, 'Nurturing Canadian Letters,' 128, 154–7, 162–3. Hamelin cal-
    culates that Wise's thirty-one original Canadian trade books constituted
    '14%' of his total 'publications.' For an investigation of Wise's resignation,
    see McKillop, 'Mystery at Macmillan.'
9   James, 'Letters from America,' 171–8.
10 George Platt Brett to Frank Wise, 8 February, 1908, box 1, file 18.
11 Clark, 'The Publishing of School Books in English,' 338; Clark, ' "Reckless
    Extravagance and Utter Incompetence." '
12 An Act to Amend the Copyright Act, S.C. 1900, c. 25, s. 1.
13 Parker, *Beginnings of the Book Trade*, 253–5.
14 Livingston, *Bibliography of the Works of Rudyard Kipling*, 247–9; Richards,
    Rudyard Kipling: A Bibliography, 153–5 (no. A173).
15 Copy examined: University of Toronto, RBSC, call no. kip K565 K44 1901c.
16 Copy examined: University of Toronto, RBSC, call no. kip K565 K44 1901b.
17 Livingston, *Bibliography of the Works of Rudyard Kipling*, 247; Richards,
    Rudyard Kipling: A Bibliography, 155–6 (no. A174), 154 (no. A173).
18 'Books and Periodicals,' *Bookseller and Stationer*, June 1901, 5.
19 Copies examined: University of Toronto, RBSC, call no. kip K565 K44 1901d
    (ten plates); Library and Archives Canada, call no. PR4854 K4 1901 Juv copy
    1 (new casing, first gatherings resewn, only two plates ['Zamzamah,' 'Kim &
    the Lama']), copy 2 (blue casing, ten plates), and copy 3 (ten plates).
20 Frank Wise to A.P. Watt, 20 August 1908, file 12, box 9.
21 Advertisement, *Bookseller and Stationer*, September 1901, 11.
22 'Books and Periodicals,' *Bookseller and Stationer*, November 1901, 5.
23 Frank Wise to Alexander Pollock Watt, 2 July 1908 [a], file 12, box 9.
24 Alexander Strahan Watt to Frank Wise, 11 July 1908, file 12, box 9.
25 Frank Wise to A.P. Watt, 20 August 1908, file 12, box 9.
26 Livingston, *Bibliography of the Works of Rudyard Kipling*, 282–5; Richards,
    Rudyard Kipling: A Bibliography, 176–8 (nos. A205–6).
27 Copy examined: University of Toronto, RBSC, call no. kip K565 P83 1906a.
28 Copies examined: McMaster University, William Ready Division of
    Archives and Special Collections, call no. PR4854 P9; University of
    Toronto, RBSC, call no. kip K565 P83 1906 copy 1.
29 'Among the Publishers,' *Bookseller and Stationer*, June 1906, 9.
30 'Among the Publishers,' *Bookseller and Stationer*, August 1906, 66–8.
31 Copies examined: McMaster University, William Ready Division of
    Archives and Special Collections, call no. PR4854 P9 1906; University of
    Toronto, RBSC, call no. kip K565 P83 1906e; University of Toronto, Robarts
    Library, call no. PR4854 P8 1906.
32 Frank Wise to A.P. Watt, 25 July 1908, file 12, box 9.

33 Advertisement, *Bookseller and Stationer,* September 1906, 14.
34 'Best Selling Books of the Past Month,' *Bookseller and Stationer,* December 1906, 35.
35 'New Canadian Copyrights,' *Bookseller and Stationer,* November 1906, 53.
36 Frank Wise to A.P. Watt, 2 July 1908 [b], file 12, box 9.
37 Frank Wise to A.P. Watt, 2 July 1908 [a], file 12, box 9.
38 Frank Wise to A.P. Watt, 10 July 1908, file 12, box 9.
39 A.S. Watt to Frank Wise, 11 July 1908, file 12, box 9.
40 A.S. Watt to Frank Wise, 22 July 1908, file 12, box 9.
41 A.S. Watt to Frank Wise, 24 July 1908, file 12, box 9.
42 Frank Wise to A.P. Watt, 7 August 1908, file 12, box 9.
43 A.S. Watt to Frank Wise, 5 September 1908, file 12, box 9.
44 Frank Wise to John H. Moss, 17 September 1914 [b], file 8, box 1.
45 Ibid.; Frank Wise to J.H. Moss, 21 September 1914, file 8, box 1.
46 J.H. Moss to Frank Wise, 17 September 1914 and 22 September 1914, file 8, box 1. *Morang v. Publishers' Syndicate* (1900), 32 Ontario Reports 393, had recently driven home the indispensability of registration to litigating under imperial copyright: 'But the plaintiffs had no right to maintain this action or proceeding, for, although they were the assignees of the proprietorship and ownership of the book, they had not complied with sec. 24 of 5 & 6 Vict. ch. 45 by causing an entry of their proprietorship to be made in the book of registry of the Stationers Company, the word "proprietor" in sec. 24 meaning the person who is the present owner of the work' (393).
47 Frank Wise to J.A. Thompson, 1 October 1915, file 9, box 1.
48 Prohibition Order re: A Far Country, 29 September 1915, box 146.

6. *Black Rock* and the Magnification of 'Ralph Connor'

1 Canada, Royal Commission on Patents, Copyright, Trade Marks and Industrial Designs, *Report on Copyright,* 16.
2 Roper, Beharriell, and Schieder, 'Writers of Fiction, 1880–1920,' 336.
3 Karr, *Authors and Audiences,* 53.
4 Gordon, *Postscript to Adventure,* 150.
5 Montgomery kept meticulous records of her sales, and I have arrived at this estimate by adding up the worldwide totals of her twelve most popular novels as she calculated them. Book Sales Record Book, 1908–1942, box 006A, L.M. Montgomery Collection, McLaughlin Library, University of Guelph.
6 Gordon, *Postscript to Adventure,* 156, 295, 376–89.
7 Wood, 'Ralph Connor and the Tamed West,' 203–4.

8 Watt, 'Western Myth,' in *Writers of the Prairies,* 12–13.
9 Karr, *Authors and Audiences,* 80–1.
10 Gordon, *Postscript to Adventure,* 150.
11 Karr, *Authors and Audiences,* 81 and 81n4.
12 Mott, *Golden Multitudes,* 197–8.
13 Ibid., 193–7.
14 St Clair, *The Reading Nation in the Romantic Period,* 443.
15 Gordon, *Postscript to Adventure,* 112, 130, 138, 146–9; Karr, *Authors and Audiences,* 46–7.
16 Macdonald to Gordon, 5 January 1897, folder 10, box 32, Charles William Gordon (Ralph Connor) Papers, MSS 56, PC 76, Elizabeth Dafoe Library, University of Manitoba (hereafter cited as Gordon Papers).
17 Gordon, *Postscript to Adventure,* 148–9.
18 Ralph Connor, 'Tales from the Selkirks,' *The Westminster: A Paper for the Home* (Toronto), January 1897, 15.
19 Macdonald to Gordon, 23 January 1897, folder 10, box 32, Gordon Papers.
20 Connor, 'Tales from the Selkirks,' February 1897, 63.
21 Karr, *Authors and Audiences,* 47.
22 Gordon, *Postscript to Adventure,* 149.
23 Macdonald to Gordon, 23 January 1897, folder 10, box 32, Gordon Papers.
24 International Copyright Act, 1886 (UK), 49 & 50 Vict., c. 33, s. 8.
25 The lists of new Canadian copyrights reported monthly in *Bookseller and Stationer* make no mention of the 'Tales' in February 1897, when one would expect to see a January registration, nor in any other month, although temporary copyrights for other serialized texts appear. 'New Canadian Copyrights,' *Bookseller and Stationer,* February 1897, 20.
26 Copyright Act 1891, c. 565, §3, 26 Stat. 1106 at 1107.
27 Gordon, *Postscript to Adventure,* 149.
28 'Ralph Connor's "Tales,"' *The Westminster: A Paper for the Home,* 2 July 1898, 35.
29 Minutes, 18 October 1898 (p. 43), Minute Book 1897–1915, box 1, The Westminster Company Limited Fonds, United Church / Victoria University Archives, University of Toronto. Summarized in Allison, 'The Westminster Company,' 28.
30 Allison, 'The Westminster Company,' 27.
31 Gordon, *Postscript to Adventure,* 149.
32 See the imprint of the 1898 Westminster issue of the Hodder and Stoughton edition: 'First Impression, Nov. 4th. Second Impression, Dec. 15th.' Copy examined: University of Toronto, RBSC, call no. canlit C65 B53

1898c. Allison, 'The Westminster Company,' 30, writes that the first advertisement of *Black Rock* in *The Westminster* appeared on 12 November 1898.

33 Copies examined: University of Toronto, RBSC, canlit C65 B53 1898a, copies 1 and 2.

34 Macdonald to Gordon, 23 January 1897, folder 10, box 32, Gordon Papers.

35 Copy examined: Eli MacLaren, personal copy.

36 Copy examined: University of Toronto, RBSC, canlit C65 B53 1898c.

37 'New Canadian Copyrights,' *Bookseller and Stationer,* December 1898, 24.

38 Mott, *Golden Multitudes,* 197.

39 Copyright Act 1842 (UK), 5 & 6 Vict., c. 45, s. 3. In the case of a book first published in Canada, this term superseded the Canadian term of twenty-eight years in 1886, when all the benefits of imperial copyright were extended to the empire. International Copyright Act, 1886 (UK), 49 & 50 Vict., c. 33, s. 8.

40 'Book Chat,' *St. Louis Globe-Democrat,* 6 August 1899, part third.

41 Doran, *Chronicles of Barabbas,* 202.

42 Copy examined: University of Toronto, RBSC, canlit C65 B53 1899b.

43 Copy examined: Eli MacLaren, personal copy.

44 Doran, *Chronicles of Barabbas,* 202.

45 'Book Chat,' *St. Louis Globe-Democrat,* 6 August 1899, part third.

46 'Weekly Record of New Publications,' *Publishers' Weekly,* 19 August 1899, 253, and 16 September 1899, 353.

47 Copy examined: Eli MacLaren, personal copy.

48 Copy examined: University of Toronto, RBSC, canlit C65 B53 1900c.

49 Copy examined: University of Toronto, RBSC, canlit C65 B53 1910.

50 Mott, *Golden Multitudes,* 197.

51 Doran, *Chronicles of Barabbas,* 202.

52 Gordon to Editor, Ridgewood, NJ, 27 May 1912, Gordon Papers, box 33, folder 4; quoted in Karr, *Authors and Audiences,* 30n29.

53 McAinsh to Gordon, 22 December 1899, folder 10, box 32, Gordon Papers.

54 Copy examined: University of Toronto, RBSC, canlit C65 B53 1900e. The price is printed on the spine.

55 Copy examined: University of Toronto, RBSC, canlit C65 B53 1900a.

56 Copies examined: University of Toronto, RBSC, canlit C65 B53 1900b, copies 1 and 2.

57 McAinsh to Gordon, 22 December 1899, folder 10, box 32, Gordon Papers.

58 McAinsh to Gordon, 13 January 1900, folder 10, box 32, Gordon Papers.

59 Copy examined: University of Toronto, RBSC, canlit C65 B53 1902a.

60 Allison, 'Westminster Company,' 29.

61 Copies examined: Eli MacLaren, personal copies 1 and 2.

62 Copies examined: University of Toronto, RBSC, canlit C65 B53 1900c and 1901a.
63 Copies examined: University of Toronto, RBSC, canlit C65 B53 1901b; University of Toronto, Knox College Library, call no. PS8463 O7 B5; University of Toronto, Robarts Library, call no. PS8463 O7 B5.
64 Advertisement, *Publishers' Weekly,* 25 November 1899, Christmas Bookshelf, 208.
65 These prices and the ones following come from advertisements in the books. Copy examined: University of Richmond (Virginia) Library, call no. PR6013 O5 b5.
66 Copy examined: University of Toronto, RBSC, canlit C65 B53 190-c.
67 Copy examined: University of Toronto, RBSC, canlit C65 B53 1902b.
68 Copy examined: University of Toronto, RBSC, canlit C65 B53 1902c.
69 Copy examined: University of Toronto, RBSC, canlit C65 B53 190-a.
70 Copy examined: University of Alberta, Book and Record Depository, call no. PS8463 O66 B6 A1 S64 (Children's Historical Collection, no. A20420).
71 'Book Talk,' *The Westminster: A Magazine for the Home,* September 1902, 193; quoted in Allison, 'The Westminster Company,' 29.
72 Copy examined: Eli MacLaren, personal copy.
73 Copy examined: University of Toronto, RBSC, canlit C65 B53 1901b.
74 'Book Talk,' *The Westminster,* September 1902, 193; quoted in Allison, 'The Westminster Company,' 29.
75 Westminster royalty statements, 31 December 1902, 30 June 1903, and 31 December 1903, folder 12, box 32, Gordon Papers.
76 Allison, 'The Westminster Company,' 44.

Conclusion

1 For example, *A Daughter of Today* (Ottawa: Tecumseh Press, 1988) and *Set in Authority* (Peterborough: Broadview, 1996).
2 Bentley, *The Confederation Group of Canadian Poets,* 24–36, 46; Robert L. McDougall, 'Lampman, Archibald,' 513–18.
3 Doyle, 'The Confederation Poets and American Publishers,' 63; Lynn, introduction to *An Annotated Edition of the Correspondence between Archibald Lampman and Edward William Thomson,* lxi–lxii.
4 Archibald Lampman to Edward William Thomson, 28 March 1890, letter 1, in Lynn, *Annotated Edition,* 1; Lampman to Thomson, 18 August 1897, letter 113, in Lynn, *Annotated Edition,* 189.
5 Lampman, 'Among the Timothy,' in *Among the Millet,* 15.

6 Gostwick Roberts to Lorne Pierce, 28 January 1925, Lorne Pierce Papers, Queen's University Archives, Kingston.

7 A.J.M. Smith, 'A Rejected Preface' [1934], *Canadian Literature* 24 (1965): 6–9. Janet B. Friskney analyses the conflict over the selection of works for inclusion in McClelland and Stewart's New Canadian Library as one of Romantic nationalism versus liberal humanism: *New Canadian Library*, 10–13.

8 According to Statistics Canada, 20 per cent of the books sold in Canada in 2006 were exclusive agencies, 22 per cent were published by Canadian publishers, 13 per cent were published by foreign-controlled firms operating in Canada, and 46 per cent were imports. Vincent and MacLaren, 'Book Policies and Copyright in Canada and Quebec,' 64.

9 Toews, *A Complicated Kindness*, 6.

10 Laura Murray, 'Protecting Ourselves to Death.'

Bibliography

Archives

A.P. Watt and Company Records, 11036. Southern Historical Collection. Manuscripts Department, Wilson Library, University of North Carolina at Chapel Hill.

Belford, Charles, Fonds. MG29-D98, R7834-0-7-E. Library and Archives Canada.

Board of Trade Papers (BT). 22/16 Canadian Copyright Part 1. 22/17 Canadian Copyright Part 2. National Archives of the United Kingdom.

Gordon, Charles William, (Ralph Connor) Papers. Elizabeth Dafoe Library, Archives and Special Collections, University of Manitoba.

Hunter Rose Papers. MS Coll 217. Thomas Fisher Rare Book Library (RBSC), University of Toronto.

Macmillan Company of Canada Fonds. William Ready Division of Archives and Special Collections. Mills Memorial Library, McMaster University.

Montgomery, L.M., Collection. McLaughlin Library, Archival and Special Collections. University of Guelph.

Ontario Publishing Partnership Collection. William Ready Division of Archives and Special Collections. Mills Memorial Library, McMaster University.

Pierce, Lorne, Papers. Queen's University Archives, Kingston.

United Church of Canada Board of Publication Papers. United Church / Victoria University Archives. University of Toronto.

The Westminster Company Limited Fonds. United Church / Victoria University Archives. University of Toronto.

Published Sources

Allison, Gordon H. 'The Westminster Company.' Master's thesis, University of Toronto, 1962.

Altbach, Philip G., and Eva-Maria Rathgeber. *Publishing in the Third World: Trend Report and Bibliography.* New York: Praeger, 1980.

Athey, Joel. 'Leland, Charles Godfrey.' In *American National Biography,* ed. John A. Garraty and Mark C. Carnes, vol. 13, 462–3. New York: Oxford University Press, 1999.

Bannerman, Sara. 'Canada and the Berne Convention, 1886–1971.' PhD diss., Carleton University, 2009.

Barnes, James J. *Authors, Publishers and Politicians: The Quest for an Anglo-American Copyright Agreement, 1815–1854.* London: Routledge and Kegan Paul, 1974.

Bentley, D.M.R. *The Confederation Group of Canadian Poets, 1880–1897.* Toronto: University of Toronto Press, 2004.

Blanck, Jacob. *Bibliography of American Literature.* 9 vols. New Haven, CT: Yale University Press, 1955–91.

Bourinot, John George. *Our Intellectual Strengths and Weakness.* Literature of Canada: Poetry and Prose in Reprint, ed. Clara Thomas. Toronto: University of Toronto Press, 1973.

Bowers, Fredson. *Principles of Bibliographical Description.* 1949. New York: Russell and Russell, 1962.

Cambron, Micheline, and Carole Gerson. 'Literary Authorship.' In Fleming and Lamonde, *History of the Book in Canada,* vol. 2, 119–34.

Canada. Parliament. 'Correspondence Respecting the Copy-Right Law in Canada.' In *Sessional Papers,* no. 11 (1869).

– 'Return to an Address to the Senate, dated 16th March, 1870.' In *Sessional Papers,* no. 50 (1870).

– 'Return to an Address of the Senate, dated 28th February, 1871.' In *Sessional Papers,* no. 43 (1871).

– 'Return to an Address of the Senate, dated 23rd April, 1872.' In *Sessional Papers,* no. 54 (1872) (not printed).

Canada. Royal Commission on Patents, Copyright, Trade Marks and Industrial Designs. *Report on Copyright.* Ottawa: Queen's Printer, 1957 (Chair: James L. Ilsley).

Canadian Biographical Dictionary and Portrait Gallery of Eminent and Self-Made Men. 2 vols. Toronto: American Biographical Publishing Company, 1880–1.

Cavallo, Guglielmo, and Roger Chartier, ed. *A History of Reading in the West.* Trans. Lydia G. Cochrane. Amherst: University of Massachusetts Press, 1999.

Clark, Penney. 'The Publishing of School Books in English.' In Fleming and Lamonde, *History of the Book in Canada,* vol. 2, 335–40.

– ' "Reckless Extravagance and Utter Incompetence": George Ross and the Toronto Textbook Ring, 1883–1907.' *Papers of the Bibliographical Society of Canada / Cahiers de la Société bibliographique du Canada* 46, no. 2 (2008): 185–236.

Cook, Ramsay. *The Regenerators: Social Criticism in Late Victorian English Canada.* Toronto: University of Toronto Press, 1985.

Copyright Association. *Report of the Copyright Association for the Year 1874–5.* London: Longmans, Green, 1875.

Daniells, Roy. 'Glengarry Revisited.' 1967. In Stephens, *Writers of the Prairies,* 17–25.

Davey, Frank. 'Economics and the Writer.' In Fleming and Lamonde, *History of the Book in Canada,* vol. 3, 103–13.

Donaldson, Islay Murray. *The Life and Work of Samuel Rutherford Crockett.* Aberdeen: Aberdeen University Press, 1989.

Doran, George H. *Chronicles of Barabbas, 1884–1934; Further Chronicles and Comment 1952.* New York: Rinehart, 1952.

Doyle, James. 'The Confederation Poets and American Publishers.' *Canadian Poetry: Studies, Documents, Reviews* 17 (1985): 59–67.

Duncan, Sara Jeannette. *A Daughter of Today.* 1894. Ed. Misao Dean. Early Canadian Women Writers. Ottawa: Tecumseh Press, 1988.

– *The Imperialist.* 1904. Ed. Misao Dean. Peterborough, ON: Broadview, 2005.

– *Set in Authority.* 1906. Ed. Germaine Warkentin. Peterborough, ON: Broadview, 1996.

Ferré, John P. *A Social Gospel for Millions: The Religious Bestsellers of Charles Sheldon, Charles Gordon, and Harold Bell Wright.* Bowling Green, OH: Bowling Green State University Popular Press, 1988.

Fleming, Patricia Lockhart, and Yvan Lamonde, ed. *History of the Book in Canada.* 3 vols. Toronto: University of Toronto Press, 2004–7.

Fraser, Angus. 'John Murray's Colonial and Home Library.' *Papers of the Bibliographical Society of America* 91, no. 3 (1997): 339–408.

Friskney, Janet B. 'Beyond the Shadow of William Briggs, Part I: Setting the Stage and Introducing the Players.' *Papers of the Bibliographical Society of Canada / Cahiers de la Société bibliographique du Canada* 33 (1995): 121–63.

– 'Beyond the Shadow of William Briggs, Part II: Canadian-Authored Titles and the Commitment to Canadian Writing.' *Papers of the Bibliographical Society of Canada / Cahiers de la Société bibliographique du Canada* 35 (1997): 161–207.

– *New Canadian Library: The Ross-McClelland Years, 1952–1978.* Toronto: University of Toronto Press, 2007.

– 'Towards a Canadian Cultural Mecca: The Methodist Book and Publishing House's Pursuit of Book Publishing and Commitment to Canadian Writing, 1829–1926.' Master's thesis, Trent University, 1994.

Frye, Northrop. Conclusion. In Klinck, *Literary History of Canada,* vol. 2, 333–61.

Gaskell, Philip. *A New Introduction to Bibliography.* 1972. New Castle, DE: Oak Knoll, 1995.

Genzmer, George Harvey. 'Leland, Charles Godfrey.' In *Dictionary of American Biography,* ed. Dumas Malone, vol. 11, 158–60. New York: Charles Scribner's Sons, 1933.

Gerson, Carole. ' "Dragged at Anne's Chariot Wheels": L.M. Montgomery and the Sequels to *Anne of Green Gables.' Papers of the Bibliographical Society of Canada / Cahiers de la Société bibliographique du Canada* 35 (1997): 143–59.

Gordon, Charles W. *Postscript to Adventure: The Autobiography of Ralph Connor.* New York: Farrar and Rinehart, 1938.

Gundy, H.P. 'Belford, Charles.' In *Dictionary of Canadian Biography,* ed. Francess G. Halpenny et al., vol. 10, 43–44. Toronto: University of Toronto Press, 1972.

– *Book Publishing and Publishers in Canada before 1900.* Toronto: Bibliographical Society of Canada, 1965.

Hamelin, Danielle. 'Nurturing Canadian Letters: Four Studies in the Publishing and Promotion of English-Canadian Writing, 1890–1920.' PhD diss., University of Toronto, 1994.

Hamilton, Thomas. 'Macleod, Norman (1812–1872).' Rev. H.C.G. Matthew. *Oxford Dictionary of National Biography.* Oxford: Oxford University Press, 2004. doi:10.1093/ref:odnb/17679. http://www.oxforddnb.com/view/article/17679 (accessed 10 November 2005).

Handa, Sunny. *Copyright Law in Canada.* Markham, ON: Butterworths, 2002.

Handley, William R. 'Western Fiction: Grey, Stegner, McMurty, McCarthy.' In *The Oxford Encyclopedia of American Literature,* ed. Jay Parini, vol. 4, 334–43. New York: Oxford University Press, 2004.

Hill, Hamlin, ed. *Mark Twain's Letters to His Publishers.* Berkeley and Los Angeles: University of California Press, 1967.

Hulse, Elizabeth. *A Dictionary of Toronto Printers, Publishers, Booksellers and the Allied Trades, 1798–1900.* Toronto: Anson-Cartwright, 1982.

James, Elizabeth. 'Letters from America: The Bretts and the Macmillan Company of New York.' In *Macmillan: A Publishing Tradition,* ed. Elizabeth James, 170–91. Houndmills, Basingstoke, UK; New York: Palgrave, 2002.

Jaszi, Peter, and Martha Woodmansee. 'Copyright in Transition.' In *A History of the Book in America,* vol. 4, *Print in Motion: The Expansion of Publishing and Reading in the United States 1880–1940,* ed. Carl F. Kaestle and Janice

A. Radway, 90–101. Chapel Hill: University of North Carolina Press / American Antiquarian Society, 2009.

Johns, Adrian. *Piracy: The Intellectual Property Wars from Gutenberg to Gates.* Chicago: University of Chicago Press, 2009.

Karr, Clarence. *Authors and Audiences: Popular Canadian Fiction in the Early Twentieth Century.* Montreal and Kingston: McGill-Queen's University Press, 2000.

Klinck, Carl, ed. *Literary History of Canada: Canadian Literature in English.* 1965. 2nd ed. 4 vols. Toronto: University of Toronto Press, 1976–90.

Lampman, Archibald. *Among the Millet.* Ottawa: J. Durie, 1888.

Livingston, Flora V. *Bibliography of the Works of Rudyard Kipling.* New York: Edgar H. Wells, 1927.

Longtin, Ray C. 'Joaquin Miller.' In *Three Writers of the Far West: A Reference Guide,* 3–117. Boston: G.K. Hall, 1980.

Lovell, John, and Graeme Mercer Adam. *A Letter to Sir John Rose, Bart., K.C.M.G., on the Canadian Copyright Question by Two Members of the Native Book Trade.* London: 15 August 1872.

Lynn, Helen, ed. *An Annotated Edition of the Correspondence between Archibald Lampman and Edward William Thomson (1890–1898).* Ottawa: Tecumseh Press, 1980.

MacMechan, Archibald. *Headwaters of Canadian Literature.* Toronto: McClelland and Stewart, 1924. Reprinted with introduction by M.G. Parks, 1974.

Madison, Charles A. *Book Publishing in America.* New York: McGraw-Hill, 1966.

Matthew, H.C.G. 'Smiles, Samuel (1812–1904).' In *Oxford Dictionary of National Biography,* ed. H.C.G. Matthew and Brian Harrison. Oxford: Oxford University Press, 2004. doi:10.1093/ref:odnb/36125. http://www.oxforddnb.com/view/article/36125 (accessed 30 November 2005).

McCalla, Douglas. 'Beaty, James.' In *Dictionary of Canadian Biography,* ed. Francess G. Halpenny et al., vol. 12, 71–4. Toronto: University of Toronto Press, 1990.

McDougall, Robert L. 'Lampman, Archibald.' In *Dictionary of Canadian Biography,* ed. Francess G. Halpenny et al., vol. 12, 513–18. Toronto: University of Toronto Press, 1990.

McDougall, Warren. 'Copyright Litigation in the Court of Session, 1738–1749, and the Rise of the Scottish Book Trade.' *Edinburgh Bibliographical Society Transactions* 5, no. 5 (1988): 2–31.

McGill, Meredith. *American Literature and the Culture of Reprinting, 1834–1853.* Philadelphia: University of Pennsylvania Press, 2003.

McKillop, A.B. 'Mystery at Macmillan: The Sudden Departure of President Frank Wise from Macmillan of Canada in 1921.' *Papers of the Bibliographical Society of Canada / Cahiers de la Société bibliographique du Canada* 38, no. 1 (2000): 73–103.

McLaren, Scott. 'Books for the Instruction of the Nations: Shared Methodist Print Culture in Upper Canada and the Mid-Atlantic States, 1789–1851.' PhD diss., University of Toronto, 2011.

Michon, Jacques. 'Book Publishing in Quebec.' In Fleming and Lamonde, *History of the Book in Canada,* vol. 3, 199–205.

Moodie, Susanna. *Roughing It in the Bush; or Life in Canada.* Edited by Carl Ballstadt. Centre for Editing Early Canadian Texts. Ottawa: Carleton University Press, 1988.

Mott, Frank Luther. *Golden Multitudes: The Story of Best Sellers in the United States.* New York: Macmillan, 1947.

Mount, Nick. *When Canadian Literature Moved to New York.* Toronto: University of Toronto Press, 2005.

Murray, Heather. *Come, Bright Improvement! The Literary Societies of Nineteenth-Century Ontario.* Toronto: University of Toronto Press, 2002.

Murray, Laura J. 'Protecting Ourselves to Death: Canada, Copyright, and the Internet.' *First Monday* 9, no. 10, 4 October 2004, http://firstmonday.org/ (accessed 30 June 2010).

Murray, Laura J., and Samuel E. Trosow. *Canadian Copyright: A Citizen's Guide.* Toronto: Between the Lines, 2007.

Nadeau, Jean-Guy. 'Taché, Joseph-Charles.' In *Dictionary of Canadian Biography,* ed. Francess G. Halpenny et al., vol. 12, 1012–16. Toronto: University of Toronto Press, 1990.

Nair, Meera. 'The Copyright Act of 1889: A Canadian Declaration of Independence.' *Canadian Historical Review* 90, no. 1 (2009): 1–28.

Panofsky, Ruth. 'A Bibliographical Study of Thomas Chandler Haliburton's *The Clockmaker,* First, Second, and Third Series.' PhD diss., York University, 1991.

Parker, George L. *The Beginnings of the Book Trade in Canada.* Toronto: University of Toronto Press, 1985.

– 'Distributors, Agents, and Publishers: Creating a Separate Market for Books in Canada, 1900–1920. Part I.' *Papers of the Bibliographical Society of Canada / Cahiers de la Société bibliographique du Canada* 43, no. 2 (2005): 7–65.

– ed. Introduction to *The Clockmaker: Series One, Two, and Three,* by Thomas Chandler Haliburton. Centre for Editing Early Canadian Texts. Ottawa: Carleton University Press, 1995.

Peterman, Michael A., and Janet B. Friskney. ' "Booming" the Canuck Book: Edward Caswell and the Promotion of Canadian Writing.' *Journal of Canadian Studies* 30, no. 3 (1995): 60–90.

Pierce, Lorne. *The House of Ryerson, 1829–1954.* Toronto: Ryerson, 1954.

Pollard, M. *Dublin's Trade in Books, 1550–1800.* Lyell Lectures, 1986–7. Oxford: Clarendon, 1989.

Rice, Grantland S. *The Transformation of Authorship in America.* Chicago: University of Chicago Press, 1997.

Richards, David Alan. *Rudyard Kipling: A Bibliography.* New Castle, DE: Oak Knoll Press; London: The British Library, 2010.

Roper, Gordon. 'Mark Twain and His Canadian Publishers: A Second Look.' *Papers of the Bibliographical Society of Canada / Cahiers de la Société bibliographique du Canada* 5 (1966): 30–89.

Roper, Gordon, S. Ross Beharriell, and Rupert Schieder. 'Writers of Fiction, 1880–1920.' In Klinck, *Literary History of Canada*, vol. 1, 327–53.

Rose, Mark. *Authors and Owners: The Invention of Copyright.* Cambridge, MA: Harvard University Press, 1993.

Schmidt, Barbara. 'A Closer Look at the Lives of True Williams and Alexander Belford.' Paper presented at the Fourth International Conference on the State of Mark Twain Studies, Elmira, NY, 18 August 2001. http://www.twainquotes.com/TWW/TWW.html (accessed 3 November 2005).

Seville, Catherine. *The Internationalisation of Copyright Law: Books, Buccaneers and the Black Flag in the Nineteenth Century.* Cambridge Studies in Intellectual Property Rights. Cambridge: Cambridge University Press, 2006.

Smith, A.J.M. 'A Rejected Preface.' 1934. *Canadian Literature* 24 (1965): 6–9. Reprinted in *Canadian Literature in English: Texts and Contexts*, ed. Laura Moss and Cynthia Sugars, vol. 2, 99–102. Toronto: Pearson Longman, 2009.

Smith, Allan. 'American Publications in Nineteenth-Century English Canada.' *Papers of the Bibliographical Society of Canada / Cahiers de la Société bibliographique du Canada* 9 (1970): 15–29.

Spadoni, Carl. 'A Bibliography of Macmillan of Canada Imprints, 1906–1980: First Supplement with Corrigenda.' *Papers of the Bibliographical Society of Canada / Cahiers de la Société bibliographique du Canada* 28 (1989): 38–69.

St Clair, William. *The Reading Nation in the Romantic Period.* Cambridge: Cambridge University Press, 2004.

Stephens, Donald G., ed. *Writers of the Prairies.* Canadian Literature Series. Vancouver: University of British Columbia Press, 1973.

Stern, Madeleine B. *Imprints on History: Book Publishers and American Frontiers.* Bloomington: Indiana University Press, 1956.

Tanselle, G. Thomas. 'The Bibliographical Concepts of *Issue* and *State.'* *Papers of the Bibliographical Society of America* 69 (1975): 17–66.

– 'A Sample Bibliographical Description with Commentary.' *Studies in Bibliography* 40 (1987): 1–30.

Tebbel, John. *A History of Book Publishing in the United States.* 4 vols. New York: R.R. Bowker, 1972–81.

Toews, Miriam. *A Complicated Kindness.* Toronto: Alfred A. Knopf Canada, 2004.

Trevelyan, C.E. *The Compromise Offered by Canada in Reference to the Reprinting of English Copyright Works.* London: Bell and Daldy, 1872.

United Kingdom. House of Commons. 'Colonial Copyright: Copies or Extracts of Correspondence Between the Colonial Office, the Board of Trade, and the Government of Canada' (339). In *Sessional Papers,* vol. 43 (1872), 277. *House of Commons Parliamentary Papers.* Cambridge: Chadwyck-Healey, 2005–.

– 'Copyright (Colonies): Copies of or Extracts from Any Correspondence Between the Colonial Office and Any of the Colonial Governments on the Subject of Copyright' (144). In *Sessional Papers,* vol. 51 (1875), 635. *House of Commons Parliamentary Papers.* Cambridge: Chadwyck-Healey, 2005–.

– 'Copyright Commission: The Royal Commissions and the Report of the Commissioners.' C. 2036. In *Sessional Papers,* vol. 24 (1878). *House of Commons Parliamentary Papers.* Cambridge: Chadwyck-Healey, 2005–.

– 'Correspondence Respecting Colonial Copyright.' C. 1067. In *Sessional Papers,* vol. 44 (1874), 539. *House of Commons Parliamentary Papers.* Cambridge: Chadwyck-Healey, 2005–.

Vincent, Josée, and Eli MacLaren. 'Book Policies and Copyright in Canada and Quebec: Defending National Cultures.' *Canadian Literature* 204 (2010): 63–82.

Wallace, W. Stewart. *The Ryerson Imprint: A Check-list of the Books and Pamphlets Published by The Ryerson Press since the Foundation of the House in 1829.* Toronto: Ryerson, 1954.

Watt, F.W. 'Western Myth: The World of Ralph Connor.' In Stephens, *Writers of the Prairies,* 7–16 (originally published in *Canadian Literature* 1 [1959]: 26–36).

Whiteman, Bruce. 'The Early History of the Macmillan Company of Canada, 1905–1921.' *Papers of the Bibliographical Society of Canada / Cahiers de la Société bibliographique du Canada* 23 (1984): 68–83.

Whiteman, Bruce, Charlotte Stewart, and Catherine Funnel. *A Bibliography of Macmillan of Canada Imprints, 1906–1980.* Toronto: Dundurn, 1985.

Wiseman, John A. 'Silent Companions: The Dissemination of Books and Periodicals in Nineteenth-Century Ontario.' *Publishing History* 12 (1982): 17–50.

Wood, Susan. 'Ralph Connor and the Tamed West.' In *The Westering Experience in American Literature: Bicentennial Essays,* ed. Merrill Lewis and L.L. Lee, 199–205. Bellingham, WA: Bureau for Faculty Research, Western Washington University, 1977.

Index

Studies in Book and Print Culture

GENERAL EDITOR: LESLIE HOWSAM

Elizabeth Driver, *Culinary Landmarks: A Bibliography of Canadian Cookbooks, 1825–1949*

Benjamin C. Withers, *The Illustrated Old English Hexateuch, Cotton Ms. Claudius B.iv: The Frontier of Seeing and Reading in Anglo-Saxon England*

Mary Ann Gillies, *The Professional Literary Agent in Britain, 1880–1920*

Willa Z. Silverman, *The New Bibliopolis: French Book-Collectors and the Culture of Print, 1880–1914*

Lisa Surwillo, *The Stages of Property: Copyrighting Theatre in Spain*

Dean Irvine, *Editing Modernity: Women and Little-Magazine Cultures in Canada, 1916–1956*

Janet Friskney, *New Canadian Library: The Ross-McClelland Years, 1952–1978*

Janice Cavell, *Tracing the Connected Narrative: Arctic Exploration in British Print Culture, 1818–1860*

Elspeth Jajdelska, *Silent Reading and the Birth of the Narrator*

Martyn Lyons, *Reading Culture and Writing Practices in Nineteenth-Century France*

Robert A. Davidson, *Jazz Age Barcelona*

Gail Edwards and Judith Saltman, *Picturing Canada: A History of Canadian Children's Illustrated Books and Publishing*

Miranda Remnek, ed., *The Space of the Book: Print Culture in the Russian Social Imagination*

Adam Reed, *Literature and Agency in English Fiction Reading: A Study of the Henry Williamson Society*

Bonnie Mak, *How the Page Matters*

Eli MacLaren, *Dominion and Agency: Copyright and the Structuring of the Canadian Book Trade, 1867–1918*